D1320304

ORIGINS OF MODERN BIOLOGY

URL LANHAM

Origins of
Modern Biology

COLUMBIA UNIVERSITY PRESS

NEW YORK AND LONDON *1968*

Url Lanham is Curator of Entomology at the
University of Colorado Museum in Boulder
and is the author of *The Fishes* and *The Insects.*

Copyright © 1968 Columbia University Press
Library of Congress Catalog Card Number: 68-24478
Printed in the United States of America

[CONTENTS]

[INTRODUCTION]

THIS ACCOUNT OF THE DEVELOPMENT of the main lines of biology takes the story up to the beginning of the twentieth century. Although this dividing line between "modern" and "traditional" biology is somewhat arbitrary, the founding of genetics in 1900, with its use of mathematical techniques and its strategic relationship to other areas of biology, was a qualitatively new development. Genetics has opened the way for the characteristic biological subscience of the mid-twentieth century, molecular biology. Also, by the middle of the century, science began to take on its present role as a large-scale professional activity, completely changing the conditions under which scientists work.

The scientist of the nineteenth century was often an amateur, in the sense that he was not paid to be a scientist, and he rarely worked as a member of a highly organized group. He was highly individualistic, and often his strongest motivation was the desire for credit for his discoveries, so that struggles over priority are conspicuous in the biographical landscape of the history of biology. The population of scientists in the mid-twentieth century is relatively large, and they tend to be crowded together in institutions and laboratories, where administrative matters and interpersonal relationships may dominate the situation. Aside from the pleasures of intellectual craftsmanship that reward scientists of all times, motivation chiefly involves questions of position and financial reward.

The overall trend in the huge establishment of modern science is toward anonymity, as science becomes increasingly socialized. This book therefore is concerned with a bygone romantic, individualistic phase of biology. Although, because of the sparsely scattered nature of its efforts, it is dwarfed by modern science in rate of output, the older era of science, with its literature of penetrating and wide-ranging concepts that were produced by solitary and persistent thought, has been a powerful influence in shaping the structure of modern science, and its study is essential to an understanding of the concepts of twentieth-century biology.

The history of science is concerned in large part with the interaction of three sets of factors. First is the inertia or momentum of scientific concepts themselves, which act as impediments or as aids in the exploration of nature and in the interpretation of new facts thus discovered. Second is technology, which, with its complex of social and material factors, goes a long way toward determining the structure of science, and is in turn influenced by scientific developments. Of particular significance is the mode of communication characteristic of the time, whether speech, writing, printing, or the electronic modes. Third, but not last in importance, are the gifted men of science who have had the energy, range, and sensitivity both to command respect in traditional areas of science and to be responsive to new forces. They have shaped with unique vigor and artistic insight the concepts that are central to the development of science. These men have become legends, and the history of science quite properly centers about them. All of these sets of factors are taken into account in this book, but there is emphasis on the biographical side of the history of biology, and the scientists themselves are quoted extensively to give the flavor of their thinking and writing.

The development of biology falls into stages that correspond to the developmental stages of science in general: first, the very long preliterate phase; second, the phase of classic Greek science, which is based on the use of written language; and third, Renaissance science, which begins with the use of printing to record and spread ideas. Modern science, which is approximately a twentieth-century phenomenon, also is developing its characteristic electronic methods of storing and communicating information. These changes in mode of communication are more or less contemporaneous with the great revolutions in social structure: writing with the founding of the great cities based on agricultural societies; printing with the emergence of capitalism out of medieval society; the electronic modes with the intensive technological organization of society that is now going on.

After its premature but significant development in classical Greece, Western science got underway as a continuing endeavor in Renaissance times, so that this book concerns itself mainly with the events of four centuries, the sixteenth through the nineteenth.

The historical section of this book is prefaced by three chapters which will serve to place the development of biology in perspective for the reader. The first is a brief description of that aspect of the living world which, until near the end of the era of traditional biology, had escaped scientific explanation. This is the adaptiveness, or apparent purpose in living nature—the usefulness and goal-directedness shown by the structure, development, and behavior of living things. In a sense, all of biology centers about organic adaptation, and there are wide implications for the history of thought in the study of this aspect of nature. The second of the introductory chapters concerns the origin of man, with emphasis on the information-acquiring and information-organizing processes that distinguish him from other animals and make science possible. The third concerns the nature of science itself, as distinguished from other human activities, and in relation to human desires and to the real world outside human life.

ORIGINS OF MODERN BIOLOGY

[CHAPTER 1]

Adaptation

in the Living World

THE CHILD OF A SAVAGE RACE finds in his human environment
purpose and care. He then grows into an awareness of a natural
world where animals have structures and abilities that fit them
for their ways of life, just as he and his tribe are so gifted as to
be able to live as a part of nature. So strong is his appreciation
of the purposiveness, the adaptiveness, of living things and their
close relationship to their environment that he extends purpose
to the nonliving world, to the land and the sky, which are, to the

savage, instinct with life. His is a world view that is hundreds of thousands of years old, as old as the human species.

This unity of man with nature was destroyed, in the Western world, by the technological advances made some ten thousand years ago when revolutionary improvements in agriculture made possible the production of surplus wealth, the appearance of cities, and the development of exploiting classes. The unity of the world view of the savage was destroyed when human unity within peoples and nations was destroyed. The chief occupation of the most energetic men became the exploitation of other human beings, while for the average man, an adaptive natural environment had disappeared, and justice had been officially postponed to the hereafter. The purpose that primitive man saw in nature was torn from its natural abode, and was now to be imposed on nature from supernatural realms. Civilized man was alienated from nature both by his mode of life—in the world of the savage, every man was a biologist—and by the violent distortion and dismemberment of the primitive world view into the ideologies of economic classes.

Along with the continuous growth of the most important of human nonexploitive activities—art—there developed a kind of intellectual activity, expressed in writing, and essentially a branch of art, which became literate science. Reaching an early climax in ancient Greece, then extinguished in Europe by the thousand-year-long episode of European Christianity, it revived as a part of the Renaissance, and while it developed mainly in association with industry and war, it took up again the study of living nature. By the nineteenth century the adaptive, purposeful character of all life, which had been obvious to primitive man, was brought vividly to the attention of literate society. And in the most dramatic development of the history of biology, Charles Darwin, in the middle of the nineteenth century, showed that this adaptiveness was integral to nature—was not imposed on it from the outside by a supernatural agency, but rather was a consequence of the operation of natural forces. He thus took a great step toward resurrecting the primitive world view of the unity of all life with nature.

One of the places in which an awareness of organic adaptation emerged to the conscious level in unusually explicit form was in the theological literature of early nineteenth-century England. Here the Church, endangered by its deep involvement in the political struggles of the time, was attempting to shore up its intellectual authority by appropriating some of the ideas of science (including the new appreciation of the adaptiveness of organic nature) as arguments in favor of its doctrines. By far the most influential theological writer of this place and time, whose writings became required reading in many of the British universities, was the liberal and thoughtful William Paley, an archdeacon of the Church, an enemy of slavery, and the author of the remarkable *Natural Theology; or, Evidences of the Existence and Attributes of the Deity, Collected from the Appearances of Nature*, published in 1802. "Paley's Theology," as it is often called, actually could be used as an excellent introduction to functional anatomy, especially that of man. Charles Darwin learned his elementary biology from this book. It is not at all a dry recital of anatomical facts; at every point structure is brought to life by explaining its relation to function. Paley begins his argument with the well-known passage:

In crossing a heath, suppose I pitched my foot against a *stone,* and were asked how the stone came to be there, I might possibly answer that, for anything I knew to the contrary, it had laid there forever; nor perhaps would it be very easy to shew the absurdity of this answer. But suppose I had found a watch upon the ground, and it should be inquired how the watch happened to be in that place, I should hardly think of the answer which I had before given, that for anything I knew, the watch might have always been there. Yet, why should not this answer serve for the watch, as well as for the stone? . . . For this reason, and for no other, viz. that, when we come to inspect the watch, we perceive (what we could not discover in the stone,) that its several parts are framed and put together for a purpose, e.g., that they are so formed and adjusted as to produce motion, and that motion so regulated as to point out the hour of the day.

As to the origin of the contrivance, the watch:

This mechanism being observed . . . the inference, we think, is inevitable; that the watch must have had a maker; that there must have existed, at some time and at some place or other, an artificer or artificers who formed it for the purpose, which we find it actually to answer; who comprehended its construction, and designed its use.

Paley sees the solar system as a gigantic contrivance, but does not devote much space to its description:

My opinion of astronomy has always been, that it is not the medium through which to prove the agency of an intelligent Creator. . . . The very simplicity of the heavenly bodies is against them. . . . Now we deduce design from relation, aptitude, and correspondence of *parts*. Some degree therefore of *complexity* is necessary to render a subject fit for this species of argument.

So that Paley turns to a discussion of structures of living things which "surpass the contrivances of art in the complexity, subtlety, and curiosity of the mechanism," although this may not

4

have been obvious to his mechanically minded compatriots of the England of the Industrial Revolution:

> I have sometimes wondered why we are not struck with mechanism in animal bodies, as readily and as strongly as we are struck with it, at first sight, in a watch or a mill. One reason for the difference may be that animal bodies are, in a great measure, made up of soft, flabby substances, such as muscles and membranes; whereas we have been accustomed to trace mechanisms in sharp lines, in the configuration of hard materials.

We can select one brief example from the many that make up the main body of his argument:

> The following is often the case with the muscles. Their action is wanted where their situation would be inconvenient. In which case the body of the muscle is placed in some commodious position at a distance, and made to communicate with the point of action, by slender strings or wires. If the muscles, which move the fingers, had been placed in the palm or back of the hand, they would have swelled that part to an awkward and clumsy thickness.—The beauty, the proportions, of the part, would have been destroyed. They are therefore disposed in the arm, and even up to the elbow; and act by long tendons, strapped down at the wrist, and passing under the ligaments to the fingers, and to the joints of the fingers, which they are severally to move.

Paley's idea was not at all new. The British zoologist John Ray had made it familiar a hundred years before, and the Dutch philosopher Niewentyt had already used even the analogy of the watch. The idea had been expressed in pagan times by Cicero, and in a more diffuse philosophical form by the Greeks.

So rich in variety is the living world that we can see in it adaptations that mirror our latest technological advances. One of the favorite examples among modern biologists of a sophisticated evolutionary invention is to be found in a group of insect-eating bats that live in the northern hemisphere. Bats of the kinds that pursue insects through dark skies have eyes too small and otherwise too poorly constructed to be of any use in catching their prey. This, together with the fact that they expertly dodge obstacles when flying in restricted spaces in the dark, has long made it plain that bats must get some signal other than light from distant objects. Experimental work done long ago indicated that it was sound: bats have large—sometimes fantastically large—ears, and when artificially deafened, they tended to lose their ability to maneuver in the dark. But just what this sound was awaited the inventions of electronic techniques to analyze sounds that were too complex and too high-pitched for the human ear.

One of the first clues that led students of bat behavior to understand their use of sound was the fact that a bat fluttering through an aerial maze in a darkened room emits a soft ticking sound, the ticks somewhat irregular, now in a slower, now in a faster rhythm. With the perfection of electronic recording devices, it became possible to record these ticks, each a burst of sound only a few thousandths of a second long, and play each one back as a long train of sound, or as a visible trace of sound waves. It was then evident that a large component of each was an ultrasonic squeak, of a pitch above the human range of hearing. More than this, the pitch was not constant, but slid quickly from a lower to a higher note—a range of about an octave—within each burst of sound, within each "tick." Such observations led to the hypothesis that the animal found its way about, and located objects in the air, by making sounds with its vocal chords and listening for echoes.

6

The meaning of the detailed characteristics of each micro-squeak was interpreted in the following way. The high pitch of the sound means short wavelengths, and a small object, such as a flying insect, will reflect mainly short wavelengths to produce a sharp echo; longer wavelengths go by little affected. The sliding pitch takes care of the contingency that the bat is so close to its prey that the echo comes back while the squeak is still being emitted. If the squeak were a monotone the echo would be lost, but with the upward slide, the echo is heard at a lower note than the sound being emitted. Such surmises have been partly or wholly confirmed by a variety of experiments, such as recording impulses from the auditory nerve of the bat when the ear is subjected to artificial ultrasonic sounds.

This kind of solution to the problem of finding small moving targets in the dark would do credit to a whole institute of engineering. The electromagnetic waves that are the basis of radar seem to be beyond the capacity of living substance to generate or sense, but they are at any rate too high-speed to use for very short ranges. The sound-detection device used by bats is most clearly akin to sonar, which uses underwater sound as an echo-location device.

If the echo-location apparatus of the bat is an adaptation related to a part of the living environment, then it would not be surprising to find that some of the organisms of this environment are in turn adapted to the presence of the bat, and this expectation has been realized in studies of moths, night-flying insects that make up part of the diet of bats. Many of the moths have structures on the abdomen or thorax that look like eardrums. Students of moth natural history had long been puzzled by these structures, since it seemed that moths had nothing to listen to.

With the discovery of the sounds made by bats, the obvious hypothesis as to the functional significance of the moth's ears was

7

put to experimental test. Minute electrodes placed on the nerves leading from the ear detected impulses that showed the ear was sensitive to sounds like that produced by bats; and when moths in free flight were subjected to a sound recording of the bat's hunting call, they went into violent evasive action.

The clicking noise made by some kinds of moths also can be explained by the bat–insect relationship. Minute analysis of the sounds shows that they can function so as to confuse the bat's echo-location system by producing sounds similar to the echo, sounds that arrive at the bat's ear at confusing and meaningless times. In another instance, the sounds produced by the moth are believed to be warning signals that the moth is one of the numerous kinds that have evolved distasteful or poisonous substances that discourage predators. Many kinds of insects active in the daylight have such protective substances, and these often advertise the fact with bright warning coloration. The nocturnal moth apparently accomplishes the same end with warning sounds; and just as some of the bright colors of distasteful insects are imitated by some tasty ones, so it might be expected that some moths have evolved false warning sounds.

There is a kind of mite (a diminutive relative of the woodtick) that makes its abode inside the ears of moths. In this sheltered and capacious chamber the mites rear their numerous young, and in the process destroy the ear. Now in a world infested with bats, a group of mites living in a deaf moth would have the normal perils of existence much increased. How would one prescribe for them? The obvious solution—that the mites come to an arrangement whereby only one ear on a moth is occupied—is the one actually used. When more than one househunting mite gets on a moth, the rule is that all follow the trail of the first mite to the ear, whether right or left. No mite will take a new trail if one already exists.

When modern biology penetrates deeply into the ultra-minute structure of living things—beyond the range of light, and beyond the range of the electron microscope, down to the level of molecular structure—it finds that the pattern even here is exquisitely adapted for the function and survival of the organism. Modern biology sees the activities of a plant or animal as dependent upon a very large number of chemical reactions that take place in coordinated fashion. Although many of these reactions can be duplicated in the laboratory, here they may proceed slowly, and often require high temperatures or powerful reagents that would destroy fragile living tissue. In the living substance of the organism are miniature machines that can carry out these reactions by dealing with the reacting molecules one at a time in a precise way, putting the electron shells of the constituent atoms under specific stress so that the reaction proceeds in rigidly prescribed fashion, and handling the flow of electrons that may be gained or lost by the reaction in an efficient way. The action of these machines—which are called enzymes, and are constructed of thousands of atoms, arranged in precise patterns that vary with the kind of enzyme and the kind of chemical reaction that is being facilitated—speeds up the reaction to a degree far beyond that achieved by laboratory manipulations, and does this without the use of high temperature.

Again, in this level of organization (that is the concern of "molecular biology") science finds in living things a reflection of the latest advances in human technology. The enzymes, which are essentially long chains of small molecules called amino acids linked together in single file, have to be assembled by the living cell, and this is technically a difficult matter, because the properties of the enzyme—the kind of chemical reaction it facilitates, and the rate of the reaction—are determined by the exact sequence of the twenty or so kinds of amino acids, and there are many hundreds or thousands of amino acids involved. This problem is solved by a molecular chain called DNA (deoxyribonucleic acid). The exact sequence of the four kinds of constituents of this chain is used to guide the assembly of amino acids into enzymes. DNA is thus an analogue of the computer tape, which stores information and releases it when needed. DNA also can reproduce itself in side-to-side fashion. It is handed down from generation to generation in the sperms and eggs as an essential hereditary material, and also is spread throughout the body as the individual develops from the fertilized egg by repeated cell division.

A different aspect of adaptiveness is shown by the study of embryonic development. There are now available films made by time-lapse photography that make it possible to see in a few minutes the development of a single egg cell into an embryo, a process that takes many hours or days. It is most impressive to watch the swirling gray mass of the egg divide into two separate cells, then into four, into eight, and on into the masses of tissues that arrange themselves into a definite pattern of organs. This small bit of living substance seems charged with a directing force straining toward the goal of completed development; the whole thing is reminiscent of the intentness with which the child stands on his feet and takes his first step. Embryo and child, bits of nonreasoning nature, seem imbued with the same kind of foresight, and to show the same goal-directedness that we find in planned human activity.

If we ask the question, "Why does the tiger have claws?" the embryologist can give us a ready answer. He can say that, given the physical and chemical conditions that exist at certain points in the embryo, it is inevitable that certain groups of living cells there will produce the substance of the hard, curved, sharp claws. But this answers the question only at one level; we are dissatisfied, and feel that an important element in understanding is left out. If the embryo tiger did not develop claws, the grown tiger could not survive; thus, events in the embryo are directed toward future contingencies. This kind of conquest of time, in which future needs are predicted and provided for, is characteristic of the whole biological world; and it is based, as Darwinian evolution demonstrated, on methods of storing information that record past successes and failures. Evolution marks the fall of every sparrow.

There is another kind of concept that sees purpose in nature that need be mentioned only briefly here. This is the nonscientific view that is the Teleology of the supernatural. It would ask the question, not what is the use of the tiger's claws, but rather, what is the use of the tiger? And it would answer that the tiger was put in the world, as is every other thing, for man's material use or moral edification. This sort of teleology sees the world as a stage on which is enacted a purposive drama that leads to man as a culmination, with the object of producing him set out in the beginning. This untestable concept has no scientific meaning.

The existence of purpose in living nature, and resultant design, was not explained in terms that integrated it with the language and methods of science until the nineteenth and twentieth centuries. This integration has produced the most profound revolution in man's outlook on nature in the history of modern civilization.

CHAPTER 2

The Human
Animal

IN THIS BOOK THE HISTORY of biology is in large part traced through a series of biographies of men important in the development of scientific thought. But during the preliterate, primitive, phase of science, which was hundreds of times longer than all recorded history, science was completely anonymous. What will be given here to introduce primitive science is a biography of man in the abstract, as a species of animal, outlining his evolutionary origin and the appearance of those traits that make human knowledge of the environment different from the kind of knowledge that other animals possess, traits that make science possible.

The human species, technically named *Homo sapiens,* is a remarkably varied assemblage of individuals. Structural and physiological differences coincide to some extent with geographical distribution, so that there are more or less recognizable races, but all such races are interfertile with one another, and constant interbreeding between them makes it impossible to set up a rigid classification within the species. Also, variations within the so-called races are likely to be of greater magnitude than differences between averages of different races. *Homo sapiens* has been one of those successful biological species in which the population is large and genetically variable, with geographic races which have formed, dissolved, and reformed during its history, allowing the species to adapt to a wide variety of environments on a global scale, and to maintain a store of genetic variability that has carried it through a variety of crises.

There is now a wide gap between man and other animal species. Although Charles Darwin thought this gap not very formidable from the scientific viewpoint, he thought that to try to bridge it in his *Origin of Species* would bring a storm of wrath on his head and unnecessarily endanger the acceptance of his general theory of evolution. As he says in the Introduction to *The Descent of Man,* published twenty-two years after the *Origin,* in 1871:

During many years I collected notes on the origin or descent of man, without any intention of publishing on the subject, but rather with the determination not to publish, as I thought that I should thus only add to the prejudices against my views. . . . Now the case wears a wholly different aspect . . . it is manifest that at least a large number of naturalists must admit that species are the modified descendants of other species; and this especially holds good with the younger and rising naturalists.

In the two decades intervening between the two books there had been a good deal of effective skirmishing on Darwin's behalf by his British compatriots; and in Germany the biologist Ernst Haeckel had made the theory a rallying point for liberal thinkers. So that by 1871, Darwin felt confident enough to use such arguments as:

He who rejects with scorn the belief that the shape of his own canines, and their occasional great development in other men, are due to our early forefathers having been provided with these formidable weapons, will probably reveal, by sneering, the line of his descent. For though he no longer intends, nor has the power, to use these teeth as weapons, he will unconsciously retract his "snarling muscles" (thus named by Sir C. Bell), so as to expose them ready for action, like a dog ready to fight.

There is no way of knowing how many men and women were inspired by the vistas offered up by the theory of evolution to put energy and time into one of the most challenging and difficult tasks of paleontology—to find fossil remains of extinct species of man. The ones we know about performed prodigies of patient and arduous toil—the modern anthropologist, L. S. B. Leakey, for example, combed the Pleistocene rocks of East Africa for thirty-five years before he found his first fossil man (and as he tells it, it was his wife who found it, while he was in camp with a headache). So rare are these fossils that scarcely seventy skulls—most of them represented only by one or a few fragments—of pre-Neanderthal apelike man have been discovered.

Ernst Haeckel, the German popularizer of Darwin, made his explorations into the geologic past of the human race at his desk, and in 1868 actually gave a name to the theoretical species intermediate between modern man and his primate ancestors—this without seeing a specimen. The name chosen was the rather obvious *Pithecanthropus*, or ape man.

It was the young Dutch visionary, Eugene Dubois, who found *Pithecanthropus*. On the basis of the distribution of the living great apes, and what he thought would be a climate favorable to ancient man, he decided that the East Indies was the place to look. Dubois, a lecturer in anatomy at the University of Amsterdam, could get no individual or institution to finance the project. He therefore left the university to become a doctor in the Dutch colonial army. He then managed an assignment to Sumatra, where he arrived in 1887. A correspondent sent him a promising skull fragment from nearby Java, and he got himself reassigned to that island. By 1892 he had found bones of his ape man in rocks along a tropical river; in 1894 he published an account of the discovery, naming his creature *Pithecanthropus erectus*, which came to be known as the Java ape man.

Since then, other fragments of skeletons of similar creatures have been found in localities scattered from Africa to Europe to China. But so great was the importance attached by each discoverer to his find, and so faulty was his appreciation of the variation within a species in nature (the describer was typically an anthropologist without experience in naming and classifying animals), that each find usually got a new name. The result was that by the mid-twentieth century there was a chaotic jumble of some scores of extinct species of animals thought to belong in the general area between the nonhuman and the modern human species. It is only recently that determined efforts by anthropologists and interested systematic zoologists have begun to yield a comprehensible, if perhaps tentative, picture of this vanished bridge between man and the rest of living nature.

Modern man can be placed in perspective among the tailless primates in a classification based on that of G. G. Simpson, who divides them up into three major categories, or families:

1. Family Pongidae: includes all the living great apes—gorilla, chimpanzee, gibbon, and orangutan—as well as many extinct fossil species.
2. Family Oreopithecidae: includes a chimpanzee-sized ape from Pliocene or Miocene rocks of an Italian coal mine and another type from older rocks; difficult to classify into either the preceding or following family, so that they are put in a family of their own.
3. Family Hominidae: includes the living and extinct tailless primates that walk erect. Some anthropologists call all of these forms men; others restrict the term to one or two of the most recent species.

A total of forty-two specific names that are valid according to rules of zoological nomenclature have been proposed for the living and fossil Hominidae. However, the modern conservative conception is that only three or four of these are acceptable as good biological species, and that these can be classified into two genera. This conception of the classification of the Hominidae can be outlined:

Family Hominidae
    Genus *Homo*.
        Homo sapiens. Modern man; worldwide in distribution.
        Homo erectus. An extinct species occurring only in the Old
            World.
    Genus *Australopithecus*

One or two species (*A. robustus* and *A. africanus*), both extinct, and known only from Africa.

The nearest living relative of modern man is the quite distantly related chimpanzee (*Pan troglodytes*) of equatorial Africa, while the nearest known relatives are certain fossil hominids and apes. The fossil record of modern man (by this term is meant the species *Homo sapiens*) goes back about 200,000 years, with the oldest remains known being the Stenheim and Swanscombe skulls. There does not appear to be any clear-cut trend of human evolution so far as skeletal characters are concerned during this 200,000 years. With the appearance of Stenheim and Swanscombe man, the selection pressures that had previously been producing a rapid increase in brain size seem to have been relaxed, because average brain size has not increased since. There is no direct evidence from the fossil record that modern man existed side by side with any other species of man or manlike ape. The most recent skeletal materials known of *Homo erectus* are about 400,000 years old, so that there is still a paleontological gap of some 200,000 years separating modern man from this presumed ancestral species.

Neanderthal man, known from numerous skeletons discovered in Europe, North Africa, and Turkestan, is now generally believed to belong to the species *Homo sapiens*. Interpretations of his skeleton that led to the reconstruction of a shambling, stooped gait were incorrect; he walked erect in true man-fashion. The volume of his heavy, elongate skull was somewhat higher than the average for modern man. He made flaked stone tools that do not seem to be qualitatively different from those of some other primitive human cultures. His heavy skull wall does not appear to be of fundamental significance, and this characteristic, as well as the receding chin, is said to persist in the general European population of today. Also, typical Neanderthal man (as recognized by skull characters), appears later in the fossil record than ordinary *Homo sapiens,* first appearing about 75,000 years ago, and becoming effectively extinct (perhaps being absorbed by interbreeding with more numerous races of *Homo sapiens*) about 20,000 years ago.

After Dubois' discovery, another anthropologist, G. H. R. van Koenigswald, took up the search for more fossils of ancient man in Java and, forty years after the original find, uncovered a few more skeletal fragments. The resulting conception of *Homo erectus* was that he was rather short (a little over five feet high), but could stand fully erect, like modern man, and was capable of the swinging human stride. He had a low, thick skull, with a brain volume of about 900 cc. compared with the modern average of 1,375 cc.

Finds of other specimens began to turn up elsewhere. By far the richest cache of skeletal fragments was found near Peking, where remains of at least forty individuals were recovered. The age of this find is about 400,000 years ago. Another skull fragment was discovered in Algeria. Another specimen that had been uncovered in Europe long before was now recognized as being one of these ape men. Each find was at first given a distinctive generic name, but slowly the realization dawned that all the specimens were basically alike, and probably did not differ more from one another than would be expected from the variations within a single species. So that all—the Java ape man, China ape man, and other scattered finds—are put in the single species *Homo erectus.*

More recently, J. B. S. Leakey and his associates have described another species, *Homo habilis,* from rocks about a million years old. The conservative opinion adopted here is that this also is *Homo erectus.*

The remarkably good specimens from cave deposits at Peking (they disappeared during World War II) showed that without doubt the ape man, *Homo erectus,* used fire and made simple flaked tools from stone that could be used to cut up game, scrape hides, or be used as hand axes. It would seem that this creature was more like modern man than it was like the older form that we will discuss presently. Therefore, it is often called the first man, the criteria for this rank being a true striding upright walk, and a brain size and conceptual ability (inferred from the use of fire) that would together make it possible that he was capable of true speech.

Back in time beyond *Homo erectus* is the realm of *Australopithecus,* the "southern ape." All of the fossils of these creatures (there were likely more than one species) have been found in Africa, and they extend in time from about 500,000 to 1,750,000 years ago. They were small, lightly built animals, standing about five feet tall. Although very ancient, some relatively good specimens have been found, as the result of determined and mostly solitary efforts of such individualists as Dart, Broom, and Leakey. The first find (1924) was that of the so-called Taungs skull, named after a locality near Kimberly; the most recent, those made by Leaky in the Olduvai Gorge, East Africa, and called by him a new genus, *Zinjanthropus,* although here grouped with *Australopithecus.*

Rather complete skulls, and parts of the rest of the skeleton, show an odd combination of ape and human characteristics. The skull of *Australopithecus* is low and apelike, and the range of variation in cranial capacity, which centers around 500 cc., ranges down to that of the modern gorilla. The structure of the teeth, especially that of the upper canines, and of the lower jaws —parallel to each other instead of converging anteriorly—is more like that of modern man. Very significant is the structure of the pelvic girdle. Here the ilium is much the same shape as that of modern man, which would indicate a truly erect, standing posture. This bone provides, in the main, the origin for the large gluteal muscles that produce the rounded, protruding buttocks and make possible erect posture of human beings. The detailed structure of the ischium, another part of the pelvic girdle, however, is not so human, and it is likely that *Australopithecus*, although walking erect, could not walk with the true human stride. If true, this would probably limit the endurance of this creature in long-distance walking, and perhaps in trotting or loping over level terrain.

Associated with the bones of *Australopithecus* are pebbles crudely flaked so as to produce a curved cutting edge. Leakey has shown that by using one of these so-called pebble tools he can cut open the hide of a tough-skinned mammal like an antelope and cut out manageable chunks of meat, something he could not do with his own set of teeth, which (like those of anyone else) were shaped much like the teeth of *Australopithecus*. The supposition is that *Australopithecus* was a tool-using and toolmaking primate, and that this kind of tool conferred a definite advantage in survival to its maker.

If we adopt Benjamin Franklin's characterization of man as *Homo faber*, the toolmaker, then we might be led to call *Australopithecus* the first known man. But recent observations on the behavior of living apes in the wild, which reveal that chimpanzees, for example, regularly make and use simple tools, indicate that not a very high degree of mentality is needed for this, and that the ability to make such tools may have been common or widespread among the great variety of apes that existed millions of years before the time of *Australopithecus*.

To summarize what seems to be the consensus as to kinds of men and manlike apes that were present on the earth during the past million years: 1) *Australopithecus,* the size of the African pigmy; the first primate, so far as known, that walked habitually erect; known only from Africa; became extinct about 500,000 years ago; 2) *Homo erectus,* somewhat more robust than *Australopithecus,* and with a brain size nearly twice as large, follows him in time (although the two may have overlapped toward the end of the history of *Australopithecus*); details of the structure of the ischium and femur suggest that this was the first primate with the remarkable human ability for long-distance walking and running; surmised to be the first primate that could speak; made the stone tools of a kind whose fabrication required patience and conceptual thought, and used fire; spread over the Old World, but did not reach the New World or distant islands; became extinct 250,000 years ago; 3) *Homo sapiens,* with a brain about a third again as large as *Homo erectus*; elaborate tools both effective and with artistic embellishment, and which evolve in complexity without detectable biological change in their makers; speech presumably much more complex than in *Homo erectus*; world wide in distribution.

When it is realized that we have as a basis for this picture only a few dozen pinpoints of fact in the vast expanse of a million years of time and in the whole space of the Old World, it is clear that we may well be in for surprises as more fossils and artifacts are found.

One of the crucial events in this chronology, the appearance of true speech, is placed where it is (with the appearance of *Homo erectus*) on the basis of slender evidence. There is no known way of tying this characteristic with any structural feature of the skeleton, or with any kind of artifact. Because of his small brain size—not much greater than that of living apes—it is assumed that *Australopithecus* did not have true speech. There is little that can be said about the psychological characteristics of *Homo erectus,* as compared with modern man. It does seem fairly safe to say, on the basis of the artifacts that have been discovered, that the toolmaking ability of *Homo erectus* did not improve noticeably during the quarter- or half-million years of his existence, while that of *Homo sapiens* did improve to a remarkable degree during his history, as a result of cumulative inventions. This may well be a consequence of the larger brain size of *sapiens.*

It is interesting to see that during the epoch of *sapiens,* while technology was developing rapidly, brain size did not increase. On the other hand, it is believed that during the epoch of *Homo erectus* the rapid evolution of the brain to its modern size was achieved.

Language is mentioned here as the important event in the origin of man because it is crucial in the origin and development of science, but actually a whole complex of interrelated adaptions were involved in human origins, among them upright walking and running, the use of the hands in toolmaking, and prolonged infancy, which besides making possible the development of the large central nervous system, makes for the strengthening of family and perhaps other social groupings. The relationship between such adaptations as bipedal locomotion and the use of hands is obvious—the forelimbs are freed for uses other than locomotion, hence their structure can be improved without hindrance for the delicate manipulations of toolmaking and tool using; and conversely, the use of sticks as spears or digging and prying tools would place a premium on the further improvement of bipedal locomotion, if a partially bipedal animal habitually carried about such tools.

The evolutionary origin of language also has been related, in speculative fashion, to the complex of adaptations clustered about upright locomotion. *Australopithecus* probably represents the stage in evolution in which two-legged walking and running became the norm, and in which the hands were completely free for uses other than locomotion. Since they were plains animals, the arms were not needed for climbing and moving through treetops. However, as was pointed out previously, the structure of the pelvic girdle indicates that *Australopithecus* was not a very accomplished walker or runner. The revolutionary advance that led to the appearance of *Homo*, the true men, involved the perfection of pelvic girdle and limb bones so as to produce the modern human stride, which makes man one of the best of long-distance walkers and runners over level terrain. In a pursuit lasting hours or days a man, or better a small pack of men, is probably a match for most plains mammals. It has been imagined that this evolutionary advance, by greatly increasing the range of activity and placing a premium on cooperation between roving, scouting, and hunting groups and the stationary body of the tribe, made it increasingly important that communication be effective. Thus, it is imagined, the evolution of language began and accelerated during the epoch of *Homo erectus*, which had at the beginning been furnished with true human capacities for walking and running, and during its quarter-million year reign increased brain capacity and with it language to their modern human levels.

Again, the interrelationships are complex and reversible, since increased brain size would influence toolmaking and social organization as well as language, and natural selection acting on the users of tools and the members of complex societies would favor increased brain size.

Consider the differences between the way a human being—who possesses language rich in symbols—would acquire and organize knowledge about his environment, and the way a nonhuman animal would do it.

A small-brained animal such as an insect has an array of built-in or instinctive responses that enable it to respond to environmental circumstances in ways that maximize its chances for survival. In a sense, these responses represent information stored in the central nervous system, but only in a derived sense. This information is not gained during the life of the individual as a result of interaction with its environment; rather, it has been slowly accumulated during the evolutionary history of the species, in which different behavior patterns have been either discarded or perpetuated by selectional processes. It is, therefore, a record of racial rather than individual experience.

In addition to its instinctive responses, the insect is capable of a relatively limited amount of learning; that is, it is able to accumulate additional information during its lifetime. A hunting wasp, by scouting and cruising in the vicinity of its nest, is able to learn and remember landmarks, and thus can return home quickly from forays after its prey. But in its short lifetime it would not have time, even if it had more elaborate neurological equipment, to learn, for example, the proper choice of prey, or suitable methods of attack. Such necessary responses are instinctive, and are thrown into operation automatically upon presentation of the appropriate stimuli.

The insect is thus essentially an automaton that reacts to a highly restricted set of environmental stimuli in a stereotyped way. It would be a mistake to think that this is necessarily ineffective; some insects have a way of life such that they produce no more offspring on the average than do human beings, so that the individual insect has as much chance as the human infant of reaching maturity. But in general, predominantly instinctive behavior is associated with a high reproductive rate and high mortality. The insect often finds itself in situations where its repertoire of responses is inadequate or irrelevant, and it fails to survive.

The large-brained, subhuman mammal also has a large repertoire of instinctive behavior patterns, but has in addition a well-developed capacity to store information gained from individual experience, to the extent that behavior in some mammals comes to be experience-dominated. During its lifetime the animal quickly enriches its genetic heritage with a store of "mental" information, and comes to know a great deal about its environment. As a result it can deal with a wide array of situations. Such a mammal does not react as an automaton, because it can evaluate stimuli in terms of a rich personal experience, properly rejecting some, that might have led the automaton to disaster, and correlating and using others that might have gone unnoticed and unused by the automaton.

The human being, like his fellow mammals, has a large brain, with the attendant capacity for getting and storing large quantities of information. But because of a set of circumstances that led to the correlated evolution of a large forebrain, of language, and of the kind of dexterity associated with the making and use of tools, his use of this information is of a special kind. His imagery involves verbal symbols, as well as kinesthetic imagery of a richness unmatched elsewhere in the animal world. He not only remembers—he plans for the future. He can daydream interminably, bringing to life on a mental stage a set of images that are set in motion to play their parts as rehearsals to real action. His dreaming extends his awareness over vast distances of individual and communal experience. He is a conscious animal.

Under these conditions, information about the environment takes on a new potential that places man in a different category from other animals. First, information gained from experience can be arranged in new ways, in patterns not yet encountered in nature; and second, communication by speech makes it possible to share experience to an unprecedented degree. There have been, accordingly, three processes involved in the accumulation of in-

25

formation by primitive man: the genetic accumulation of the instinctive background, the individual accumulation of experience, and the social accumulation that is transmitted by cultural devices, especially spoken language.

As we have seen, people have been talking with each other, and daydreaming in the complex languages of a "modern human" level for perhaps a quarter of a million years, back to the skull of Stenheim. Yet our way of life is immeasurably different; and we can lay this difference mainly to the circumstance that what men say and think have come to be different.

But of course the phrase "our way of life" reveals an oversimplification. There are innumerable ways of life existing in present human society. During the past hundred years or so it has seemed that the human race is moving rapidly toward a highly technological, uniform, global society, but this is not a very long time on which to base such a sweeping prophecy; for all we know, it may be some modest cultures of brown people of the backward lands that carry the species through the next phase of history.

We can find living today human societies with tools and weapons simple enough to remind us of the ways of life of *Homo sapiens* of tens or even hundreds of thousands of years ago. Two much-studied examples of such preliterate cultures are the bushmen of the Kalahari of Southeast Africa, and those of the Great Australian deserts and semideserts. The typical citizen of one of these societies can pick up everything he owns and walk off with one hand free. With no help from the civilized world he gleans a living from some of the most barren lands in the world; and without solid and fixed shelter he stays alive in some of the most ferocious climates known.

It probably is a mistake to think that this harsh life was typical of the life of early man. The living bushmen types have been pushed out into the most unpromising and inhospitable environments by peoples with greater material power. Abundant food and mild climate may once have been the lot of much of the human race. But aside from the presumed abnormal harshness of his surroundings, we can probably assume many similarities between the life of, say, the Kalahari bushmen, and that of the first *Homo sapiens*.

It should be pointed out that the bushmen of the Kalahari, as a minimum, possess bows and arrows, and make skillful use of an esoteric and potent arrow poison, which one would guess were not available during many tens of thousands of years of earliest human history. But if we balance against this the scarcity of game in the bushman habitat, the material resources of both early men and bushmen were probably of about equivalent strength in relation to the problems of getting food and shelter presented by the environment.

A most attractive account of the Kalahari bushmen is that of Elizabeth Marshall Thomas, whose *The Harmless People* depicts their life as seen by a member of an American archeological research group that worked in the Kalahari. The material fragility of the society of these "primitive" and small people is well described in her account of the end of a search lasting for several days to find the home of a small group of bushmen:

We drove for several hours and at last we came to a wide plain, grown over heavily with small trees of slender trunks, with a few short branches sprouting leaves, like fence posts. Gai directed us to one of the smaller trees in the center of the plain and told us to stop. He climbed down and looked around over the veld, then bent and picked up a small pipe, a piece of the leg bone of an antelope. He asked us for a match, lit his pipe, and smoked it.

At last we noticed on the other side of the tree two shallow depressions scooped in the sand and lined with grass, like the shallow, scooped nests of shorebirds on the beach—the homes of families, where the people could lie curled up just below the surface of the plain to let the cold night wind which blows across the veld pass over them.

Other than the depressions, except for a small pile of brown, twisted bean shells, no sign would show that people lived there. . . .

We sat in the middle ground between the depressions so we wouldn't risk stepping on or crushing anybody's hidden things, for, without knowing it, a European can in a moment trample through a Bushman's cache, breaking the delicate bone or wooden objects, bending the reed arrows, or crushing eggshell beads.

In this region of scanty vegetation cover and animal life, it might be expected that making a living would be a tense business that took up essentially all of the bushmen's energy and time. But just as the efficiency-expert approach to the life of animals is frustrated by the amount of time that an animal spends doing nothing, or merely playing, so the cost-accountant analysis of the bushman's activities would seem to be not very rewarding, unless one wanted to count the interminable conversations in which the bushmen tie together their past experiences, the hours-long songs they contrive and play on their simple instruments, and the hours they spend dancing as psychically or physiologically necessary activities to prime these peoples for their next food hunt, although the distinction between work and play, between productive and nonproductive activity, is perhaps only a bias brought in by the observer from an industry-dominated society.

The bushman holds in his head the detailed geography of hundreds of square miles. Once when a small party of bushmen and archeologists had been driving for some hours across the trackless veldt, a bushman called a stop, having seen a few broken ostrich shells in the sand. But a conference led to the conclusion that these shells probably were the ones described some time back by a certain individual, and were his property, so they had better leave them there. Individual trees have names, and a bushman will relate who climbed it, who caught what animal in its branches, and who ate what part of the animal. The mind, like the muscles of a healthy individual, demands to be used, and boredom is the most feared of human afflictions.

There are two main circumstances that make possible what we could call science among these preliterate bushmen. First of all is language. By definition science has to be a social phenomenon. It is more than what a single individual can learn about the environment from his own direct experience. His conceptions are shaped by what is communicated to him from innumerable exchanges with other human beings. Communication of intricately complex information and its codification into concepts requires complex language. The second circumstance is the contact that the bushmen have with a wide range of natural materials—animals and plants used for food, and others encountered in the search for food; substances used for tools, weapons, and ornaments; intimate exposure to climate, season, and the natural landscape. The contact is far more vivid, varied, and wide ranging than that experienced by our mythical average modern citizen. Such experience with nature is the most fundamental of the requirements for science.

When the Americans asked a young hunter to describe the parts of a dissected springbok, he was reticent, apparently not wishing to speak of such matters in the presence of women, but Thomas says of the older Ukwane:

The cold night had come, and Ukwane in the frosty grass was shivering, yet he sat for an hour keeping his patience, putting his hand into the cold blood of the springbok to trace veins to their source, prefacing all his answers with positive, qualifying remarks. "I am an old man," he would say, "and I know that the diaphragm separates the heart and lungs from the stomach," or "I am Ukwane, and I know that when the heart is gone the animal cannot live, or a person either, because the heart is that animal's life."

Ukwane knew a great deal. He named every major part, inside and out, of the animal, even naming the major veins and arteries that lead to and from the heart. We were not surprised to find that Bushmen, who prefer to be specific rather than general when dealing with minute things, distinguish more exterior parts of the body than we do. They have names, for example, for the inside of the elbow and the back of the knee. The *leg* of an animal means the hind leg, the front leg is the *arm,* and these are called by the same names as the arms and legs of human beings. Birds, too, fly with their arms and land on their legs, but I could never discover what insects do.

Ukwane went on to explain the various systems of the body, saying in the case of the urogenital system that liquid, which was "the little springboks," ran from the testicles into the kidneys, then down again and out the penis. He stuck to this version, too, even when Bill suggested that it might be otherwise. . . .

Ukwane understood the course of food and water through the digestive system, but said that food and water spread out like sweat to all the body. He did not understand what the lungs did, or that air went into them, or that air went through the trachea. Breathing, said Ukwane, is air going down into the stomach, where it makes belches. Ukwane did not know about the circulation of the blood, believing that the blood ebbs and flows, nor did he recognize pulses in the body except the pulse at the V of the throat, noticeable in people who wear little clothing, which is known as "the place of the heart."

This account is reminiscent of some of Aristotle's descriptions. There seems no reason to doubt that knowledge at Ukwane's level of sophistication existed many tens of thousands of years ago.

The various ways of designating a critical stage at which the human level was reached—walking, speech, or toolmaking—each have some usefulness or validity. There is yet another, that seems to lie more or less unconsciously in the minds of artists who draw a series of portraits of apes, ape men, and man. The reflective, sadder-but-wiser look of the first man is perhaps the result of the artist's recognition that this conscious animal is aware of death.

Some one has said that an animal lives for an eternity. In a death struggle with a victorious enemy, the last moments are filled with the sensations of the battle, and even fading consciousness is itself a sensation. Death is something observed in others, and is a concept only possible in thinking and social man. By inventing a concept of time that is independent of his own existence, man has lost the eternal life of his biological heritage, and this is one of the circumstances that makes him human, and profoundly shapes his endeavors.

[C H A P T E R 3]

The Nature of

Science

MODERN SCIENCE COULD BE DEFINED as generally accepted knowledge about the physical and biological worlds that is organized with respect to the discovery and formulation of general truths. Or it could be defined as the activity that produces and sustains such a body of knowledge. In different periods of history, the activity that in hindsight we call science has different characteristics; in particular, it seems to take on its identity in relation to one or another competing activity that is important at a given time. Thus, in Renaissance times, scientific knowledge, derived from a study of nature, might stand in contrast to the bookish knowledge of the Scholastics. Or science might have partisans antagonistic to the priests who claimed the superiority of revealed knowledge. In another era, science might seem to need defining and defending in relation to technology. A truly historical analysis of science would have to take into account shifting values and viewpoints.

Knowledge cannot be generally accepted as true, and therefore qualify as scientific knowledge, unless statements about it can be set up in such a way that they can be repeatedly proved or disproved. This tends to restrict science to relatively simple phenomena, or to mass phenomena, where averages or probabilities are predicted, rather than individual behavior. It is characteristic of some theories that they have to be restated or qualified each time experimental proof is wanting, as that of the magician who says that spearing a drawing of an antelope insures killing a live one next day, then explains failure by error in some detail of the rite. Or, for example, a theory of extra sensory perception that appeals to the boundless qualification that the subject fails because he is not in the right mood. Protean theories like these lie beyond the realm of science; they forever escape disproof because of built-in protective mechanisms. Science is fundamentally modest: it claims jurisdiction over a relatively limited area of human activity in which propositions can be stated in simple and stable form and tested for falsity in rather simple ways. In practice, of course, there is wide variation in the complexity and testability of scientific theories.

Science is not competent to examine even the most elementary questions of morality or of value judgment, although it is both feared and praised for its ability to provide novel information used to make such judgments.

Differences between scientific knowledge and what Thorstein Veblen calls "pragmatic lore" are discussed in his essay on "The Place of Science in Modern Civilization":

> The pragmatic knowledge of the early days differs scarcely at all in character from that of the maturest phases of culture. Its highest achievements in the direction of systematic formulation consist of didactic exhortations to thrift, prudence, equanimity, and shrewd management—a body of maxims of expedient conduct. In this field there is scarcely a degree of advance from Confucius to Samuel Smiles. Under the guidance of the idle curiosity, on the other hand, there has been a continued advance toward a more and more comprehensive system of knowledge. . . .
>
> The modern scheme of culture comprises a large body of worldly wisdom, as well as of science. This pragmatic lore stands over against science with something of a jealous reserve. . . . They feel the inherent antagonism between themselves and the scientists. . . . The reasoning in these fields turns about questions of personal advantage of one kind or another, and the merits of the claims canvassed in these discussions are decided on grounds of authenticity. Personal claims make up the subject of the inquiry, and these claims are construed and decided in terms of precedent and choice, use, and wont, prescriptive authority, and the like. The higher reaches of generalisation in these pragmatic inquiries are of the nature of deductions from authentic tradition, and the training in this class of reasoning gives discrimination in respect of authenticity and expediency. . . . Of this character was the greater part of the "science" cultivated by the Schoolmen, and large remnants of the same kind of authentic convictions are, of course, still found

among the tenets of the scientists, particularly in the social sciences.

Veblen's "pragmatic lore" concerns knowledge that is useful for survival in relation to the human environment, rather than the natural environment. This kind of knowledge clearly is not a joint human enterprise. Its strategy and tactics depend on one's place in society, and the place one wishes to attain. Its concepts, concerned mostly with force and fraud, are varied and fluid, limited only by the bounds of human gullibility.

Primitive peoples would seem to have a better working knowledge of their natural environment than civilized ones, because they have no social classes supported by others in such a way as to insulate them from nature. So that if we were to say that science is simply usable knowledge about nature, then primitive preliterate societies would be the most scientific of all, since their direct and nearly universal confrontation with nature would be the dominant social activity. In the civilized societies, the farmers, fishermen, and artisans somehow get pushed out of the written record, so that the culture seems to have little to do with scientific matters, and even until rather recent times, there were only a few areas of technology that were considered proper for lettered gentlemen: medicine, warfare, navigation, or architecture, for example.

The practical knowledge of savages could be said not to be science at all on two counts: that it is not organized (that there is no theory) and that the savage has no curiosity about nature that leads him on to new discovery. A more reasonable judgment would seem to be that both traits of science exist in savage society in at least rudimentary form. The existence of language itself guarantees that there will be a degree of organization of knowledge into categories and concepts. Savages draw maps, and use simple memory devices such as notched sticks for recording information. It may be that certain individuals in the community are especially noted for their knowledge of animals and plants, and serve as repositories for information which they have to arrange in some fashion, and thus function as prototypes of the modern scientist.

Anthropologists often comment that the savage shows no drive towards understanding his natural surroundings or learning more about them. It may well be that periods of innovation and inventiveness were few and widely scattered in the quarter of a million years of preliterate human history, and that the chances are that the anthropologist will encounter a society that is essentially stable so far as scientific advance is concerned, except for the changes brought about by impact with civilization. Very likely there were places and times when remarkable men and remarkable circumstances gave to primitive societies something very like the Renaissance spirit of scientific discovery, even though they may have been concerned only with the discovery of a new weapon, or of the plants and animals of a new territory.

It has been said that the savage is so incapable of an objective view of nature that even his so-called practical knowledge has no tinge of science. In his *Magic, Science, and Religion,* the anthropologist Bronislaw Malinowski summarized this view (which opposes his own): "primitive man has no sober moods at all . . . he is hopelessly and completely immersed in a mystical frame of mind." That is, the belief in and practice of magic so thoroughly permeates the primitive mind that objective knowledge is impossible. Malinowski himself thinks otherwise; from his observations on the Melanesians of the Tobriand Islands, he comes to the conclusion that the native is perfectly aware of when he uses rational knowledge, and when he uses magic.

If you were to suggest to a native that he should make his garden mainly by magic and scamp his work, he would simply smile on your simplicity. He knows as well as you do that there are natural conditions and causes, and by his observations he knows also that he is able to control these natural forces by mental and physical effort.

But the native knows also that there are agencies that

> bring ill luck and bad chance, pursue him from beginning till end and thwart all his most strenuous efforts and his best-founded knowledge. To control these influences and these only he employs magic.

Malinowski found the division between magic and scientific technology to be especially clear cut when it came to fishing. In the Trobriand Islands, fishing inside the reef is a safe and certain venture, where by poisoning the water one can easily get a catch. Deep-sea fishing, by contrast, is a dangerous and uncertain affair, subject to storms and the erratic movements of schooling fish. For quiet lagoon fishing, no magic is used; but before putting out to sea, the fishermen use elaborate and extensive ritual magic.

Magic, like science, supposes the individual can control nature by his own and unaided efforts. Both have a materialistic outlook on the universe. Both suppose that all the material forces of nature are interconnected to form a unified whole. A mock slaying of an animal one day is somehow connected with its real slaying on the next. The astrologer, who believes in magic, has the theory that the sun and the planets influence events on earth—not at all an unscientific theory, since from the theory of gravitation it follows that the earth's orbit is determined by the joint effect of all the planets and the sun, and since it is a tenet of biology that the sun provides the energy for all the affairs of life. The difference is that the magician (like the astrologer) greatly oversimplifies the universe, and bypasses the immense diversity of cause and effect that lies between the general and the particular with his own special kind of wishful thinking.

Religion differs from both science and magic in taking for granted that nature is controlled, or at least influenced, by powerful beings that live in a supernatural realm beyond direct human observation. This realm of the supernatural is associated with human life after death, and the concept becomes a most powerful one in all human societies. In primitive societies religion is concerned mostly with the relation of the individual to the crises of birth and maturity and death, but sometimes, where the control of nature is at stake, the savage society admits its impotence in certain matters, and appeals to the gods for help. It may be that primitive religion differs from magic in that it is more generally a social rather than an individual matter. Some anthropologists describe rigid systems of religious beliefs held to tenaciously by every member of the community; others tell of a more happy-go-lucky situation where new ideas on religious observance are quickly adopted, and old ones easily dropped.

Primitive science exists in a form that is almost inseparable from technology, since its theoretical side is extremely rudimentary. The technology itself, with its scientific aura, exists side by side with a well-developed magical practice, which the savage recognizes as something different from rational technology. And finally, in primitive societies there is a body of religious knowledge, administered by the whole society rather than by a custodian class, which with its mythology grades more or less imperceptibly into the more theoretical kinds of scientific explanation.

Thorstein Veblen, in his essay on "The Place of Science in

Modern Civilization," thinks that the theoretical creations of sav-age cultures "are chiefly of the nature of mythology shading off into folklore" and terms this myth-making a "genial spinning of apocryphal yarns." He thinks that it is

a quest of knowledge, perhaps of systematic knowledge, and it is carried on under the incentive of the idle curiosity. In this respect it falls in the same class with the civilized man's science; but it seeks knowledge not in terms of opaque matter-of-fact, but in terms of some sort of spiritual life im-printed to the facts. . . . It is like science in that it has no ulterior motive beyond the idle cravings for a systematic cor-relation of data.

The fact that in primitive societies there are no well-marked classes that skim off wealth from the producers, that individuals tend to be equally rich (or poor), gives to them idyllic quality ever appealing to social reformers and revolutionaries. It proba-bly is true that the most significant change in the human condi-tion is that which took place in the Neolithic revolution, a com-plex and rather drawn out change in the mode of food production which took place (in the cultures concerned with the origin of Western civilization) between about 9000 and 4000 B.C. The re-sult of domesticating plants and animals was that a man could produce more than enough to keep himself alive. The subsequent history of mankind—the history of civilization—has been colored by the question of the distribution of the resulting surplus wealth.

A savage, as an edible animal, is hardly worth the effort it takes to kill him, since he is an uncommonly dangerous creature. But a civilized man is a potential source of wealth, or even an owner of wealth. With this circumstance, human strife becomes more than casual entertainment, and comes to occupy a central position in the historical record, both as warfare and as class conflict. With the development of class structure, many of the intellectual occupations that seem playful in the savage society take on quite a different character. Mythology becomes anything but genial. Some aspects of it are taken over by ruling groups, and rivers of blood are shed over doctrine—myths become official dogma. In the earliest civilized societies, it is the priestly class that assumes responsibility for the myths of most general and theoretical character. Gordon Childe, in his *What Happened in History,* says that "By the beginning of the historical records the Sumerian priests formed corporations as eternal as the gods they served and maintained. . . . Presumably these had already by the Fourth Millennium undertaken the not unprofitable task of administering the god's estates and directing the works on which their surplus wealth was expended."

The transition of savagery into barbarism, and then into civilization, meant little for the development of science as a specialized theoretical associate of technology, this because of the appropriation of the "higher learning" by the priesthood. There are in ancient Sumerian writings some records of astronomical information, and of geometry and arithmetic, but these appear to concern strictly technological matters. For some several millennia after the invention and widespread use of writings, science was to remain almost completely hidden in technology, as it had during savagery. Technology was itself enormously enriched by the new experience with nature and physical forces made necessary by agriculture, by the intensive cultivation of the same irrigated lands year after year, and by the construction of cities.

But along with a rich and varied technology was a highly organized social structure for control of dense populations that had to share limited supplies of water and land and do the work of production and construction in precisely coordinated fashion. In this fixed agricultural society, a class structure was established in which there was no room for the development of a literature of theoretical science.

As is described in the chapter on classical and medieval science, it was in Greece of the first five or six centuries before Christ that science breaks into literature as a kind of writing that is consistently distinct from technology—where the division between "pure" and "applied" science comes to have real meaning —and is of a kind that has nothing to do with theology. Instead of being a fixed agricultural society, Greece was a collection of mercantile states, where the pressures for maintaining written dogma were relaxed. Under these circumstances, a rich literary tradition developed which included literary science. Unlike the priests, the Greek scholars discussed the larger theoretical question of the universe and natural forces in completely materialistic fashion, leaving out the personal dieties served by the priesthood.

As it happened, the highly developed Greek science, with its beautifully distinctive theoretical side, was many centuries ahead of its time, and when science in a form recognizably separate from technology did reappear in the European Renaissance, it differed from Greek science in that it developed in the direction of strengthening its ties with technology. It may be that the later Greek science of the Alexandrian era also was developing in this direction, but if so, the trend was cut short by the larger historical events in the Mediterranean basin—the growth of Roman civilization, and its disappearance into medieval Europe.

It is in Greek times, then, that science of a fully developed kind first appears. Science depended upon the existence of writing (the Greeks had a flexible phonetic alphabet) to attain the stability and richness needed to organize the vast amount of experience that had been accumulated by their predecessors. The potential for science that had been built up by a complex technology, and by the development of Greek literature, was realized with almost explosive suddenness in Greece of the fifth and fourth centuries B.C., and the results still command the admiration of the world.

In the Dark Ages of Europe, science relapsed to the form it had before Greek times—almost completely buried in technology, and rarely expressed in literature. When Greek literary science began to pour into Europe via the Arab world, in the twelfth century, there occurred the strange reaction that came from mixing a highly evolved Christian theology with a similarly sophisticated theoretical science: Scholasticism, which studied books, not nature, and whose main function was to assimilate as much of the Greek writings into theology as possible.

The science of the sixteenth and seventeenth centuries, the time of the true scientific Renaissance, appeared, like the Greek science of a thousand years before, with explosive force. There were three main predisposing factors: a steady development of technology in medieval Europe, the political upheavals associated with the Protestant Reformation, and the debates of Scholasticism, which made certain that when science did revive, it would concern itsef to a considerable extent with theory. These factors gave it the traits that characterize science in its most highly developed form: its concern with technology helped insure that it would constantly be shaped by the test of nature; the emergence of powerful new economic groups fostered actual and figurative voyages of discovery into unknown nature; and the four centuries of study of the literary remains of Greek science gave to the new science an emphasis on the organization of the new knowledge, rather than simple rote recording of facts.

However, the fact that the physical sciences dominated this era gave it a parochial, limited character. There developed a tendency to look to the physical sciences, with their use of mathematics and the experimental method, as models for the other sciences. In fact, some philosophers and scientists admit to the status of true science only those branches of knowledge that are predominantly mathematical in character.

Be that as it may, Darwin, innocent of mathematics, created a revolution in thought with observations on natural history; and thousands of biologists and geologists go their way with, perhaps, the aid of simple arithmetic.

It is an economic fact that the technologies associated with the physical sciences are the fields in which capital investment is most feasible, at least up until the mid-twientieth century, and this historical circumstance largely accounts for the dominance of the physical sciences. The success of the quantitative approach in the physical sciences is related more to their simplicity rather than to the superiority of mathematics as a language in any scientific endeavor.

Instead of the nineteenth-century vision of a unified science, stretching all the way from atoms at one extreme, through living things, man, to society at the other, science of the twentieth century has seen the development of the concept of integrative levels, which divides up the vast range of phenomena into more or less isolated segments, each with its own terminology, methods, and theory. The laws of behavior of atomic nuclei are different from those of atoms. Living things, although composed of atoms, behave in ways that have nothing to do with the science of chemistry. True, it is possible to alter, say, the sexual behavior of a laboratory animal in a predictable way with a hormone of a specified molecular structure, but behavior is not chemistry, and molecular interaction is not animal behavior.

There is a reductionist view which holds that it is always possible—and also desirable—to explain the happenings at one level of integration in terms of the lower level. This is an expression of the belief in the primacy of the physical sciences, since ultimately any level of complexity could be explained in terms of chemistry, which in turn would be explained by physics. The reductionist view could also seem to imply that one can predict the properties of the higher level from those of the lower. It would say that knowing the properties of atoms, one could predict a bacterium. This is an imaginary experiment which can never be put to the test. We already know about bacteria, and have a ready-built terminology to describe them. Given a bacterial structure or process, we can say a good deal about it in terms of chemistry. But if we knew only chemistry, would we deduce the existence of bacteria? It would seem that if we considered all possible atomic interactions we would be led off into limitless complexities, which would give us no useful information that we could seize upon, in the absence of any preconceived ideas. It is the unique evolutionary history of the earth, involving natural selection of competing self-reproducing entities, that produced bacteria. Such processes are foreign to the terminology and outlook of chemistry.

Prediction of individual events (chemistry, is, of course, the prediction of mass events, involving billions of atoms) is notoriously uncertain. Sometimes it is said that the goal of science is absolute prediction of all unique, individual events; but no one really wants this—as Mark Twain pointed out, if it were not for differences of opinion, horse racing would be impossible.

Thus it would seem that it would be a repetition, in a sense, of the error of the outlook of the magician or astrologer, to expect to construct a science of nature based on the physical sciences. The world is more complicated than this, and meaningful questions about life that we put to the physical world for answer have to be based on a sophisticated knowledge of life.

The rather large kernel of truth in the reductionist view is that, once one builds up a terminology and a list of problems by study of the higher level of integration, it is not only informative, but absolutely necessary to refer back to the lower level to understand better the higher level. In the twentieth century an adequate understanding of biology, for example, is impossible without chemistry; but one can understand chemistry quite well without reference to biology. This is perhaps analogous to the relationship between bricks and buildings: the architect has to know a lot about the properties of bricks, but the brickmaker does not have to know anything about architecture.

The evolutionary outlook, which rather quickly permeated all the sciences during the nineteenth century, is related to the integrative level concept in that the levels can be visualized as actual temporal sequences, reached one after another in the physical evolution of the universe, or for biological systems, during organic evolution on the earth. If we say that one cannot initially predict from a lower to a higher level, it would follow that it is essentially impossible to predict the future in an evolutionary situation. The best that can be hoped for is the prediction of a probable result—a high probability for predicting the outcome in the next instant of time, but quickly vanishing to near zero as one goes out into the more distant future.

In cultural evolution, which concerns thinking human beings, prophecy becomes even more difficult. When, on the basis of the dynamics of the existing situation, a convincing prediction is made, this prediction itself is seized upon to become a powerful social force which in turn alters the situation.

It has long been said that the goal of science is final Truth, or complete description and understanding of nature. When the early Renaissance scientists began checking the writings of the ancients against nature, it must have seemed to them that they were making good progress in this direction. One error after another was detected and set right. The ages-long mystery of the operation of the solar system was thoroughly cleared up by Newton and Laplace—complete explanation in terms of simple laws of motion and gravity, except for some seemingly unimportant details, such as the motion of Mercury, near the sun. But as investigations of nature carried students into new areas—electromagnetic fields, distribution of organisms in space and time, radioactivity—science began to take on a new appearance. Each new major discovery opened up a new set of problems. To draw a geometric analogy, the scientists were busily working inside a sphere, tidying up the organization of knowledge already gained, while constantly exploring its periphery, working farther out into the unknown. But if the surface of the sphere is boundary of the unknown, the result of scientific activity is merely to increase its area, and there is nothing in our experience so far to show that we are going to run out of space outside our sphere of knowledge.

Thus, science keeps on finding new truths—not the Truth, but momentary truths, that solve immediate problems. Great theoretical simplifications, like the concept of gravity, that seem at first to provide ultimate answers, eventually dissolve into new complexities, which are in turn resolved by new simplifications.

An always interesting question is that of the relation between science—our knowledge of nature—and nature itself. The historian of science E. Radl, in his *History of Biological Theories* says that "Materialists and idealists alike seem to consider that Nature is identical with our picture of Nature: the former declare that it is Nature which is real, the latter that it is our picture which is real." But in the twentieth century, the conviction has been growing that neither the materialists nor the idealists, defined in this way, are right.

The concept of organic evolution in the last half of the nineteenth century gave man a startling new estimate of his place in the world. With this revelation, there was a new look at the nature of science. This is one of the points taken up by George Gaylord Simpson in his essay on "Biology and the Nature of Science." As he describes the situation, science

is all carried on by human beings, a species of animal. It is in fact a part of animal behavior, and an increasingly important part of the species—specific behavior of *Homo sapiens*. From the functional point of view, it is a means of adapting to the environment. It is now, especially through its operating arm, technology, the principal means of biological adaptation for civilized man. It is an evolutionary specialization that arose from more primitive, pre-scientific means of cultural adaptations, which in turn had arisen from still more primitive, prehuman behavioral adaptation.

If, disregarding its esthetic aspect, we look at science as an adaptive activity which makes it possible for us to get along with and manipulate nature, it becomes clear that our scientific terms and concepts are concerned with things that we do, with operations, and have no meaning beyond this. We say that steel is hard, that marble is soft. The operational meaning of our use of the term hardness is that a steel blade will scratch marble. This is an entirely different matter from whether or not steel is "really" hard. Lightness or heaviness has to do with the way a substance affects a balance. Is it a true description of nature to say that gold has a higher specific gravity than lead? The scientist could say that it is true if equal volumes of the two metals affected a balance in the way predicted. His concepts are "true" if nature gives the expected answer when a question is put to her.

This operational view—that the terms and concepts of science are meaningful only in terms of actual operations carried out in relation to nature—should be carried to its logical conclusion:

that man is himself the ultimate operator, or instrument. Although the universe exists independently of man, his description of that universe does not. If the operator were other than man, the description would differ. The universe has this structure for one operator, that structure for another one. This consequence of the operational view means that we have to use the concept of an unstructured universe to designate ultimate reality—a concept of existence without structure. To put it another way, structure requires the existence of an operator.

Two subsidiary notions have to be mentioned in this connection. First, this operational point of view is not a solipsist view; that is, the universe is not structured uniquely (at least not in significantly different ways) by individual human beings of a given culture. Man is a social animal, and science a social enterprise, so that the "operator" is the human species (or a human society), not an individual.

Also, the operational view is not a completely relativistic one: it does not say that "anything goes." Not all structures produced by the operator as theoretical guides are equally valid. For, although the universe cannot be said to have absolute structure, it does have a quality that could be termed coherence; there are only certain ways of getting desired results out of it, and it always gives the same answer to the same question.

These considerations show again that science can in no way be regarded as the quest for absolute truth. Science grows as human experience with nature grows. It is only if this kind of experience should somehow cease to widen, and if society would turn completely in upon itself, to consider only the relation between human beings, not between man and nature, that scientific knowledge would take on the character of absolute truth.

To the "three ages of science"—preliterate, Greek literate, and

Renaissance—should be added the science of the twentieth century, which is taking on a distinctive character. It can be characterized as "socialized science" in the sense that factory production is social production, whether the factory is privately owned or state owned. The scientific enterprise has grown to such bulk that it is a profession employing hundreds of thousands, and as technology and science tend to fuse in this era, it would seem a reasonable projection that a large percentage of the population will be engaged in what will be called science. Under these conditions, scientists tend to work as members of teams. This makes possible careful and relatively error-free work on projects that have predetermined goals. Not only are techniques developed for specific applications of science, but even for research itself. The crucial question here seems to involve the difference between team work and individual work, the difference between a committee and an individual as the unit of social activity. It would seem that the subordination of the individual would tend to eliminate the somewhat erratic excursions of unique personalities into the unknowns of science, excursions which would usually, but not always, be unproductive. In other words, a source of variability that would occasionally turn up creative novelty would be eliminated.

Just how the socialization of the scientific enterprise will ultimately affect it is of course unpredictable, but among the possibilities to be considered is that professional science can evolve social mechanisms that would tend to insulate it from nature, and in the long run produce a situation more reminiscent of medieval Europe than of the twentieth century.

But history never repeats itself, for we find yet another component of the total environment that has been added during the highly socialized twentieth century. This is the machine, whose ubiquity and complexity has an overwhelming influence on all human activities.

Each scientific age has its characteristic mode of communication—the spoken word, writing, and the printed page. Twentieth-century technology has developed the so-called computer methods of recording and transmitting information which, it is said, will become the dominant mode of communication. It is perhaps significant that computer techniques are ideally designed to transmit information from one machine to another, as in the control of manufacturing processes, or in guidance systems.

It probably cannot be determined who is in charge: man or machine. Both are indissolubly bound in a symbiotic association. It could not, of course, be said that machines are alive; yet one of the criteria of life is reproduction, and machines are everywhere. The existence of an appealing automobile forces society to produce millions more like it, as a virus somehow induces its host cell to produce replicas of the virus. Like all reproducing entities, machines evolve, and pursue a more or less independent evolutionary history with great and gathering momentum. The study of nature becomes in large part the study of machines. Even granting that increasingly intimate participation in the machine–human symbiosis is the next state of man—and the probability for this may be remote—detailed prediction is not possible. The varied, contradictory, and entertaining literature of science fiction is as enlightening as any.

CHAPTER 4

Greek and Arabic Biology

ONE OF THE MOST SIGNIFICANT facts of the history of biology is that there was written in Greece in the fourth century B.C. a text-book of biology that stands isolated in time until the work of Count Buffon in eighteenth-century France. Not that Buffon was another Aristotle; but his *Natural History* is like Aristotle's work in describing a variety of animals in great detail but yet in a broadly philosophical way that related the living world to the rest of the earth and the universe. The isolation of the work of Aristotle results only in part from the imperfection of the written record of ancient times. Greek civilization itself stood for a few centuries as an island, aloof from the priest-dominated agricultural societies that prevailed from the beginnings of civilization in Mesopotamia and Egypt up until the time of the Renaissance revolutions in Europe.

Philosophy began, says Bertrand Russell, in Greece, and as a revolt against religion. It is not possible to draw a line between philosophy and science in the work of the early Greek philosophers, because they were primarily cosmologists, interested in an orderly description of a universe that operated through natural rather than supernatural forces. These philosopher-scientists were members of a fluid, mercantile society in which the power of the priestly caste was relatively limited, and were knowledgable and practical men of affairs who roamed their world as free spirits. It is characteristic of philosophy that it represents the unfettered efforts of the individual to explain the world; and this has always been true also of the more theoretical side of science. It was the Ionian Greeks, to the east, and in contact with the sophisticated civilization of the Persians, who provided these early prototypes of the Renaissance Man.

One of the first of the Ionian natural philosophers was Thales, legendary among the Greeks themselves as the father of philosophy. It is in the writings of one of his disciples, Anaximander, of the sixth century B.C., that a detailed cosmology is developed: the universe arose from a quality-less substance; water, then earth, fire, and air differentiate out; human beings first lived in the water, and were shaped like fishes.

Most of what is known of the written works of the Greeks of the Heroic Age (600–400 B.C.) is deduced from the comments of later Greek writers. The only extensive writings before the time of Socrates that have survived are those of the Greek physician Hippocrates and of the men associated with him in his medical school founded on the island of Cos, just off the southwest coast of what is now Turkey.

The novelty of the Hippocratic school was their rejection of priestcraft in healing disease. Not only did Hippocrates reject the mythology of the temple, he also had to be wary of the scientific cosmologies of the time that set out to explain the universe. There are many levels of complexity between cosmological theory and the functioning of the human body in disease and health. Nothing so infuriates the practitioner of a complex and subtle art such as medicine as the lofty and uncritical application of some universal theory to the details of his technique. Thus, the Greek philosophers thought that the universe was compounded of the four elements earth, air, fire, and water, with the corresponding pairs of qualities of cold and dry, hot and wet, hot and dry, and cold and wet. It logically follows, a philosopher might say, that a human being, who is necessarily compounded of these four elements, has these qualities in a characteristic combination. In disease, the properties become out of balance, so that heat, or cold, or dryness, or moisture have to be supplied to remedy the deficiencies characteristic of the disease.

But nature is not so simple as such a philosophical scientist would have it. One of the Hippocratic writers says: "All who attempt to discuss the art of healing on the basis of a postulate—heat, cold, moisture, dryness, or anything else they fancy—thus narrowing down the causes of disease and death among men to one or two postulates, are not only obviously wrong, but are especially to be blamed because they are wrong in what is an art or technique, and one moreover which all men use at the crises of life, highly honoring the practitioners and craftsmen in this art, if they are good." The physician is faced with the infinitely varied world brought before him by individual patients, human animals affected by many psychological, physiological, and environmental variables. He is constantly faced with the test of practice: he has to do something, and will shortly be confronted with the result. It is a different sort of thing from the philosopher speculating on the heavens: the stars and planets indifferently go their way.

This resistance to cosmological theory does not mean that the Hippocratic rejects all theory; rather, he insists that there is a hierarchy of theory grading all the way down to the technical details of medical practice, and he insists that the theory immediate to medical practice be derived by induction from facts observed in medical practice, not by deduction from the most comprehensive cosmological theories.

Probably the most useful of the general theories of Hippocratic medicine was that the human organism was by nature equipped to combat and overcome disease. The best thing for the physician to do, then, was to let nature take its course, but at the same time to aid nature skillfully at critical junctures so as to guide events toward the recovery of the patient. This aid took the form of imitating nature—such cures as exercise, variations in diet, or straightening out broken bones.

Hippocrates and his followers were not entirely successful in freeing themselves from cosmological theories. The theory of four elements—one that dominated the Western world for more than a thousand years after Asritotle—was so much a part of their intellectual equipment that they could not avoid being deeply influenced by it. So when they came to the necessary task of in some way simplifying and organizing the unwieldy mass of medical observation, they picked as the essential components, or "humors" of the human body, four entities, which have a relationship to the four elements of the pre-Aristotelian philosophers. These four humors are: blood, which contains the warm-moist qualities; yellow bile, the warm-dry qualities; black bile, the cold-dry; phlegm, the cold-moist. Until well past the Middle Ages the theory of the four humors, like the theory of the four elements, dominated scientific thought, and we still have in common speech such terms as phlegmatic, sanguine, melancholic, or bilious temperament.

Early Greek medicine, then, like modern medicine, was not purely an art, but was a science with a well-developed theoretical component. The Hippocratic tradition is medicine, seen in retrospect, is one of a healthy balance between theory and practice; other schools of ancient and medieval times can often be characterized by their emphasis of one or the other. The debt of modern medicine to Hippocrates is not so much to its factual content as to its humane and ethical approach, its rejection of supernatural explanation, and its reliance on a wide and firsthand knowledge of the living human animal.

Among the Hippocratic treatises is one on animals other than man, but this biological work is overshadowed by the towering figure of Aristotle.

Already by the fifth century B.C., the free society that had made Greek Ionia a landmark in the history of human thought had begun to freeze into a new kind of authoritarianism, the kind needed to maintain a society based on slave labor. It is possible to divide all the ancient civilizations of the West into two kinds, sacerdotal and military, the military being distinguished by the fact that the war-making machinery has as its primary function the capture of slaves. Greece of the time of Plato was beginning to be such a society, and the trend was continued and intensified on into Roman times, until the institution of slavery was destroyed by the fall of the empire and transformed into serfdom. The priestly organization continues to exist in such a society, but functions mainly to support the social structure, which is built primarily around military requirements.

In a society like this, the primary concern again becomes the relationship between man and man. This is what is meant when it is said that Socrates and Plato were philosophers who made "man the proper study of mankind." These two are main figures in the making of the modern mind: writers speak of the Socratic revolution in thought, and the philosopher Whitehead has said that European philosophy is essentially a series of footnotes to Plato.

To the scientist, it would seem that the so-called Socratic revolution would not have been as profound as that brought about by the earlier Ionian philosophers. In fact, it has all the marks of a counterrevolution, representing a reversion in many ways to a pre-Ionian level.

The universe, including human society, is for the Socratics (better, the Platonists, since they have contributed a bulky written record) a static affair that is the expression of eternal ideas in the mind of a creator. They taught immortality of the human soul, and that this soul was not a part of nature, but of the eternal celestial realm. The crudities of the earlier theologies are cleaned up, with the result that Platonism is essentially theology served up in antiseptic form as philosophy. In the words of the ancient historian Plutarch, Plato " made natural laws subordinate to the authority of divine principles." And just as theology has a practical political component, so Platonism is by and large a theoretical justification for a slave society. However, Plato was a philosopher rather than a theologian because he and his work were ostensibly not associated with a definite ruling group.

The Platonic school, continuing as the Academy, kept alive this antiscientific philosophy, and in Alexandria as well as later in medieval times contributed to the formulation of the Christian theology. It is interesting that the Platonists placed great emphasis on the study of mathematics, a language of incomparably great importance in the development of science. But where the

Platonist would call mathematics the language of nature or, more specifically, the language of a Creator that is manifested in the design of nature, the materialist would be inclined to call it a purely human language, one adapted for use in describing nature.

Aristotle, a pupil of Plato, began his career with the Academy, but broke away from it to found his own school, the Lyceum. In his intellectual development he steadily left behind the Platonic tradition. However, his earlier works particularly those dealing with the physical sciences, are dominated by the idealistic bias of his mentor; it is largely his writings on physics that gave Aristotle a bad name among scientists of more recent times, a reputation that has been reversed only within the past hundred years or so, when the true stature of Aristotle as a biologist has finally been recognized.

Aristotle was a pupil in the Academy for twenty years, not leaving it until after the death of Plato. Besides a growing disagreement with Platonic views in general, Aristotle seems to have become disillusioned with mathematics as a tool for describing the living world, which was more and more absorbing his interests. As Benjamin Farrington put it: "Fleeing from Athens and mathematics, Aristotle took refuge in Ionia and natural history."

The surviving biological writings of Aristotle make, in English translation, two average-sized volumes. The sections, or books, are usually known by their Latin titles:

1. *De Generatione Animalium.* (Reproduction.)
2. *De Motu Animalium.* (The motion of animals.) Here Aristotle takes up the "common ground" of animal movement, where he relates the topic to his theoretical physics.
3. *De Incessu Animalium.* (The locomotion of animals.) A detailed

and sophisticated discussion of how animals walk, fly, swim, etc.

4. *De Partibus Animalium.* (The parts of animals.) The structure of animals, including man, discussed from a functional point of view.

5. *De Plantis.* (Plants.)

6. *Historia Animalium.* (A natural history of animals.) A self-contained textbook of zoology that repeats many of the topics of the other books and also deals with other topics such as animal psychology and ecology. Emphasized discussion of a large number of species of animals.

Modern authorities in general agree that these books are lecture notes prepared by Aristotle for use in teaching. If they could be edited and reorganized, with the unimportant book on plants omitted, they would make a substantial zoology textbook of the general type used in modern university courses. The section on "motion" would correspond roughly to the physics and chemistry that are found in the introductory sections of most textbooks. Chapters on such functional topics as digestion, locomotion, or respiration could be pulled out of Aristotle's text. Finally, an extensive review of the animal kingdom, group by group and species by species, could be so organized. The resulting textbook would be very rich in factual detail. However, it would differ most from many modern texts in that there is a powerful and consistent drive to place facts explicitly in a theoretical framework of some kind, and it is this tendency, carried to an extreme, that makes some of Aristotle's writing ludicrous to modern eyes. Thus, in *De Partibus Animalium:*

> As for the insects that have a sting behind, this weapon is given them because they are of a fierce disposition. In some of them the sting is lodged inside the body, in bees, for ex-

58

ample, and wasps. For these insects are made for flight, and were their sting external and of delicate make it would soon get spoiled; and if, on the other hand, it were of thicker build, as in scorpions, its weight would be an incumbrance. As for scorpions that live on the ground and have a tail, their sting must be set upon this, as otherwise it would be of no use as a weapon. Dipterous insects never have a posterior sting. For the very reason of their being dipterous is that they are small and weak, and therefore require no more than two feathers to support their light weight; and the same reason which reduces their feathers to two causes their sting to be in front; for their strength is not sufficient to allow them to strike efficiently with the hinder part of their body. Polypterous insects, on the other hand, are of greater bulk —indeed it is this which causes them to have so many feathers; and their greater size makes them stronger in their hinder parts. The sting of such insects is therefore placed behind. Now it is better, when possible, that one and the same instrument shall not be made to serve several dissimiliar uses; but that there shall be one organ to serve as a weapon, which can then be of spongy texture and fit to absorb nutriment. Whenever, therefore, nature is able to provide two separate instruments for two separate uses, without the one hampering the other, she does so, instead of acting like a coppersmith who for cheapness makes a spit and lampholder in one. It is only when this is impossible that she uses one organ for several functions.

At the same time, it should be pointed out that there is a current trend even in textbook writing to present facts only in a theoretical framework, to about the same extent as this passage from Aristotle. In this context, Aristotle looks odd because of changing styles in theory, and he would not seem out-of-date had he confined himself to simple description. Thus, the defensive or offensive sting of bees and wasps is regarded as a modified ovipositor, which always occurs in the abdomen. Aristotle's "sting" of the Diptera is not a sting in the modern conception, but is a structure used for feeding, and if it causes pain to the victim, this is an unavoidable byproduct of its use, presumably even of disadvantage to the user.

Sometimes Aristotle is unreadable to any but the most determined student of the history of ideas. For example, in *De Motu Animalium*:

> Now whether the soul is moved or not, and how it is moved if it be moved, has been stated before in our treatise concerning it. And since all inorganic things are moved by some other thing—and the manner of the movement of the first and eternally moved, and how the first mover moves it, has been determined before in our *Metaphysics,* it remains to inquire how the soul moves the body, and what is the origin of movement in a living creature. For, if we except the movement of the universe, things with life are the causes of the movement of all else, that is of all that are not moved by one another by mutual impact. And so all their motions have a term or limit, inasmuch as the movements of things with life have such. For all living things both move and are moved with some object, so that this is the term of all their movement, the end, that is, in view. Now we see that the living creature is moved and intellect, imagination, purpose, wish, and appetite. And all these are reducible to mind and desire. For both imagination and sensation are on common ground with mind, since all three are faculties of judgment though differing according to distinctions stated elsewhere.

Another difference between Aristotle's text and a modern one is the larger amount of information, both theoretical and anecdotal, on sex, not only in the book on reproduction, but throughout the *Historia Animalium*. This in part is in keeping with the general folklore flavor of much of the writing, but it also is a natural consequence of Aristotle's argument that "The life of animals, then, may be divided into two acts—procreation and feeding; for on those two acts all their interests and life concentrate. Their food depends chiefly on the substance of which they are severally constituted; for the source of their growth in all cases will be this substance. And whatsoever is in conformity with nature is pleasant, and all animals pursue pleasure in keeping with their nature."

Leaving out the philosophic discussions, which, to borrow a phrase from the classicist Frederick Woodbridge, seem to be written in some sort of literary algebra, the two volumes of Aristotle's biological writings make fascinating reading. The amount of information (and entertaining misinformation) on lives, loves, and structures of animals is astonishing. Some 500 species of animals appear on these pages, many only in passing; but others are described at length. Some of the accounts indicate careful study of the animal by Aristotle, others are, as Aristotle himself sometimes says, taken from the tales of herdsmen or fishermen, or perhaps from the writings of other naturalists.

Much of the writing in the *Historia* is light and informative:

In Libya, according to all accounts, the length of the serpents is something appalling; sailors spin a yarn to the effect that some crews once put ashore and saw the bones of a number of oxen, and that they were sure that the oxen had been devoured by serpents, for just as they were putting out to sea, serpents came chasing their galleys at full speed and overturned one galley and set upon the crew. Again, lions are more numerous in Libya, and in that district of Europe that lies between the Achelous and the Nessus; the leopard is more abundant in Asia Minor, and is not found in Europe at all. As a general rule, wild animals are at their wildest in Asia, at their boldest in Europe, and most diverse in form in Libya; in fact, there is an old saying, "Always something fresh in Libya."

Or:

The crake is quarrelsome, clever at making a living, but in other ways an unlucky bird. The bird called sitta is quarrelsome, but clever and tidy, makes its living with ease, and for its knowingness is regarded as uncanny; it has a numerous brood, of which it is fond, and lives by pecking the bark of trees. The aegolius-owl flies by night, is seldom seen by day; like others we have mentioned, it lives on cliffs or in caverns; it feeds on two kinds of food; it has a strong hold on life and is full of resource. The tree-creeper is a little bird, of fearless disposition; it lives among trees, feeds on caterpillars, makes a living with ease, and has a loud clear note. The acanthis finds its food with difficulty; its plumage is poor, but its note is musical.

Aristotle discusses the problem of classifying organisms in an oblique and elliptic fashion that suggests he wrote more on it elsewhere. He did understand that there were natural groups of animals that would be broken up if one tried to classify animals on the basis of single characters. For example, to classify animals as to whether they were terrestrial or aquatic would put the dolphins with the fishes instead of with the air-breathing mammals, where they really belonged. However, there is no evidence that he ever constructed a systematic classification in the manner of Linnaeus, in the eighteenth century.

Aristotle is at his scientific best in describing marine animals, and when Cuvier, in the nineteenth century, came to describe the invertebrates of the French seacoast, he found that Aristotle knew more about these animals than anyone else who had ever written.

The impression one gets from the lecture notes is that Aristotle was an arrogant know-it-all. There is no feeling for science as a developing process, with the unknown always ahead. There seems to be no drive toward discovery. The body of knowledge the notes summarize seems finished and self-sufficient. However, this single kind of writing is a rather treacherous basis for such a sweeping judgment as this. Perhaps these considerations are too self-evident to be put in lecture notes—they are to come out in ordinary spontaneous discourse with the students. However that may be, it was the authoritarian, dogmatic interpretation of Aristotle's writing that was to be paramount when they were recovered in Europe a thousand years after the decline of Greece.

Yet, Aristotle did know everything; he was in his day a one-man university. Woodbridge writes of him: "Aristotle happens to be a man who could analyze space, time, and infinity in a rather masterful way, who knew more about animals than his successors knew for centuries, who collected the constitutions of Greek cities; who wrote on politics and ethics, and who wrote a book on poetry which critics are not yet tired of studying." Aristotle could only have lived this way in the days when the world was young.

Two notable writers headed in succession the Lyceum after Aristotle left Athens. These were Theophrastus, the botanist, and Strato, a physicist who flourished about 280 B.C.

Theophrastus, although he had a solid scientific interest in

plants, has been termed a popularizer of science. He wrote volu-
minously on a variety of subjects, but is best known as the author
of two of the oldest treatises on plants that have survived to our
time. Like the biological writings of Aristotle (who was concerned mostly with animals), those of Theophrastus on plants
had a good deal of sound and interesting factual content, as well
as an impressive organization of the subject.

The Lyceum was equipped with a good botanical garden, to
which Theophrastus evidently devoted a good deal of time and
affection. He wrote of plants, not from the standpoint of their use
in agriculture or medicine, but simply as plants, paying attention to such things as growth, development, and morphology. For
this reason—his emphasis on pure rather than applied science—
he is sometimes called the father of botany.

Strato, who was brought from Egypt to head up the Lyceum,
was a physicist, and is credited with developing the experimental
method in physics to a rather high degree. In writings apparently
based on his work there are descriptions of methods used in discovering and further demonstrating the corpuscular nature of
air, and that in the absence of air there is a vacuum.

By the time of Strato, the center of scientific activity had
shifted from Athens to Alexandria, the newly founded city in
Egypt. Under the early Ptolemies, there was established what
corresponded to a modern university—the Museum of Alexandria, equipped with a library (by far the largest at the time), ob-
servatories, and experimental laboratories. The Alexandrian Museum was the successor to the Lyceum, continuing a scientific tradition (at least until the beginning of the Christian era) instead
of the metaphysical tradition of the Academy founded by Plato.

One of the functions of the Museum was purely that of scholarship, of reviewing and making critical comment on what had al-

ready been made known during the long and illustrious Greek past, an activity that included all the literary arts as well as science. There also was experimentation and observation of a rather sophisticated kind in physics, physiology, and some other fields. The scientific treatises—the Alexandrian period has been called the Age of Textbooks—that were produced by the Museum tended to become specialized and detailed. The writer did not try to compass the whole universe of knowledge as had Aristotle and Theophrastus.

The mechanical sciences appear to have been concerned to some extent with such practical problems as pumping water and keeping time, but were in the main concerned with warfare—the construction of defenses, and of means to overcome them. An interesting sidelight on these sciences was their wide use in producing miracles for use in the temples. Magnets, steam engines, and mechanical toys were used on behalf of maintaining the state religion; enough mechanical power was already produced by slaves.

Some of the works of Euclid, whose teacher probably was a pupil of Plato, and who was one of the first eminent scholars at the Museum, have been used as schoolbooks, little changed, into the nineteenth century. Euclid's *Elements of Geometry* treats of number theory and other fundamental mathematical questions as well as geometry.

The astronomer Aristarchus was at this time attempting to determine the relative distances and sizes of the moon and sun, and it was only an error in measuring a critical angle that put his results off. Unlike most other astronomers before him, and after him until the time of Copernicus, he thought that the relatively huge sun must stay fixed, and that the earth must move about it. Archimedes, a Greek Sicilian who visited Alexandria, and was a younger contemporary of Aristarchus, made the fundamental mathematics analysis of static mechanics, just as Galileo 1,500 years later founded dynamic mechanics.

Against this impressive background of achievement in the physical sciences, that of the biological sciences is disappointing, especially in view of the promising beginning made by Aristotle and Theophrastus. Instead of branching out into a study of the entire plant and animal world, so far as is now known attention was limited mostly to human anatomy and plants of medicinal importance. With Herophilus (300 B.C.) the study of human anatomy became highly developed, and details of human structure were compared with that of other animals. Curious mistakes were made, apparently usually under the influence of fixed notions regarding function.

It was thought, for example, that the arteries carried air, not blood, and the common observation that blood spurted from a cut artery of a living mammal was explained as resulting from the air rushing out, producing a vacuum which pulled blood in from the veins by way of the capillaries. Nerves were supposed to be hollow; this might have been deduced from the observation that the largest nerve, the spinal cord, is hollow, but also probably in part from the idea that the nervous impulse was carried by a fluid that flowed the length of the nerves. Erasistratus, a contemporary Alexandrian, must have carried out rather sophisticated experiments in animal physiology, since he was able to identify sensory and motor roots of the spinal nerves, a feat not duplicated until the nineteenth century.

Although Alexandrian science after the Roman conquest in the first century never achieved the originality and brilliance of the early days of the Museum, still its record is impressive. In the first century B.C. an important innovation in botany was made by Crataeus, who illustrated a text on medicinal plants with highly naturalistic drawings of a quality not surpassed until the time of the artists of the Renaissance.

One of the most influential figures in the medicinal botany of antiquity was Dioscorides, also of the first century. He improved the descriptions of the plants that yielded drugs, and some copies of his work have been illustrated, in the manner of Crataeus. As an army surgeon, he traveled widely in the Mediterranean area, and used the opportunity to make careful observations on a large number of plants (he describes some 600 medicinal and edible plants in all, a number greater than that of his predecessors) and exhorts his readers to become familiar with the plants in nature, in all stages of growth, as he claims he did himself. Upon the rebirth of scientific inquiry in Europe during the Renaissance, the first botanies were mainly commentaries upon Dioscorides, and scholars tried, with unhappy results, to match up their northern European plants with the warmth- and drought-loving plants described a thousand years before.

Although original scientific activity continued to ebb away during the first two centuries of the Christian era at Alexandria, ancient science reached a sort of high-water mark—if by this we mean creative synthesis of a field of science by single individuals —as represented by two men of the second century A.D., Ptolemy, the astronomer and geographer, and the physician Galen.

Ptolemy's famous *Almagest* is essentially a mathematical treatment of astronomy, mostly devoted to an analysis of the motions of the planets. The work is mainly a compilation, based on the researches of such men as Hipparchus. It follows the well-worn path beaten by the adherants of the earth-centered theory of the structure of the universe, which is part of the reason for the complexity of the mathematics, since the routes taken by the planets, if the earth is assumed to be fixed, fall into an extraordinary assortment of looping orbits. Ptolemy was not merely a compiler;

he had a profound understanding of mathematical astronomy, and made original observations himself. His organization of the subject was superb, and one would have expected that it would form the basis for subsequent Roman textbook science. This, however, did not happen. The work of Ptolemy survived only in the Arabic world, not to become absorbed in Latin culture until the eleventh and twelfth centuries.

Galen's work had the same history. Although his medical writings were by far the best available in antiquity, they were by-passed in the assimilation of Greek writing by the Romans, and like the *Almagest,* were kept alive by the Arabs. By the time when Galen and Ptolemy were writing, there was already a Greek handbook literature, written largely by nonscientists, which had summarized the sciences and philosophy in a form well suited to the tastes of the Romans. When the great Roman encyclopedists such as Varro and Pliny summarized all of knowledge in their massive Latin works, they were able to draw on these handbooks, or more usually, second or third generation handbooks which had themselves been drawn from compilations that were often uncritical hack performances.

Like Ptolemy, Galen was in large part a compiler, drawing his information on human anatomy mainly from descriptions based on detailed dissections, made by such earlier Greek Alexandrians as Herophilus and Erasistratus, and their followers. It is said that by Galen's time the dissection of human bodies was no longer permitted; at any rate, Galen's own observations were based mostly on dissections of the so-called Barbary ape, not a true ape (the true apes are closely related to man), but one of the tailed monkeys. Galen had, however, rich observational experience as a practitioner of medicine, so that, like Ptolemy, he was exceptionally well fitted to write a great synthesis.

Another parallel with Ptolemy is found in the fact that his basic theories as to the physiological functioning of the human body, although consistent with his observations, and logically coherent, turned out to be of little or no use when applied to the new observations of later times, and one of the dramatic events of Renaissance science was the overthrow of Galenic authority. Exactly the same fate befell Ptolemy's geocentric cosmology, which accounted for observed phenomena and was consistent with most of what was known at the time. The overthrow of this theory by Copernicus and Galileo, dependent in large part on crucial new observations by the latter, represented one of the great revolutions is the history of human thought.

Alexandria was a truly cosmopolitan city, made up of about equal numbers of Greeks, Jews, and Egyptians. Here the Old Testament was translated into Greek, and much of Christian doctrine was hammered out in the interaction of Greek and Jewish thought. Under the Romans, the Jews were massacred in the second century; in the third century, all male citizens of the city were ordered massacred by a Roman emperor. The main part of the Alexandrian library, by far the greatest in the world, was destroyed in the third century, and in the fourth, the Christian emperor Theodosius ordered the annex of the library, housed in the pagan temple of Serapis, to be destroyed. So that when the Arabs captured the city in the seventh century, there was not much left of the great library, which apparently once had in it most of the works of antiquity, and which had been a main operational base for scholarship for hundreds of years. But before this time, many of the books had been recopied, and sent out to other centers of learning, especially in the Near East, and it is to this that we owe the survival of the fragments of Greek science known to us.

Even though the Arabic world did not fall heir to the Alexandrian library, it was nevertheless able to absorb gradually a good part of Greek science through the scattered copies disseminated from Alexandria.

The explosive spread of Islam in the seventh and eighth centuries, as far as the Pyrenees and India, brought the Arabs into contact with many different cultures, many of them far more sophisticated than their own. Among these was the Byzantine culture. In the hacking slaughter that coursed back and forth across the Mediterranean world during antiquity and medieval times, the Byzantine empire fluctuated violently in size, from a small area around Constantinople to a region encompassing most of the Mediterranean world. But throughout it remained a comparative haven for scholarly Greek writings, probably for the most part coming by way of Alexandria. Many of these were translated into Syriac, which replaced Greek as the most important language in the empire. It was from the Syriac sources that much of the absorption of Greek culture by the Moslem world took place. But by the ninth century Moslem rulers were maintaining centers of learning from which they sent out scholars to ransack the Moslem empire for Greek manuscripts, to be translated into Arabic; in Baghdad, Aristotle was first rendered into this language from the Greek. From India came important innovations in mathematics, and from Persia, many of the techniques of alchemy.

In the Moslem world, until the twelfth century, science was not merely being kept alive by the dedicated labors of a few in translating, copying, and recopying the ancient Greek sources. Rather, the quality and vigor of the written record shows that the Arabic culture was continually widening its experience with nature, and assimilating at least some of this experience into the codified record of science.

In physics, particularly in optics, the work was far in advance of anything the Greeks had done. Arabic algebra and arithmetic were equivalent in excellence to Greek geometry, although apparently they were borrowed from India, the Arabs being proficient mainly in applying these mathematical techniques to astronomy and physics. Originality and vigor were not as great as in the Heroic Age of the Greeks—but then it is possible to separate science from the supernatural only once. All in all, the picture we get of Arabic science is one of a healthy enterprise, nourished by continuing contact with nature, and expressed in a matter-of-fact, truly scientific literature. It was acceptable to the learned and scholarly world of the times because of the essentially tolerant attitude of the Moslems toward other cultures, an attitude not duplicated in Europe during this period. It was not until the twelfth century that religious dogmatism began to erode Moslem science.

Just as in the Alexandrian period, Arabic biology did not go much beyond the confines of practical medicine. More than three hundred authors in Arabic medicine are known. Rhazes, of the tenth century, apparently wrote in greater volume even than Galen, and the quality seems to have been nearly as good. The writings of Avicenna (eleventh century) were better preserved, and although marked with little originality, they became very influential in medieval Europe, even overshadowing Galen. Anatomy and physiology probably declined somewhat in the Arabic era, but even this indicates much activity and keen observation in medicine, since it takes a good deal of running even to stay in the same place in science, and without continued observation and experimentation, the decline is catastrophic.

The main contribution of Arabic medicine was in the preparation and use of drugs. It is said that the outlines of modern pharmacology were established by the Arabs. This advance was in large part made possible by importation of new drugs from the East. Also, it probably was supported by the continuing additions to chemical technique that came from the growing art of alchemy. Evidently thousands of experimenters were observing and recording the effects of heat energy poured into the most improbable mixtures of ores, metals, and organic substances, in the process laying the technical foundations for modern chemistry.

$$\left[\,\text{C H A P T E R }\, 5\,\right]$$

Roman and Medieval Science

ROMAN SCIENCE MAY BE CHARACTERIZED in this way: it represents a smooth transition from Greek science to the Dark Ages of medieval Europe.

Roman civilization produced great quantities of first-class literature, among them works like Pliny's *Natural History* and Lucretius' *Nature of Things*, which must be mentioned in any account of the history of science. But it must be stated that when these works were written, science was dead in Rome. They were written by intelligent, cultured men who were accomplished scholars, widely read in Greek literature. They observed nature with keen eyes, and although their writings were in the main based on Greek science, they were more than compilations, for facts were put in fresh contexts, and ideas were illustrated with original observations. All the same, the original observations of these writers were not well enough informed or sustained enough to qualify as science. These men were too busy to be scientists of the caliber of those in the Alexandrian Museum, some of whom were contemporaries of these Romans. They were primarily Roman citizens, active in affairs of state.

After the first century B.C., European science had two languages, Greek and Latin. In Alexandria, Greek science was to continue to develop, until the time of Galen and Ptolemy at least, and to begin to divide into specialties in a way that has characterized growing science ever since. Latin, on the other hand, was destined at this time to serve merely as the vehicle for the adaptation of Greek science to Roman needs. And the significant thing is that Roman needs did not at all include the further development of science—the disinterested pursuit of new knowledge about the world, built upon the ingenious, time-consuming, dedicated investigations of nature that had become so noteworthy in Greek culture.

So far as we know, the impressive Roman technology, the feats of engineering and the war machines, resulted in no new advances in science. Greek mathematics was far more luxuriant than was needed for architecture. There were hospitals and arrangements for medical care; but the doctors had no schooling in dissection, for example, nor did they feel the need for investigations of the workings of the body that went beyond what had already been learned by the Greeks.

Once the degree of specialization in science had been reached that characterized Alexandrian Museum science, a productive scientist had to be uncommonly devoted to his craft, and that often to a craft without visible connection with the practical requirements of social life. The question is perhaps not so much why should science have been allowed to lapse, but why should it be expected to continue to develop in the ancient world. The price of science was by now a high one.

To the Roman mind the devoted mathematician, the devoted scientist, was not a man to be emulated, but was rather an aberration to be pitied. The whole man was one active in the affairs of the empire, or if merely an educator, was one who prepared the young for the social, technological, or military requirements of the society, preserving tradition rather than producing innovation.

It would seem that a continually expanding technological base, social conditions that would allow free flow of people and ideas between technology and academic science, and a situation in which theological authority is significantly weakened, would all have been required for healthy and continued growth of science above the level reached in the Alexandrian period.

With a continually expanding technological base, the leisure that is necessary for the development of pure science can be achieved. And this leisure must be relatively abundant, for societies of even this time have many other demands upon leisure. So that in classical times, science was probably at best a highly marginal activity, a weak flame extinguished by the slightest vagaries of the social climate, and one that was not to catch and spread to a steady fire until the time of the Renaissance, when social conditions had evolved—even through the Dark Ages—to provide an overwhelmingly favorable environment.

Also with an expanding technological base, experience with nature is widened to new areas of contact. Only then does science become a dynamic, developing activity, rather than static review and preservation of what is already known.

The technological base, at a superficial level, of the Roman empire was a military one, in which armed force was used to obtain slaves and tribute. At the deeper level, it was an agricultural society in which the basic production was carried out by techniques that may have already been centuries old. Some of the classic Roman writings, such as Virgil's *Re Rustica,* are on agriculture, and show a surprising degree of sophistication in such techniques as grafting, but likely this is surprising only because of our ignorance of the state of agricultural technology before Roman times. At any rate, these writings have the flavor of summaries of existing knowledge, rather than accounts of investigation in progress.

Roman weaponry does not appear to involve any fundamentally new techniques in metalcraft or mechanics. That is, the Iron Age was already well under way by the time of the height of the Roman empire—or at least no new experiences with nature were acquired that would stir the imagination of a potential creative scientist. So far as the interchange of ideas and personnel between technology and science is concerned, it must be assumed that the slavery that provided the bulk of manual laborers made for a nearly impassable barrier between the educated classes and the kind of direct experience with nature that is involved in the production of food, weapons, and other economic necessities. True, there were the gentlemen farmers; and medicine and architecture were for various reasons given the status of professions. But in Roman society in general the wall between technology and the upper classes was a formidable one.

In neither pagan nor Christian Rome was society free of powerful and unremitting theological influence. Although pagan religion was subordinated to the requirements of a military state, it was recognized that theology provided extremely effective instruments of statecraft. Its use was flexible rather than dogmatic (rulers regularly got themselves and their favorites deified), but the pervasiveness of this rather benign religious outlook was inimical to the development of science. With the downfall of Christian Rome, the Church became the dominant political force in Europe, developing psychological methods of control that did not encourage rational study of nature among the literate classes, and creating a view of the human animal that led G. Rattray Taylor, in his *Sex in History,* to characterize medieval Europe as one vast insane asylum.

It would seem that none of the major social requirements for healthy scientific activity were present in the Roman empire, nor did they appear in the Dark Ages. In the following review of the literary figures of what is called Roman "science," we will be tracing the progressive decline of written science in Europe.

The earliest of the Latin encyclopedists was Cato the Elder (234–139 B.C.), but he is not representative of the line of writers who come later, since he fought a delaying action against the overwhelming tide of Greek scholarly influence. His writings on agriculture were chiefly how-to-do-it books, and he categorically denied the worthwhileness of any sort of theoretical science.

Although scarcely any of the writings of Varro (about 116–27 B.C.) have survived, it is evident from the work of others that he founded the line of Roman encyclopedists whose books were to dominate the classical world and the Dark Ages. He was apparently by far the most erudite of the Latins who wrote on science, and had read widely in the Greek classics. The Greek encyclopedist he drew from most heavily was a somewhat older contemporary, Posidonius of Rhodes. Posidonius' scientific strength lay in geography, but he was also an influential Stoic philosopher, and founded an important school. Because of his relationship to Varro, he can be said of all the Greeks to have had the dominant influence in determining the course of Roman literary science. Varro's work on agriculture, his only surviving scientific writing, is in three books, written as dialogues. At the age of seventy he had been commissioned by Julius Caesar to assemble a great library, but Caesar was killed shortly after, and the project was dropped. He wrote the *Re Rustica* in his eighties. It shows a profound knowledge of Aristotle and Theophrastus, but apparently this work, in places brightly and interestingly written, has no original observations.

Only one work of Pliny (23–79 A.D.) has survived, but this is the massive *Natural History,* of thirty-seven books, which was the most widely read reference book is Europe for over a thousand years. It is nearly all a compilation, usually from sources less than secondary, and represents a decline in scholarship from the work of Varro. But this disorderly collection of fact and fancy, written with the conviction that everything on the earth was placed there for the convenience of man, was eminently suited to the taste of the time, and to medieval tastes as well.

Two Roman writers on scientific subjects who were in a category entirely different from these encyclopedists were Lucretius (96?–53 B.C.), and Virgil (70–19 B.C.), whose superb didactic poems are among the finest literature of all time. Both, as poets imparting knowledge of nature, had precedents (Empedocles and Hesiod) in ancient Greek writing, dating as far back as the eighth century B.C. Lucretius is said to have been at a sort of turning point in the development of Roman philosophical writing. His preoccupation with nature, and sympathy with the outlook of the Greeks of the Heroic Age contrasts with the characteristic Roman Stoic–Platonic emphasis on man, and the importance of being a good citizen. Lucretius turned out to be on the losing side, and stands more or less isolated in the history of Roman thought. The turn away from Epicureanism, with its thoroughly materialistic view of nature, is one of the most diagnostic of the whole complex of events that led to the characteristically religious European societies of Roman and medieval times, and is intimately associated with the decline and virtual disappearance of science.

Most influential of the Roman encyclopedists was one who wrote at the end of the long period of decline of Roman "scientific writings," in the century when the empire was being overrun by the barbarians. This is Martianus Capella, lawyer in Carthage, who wrote just after the time that Rome had fallen to Alaric. His *Marriage of Philology and Mercury* is an encyclopedic treatment of the "seven liberal arts," which at that time were taken to comprehend all human knowledge. It is modeled on Varro's *Nine Books of Disciplines*, a distinctly superior work (judging from others who borrowed from it) which has not survived. Two of Varro's disciplines, medicine and architecture, were discarded, leaving a group of three subjects dealing with literary style—grammar, dialectics, and rhetoric—as the "rhetorical trivium," and four other subjects—geometry, arithmetic, astronomy, and music—as the "mathematical quadrivium." In this particular encyclopedia, musical harmony was not treated in the usual mathematical fashion.

Capello's handbook of "all existing knowledge" was a bizarre, verbose, and garbled condensation of knowledge that had been current for more than 500 years. The subject matter was tied into an elaborate, but to the modern eyes grotesquely inappropriate, allegory, and the writing was a mixture of prose and poetry. This book had a very high reputation during the Middle Ages, and its author is credited with making the trivium and quadrivium the foundation of medieval education.

The earlier of the Latin writings on science represented fairly competent and sometimes remarkably well-composed summaries, considering that they covered such a wide range of knowledge. It is tempting to blame these writings themselves for the decline of science in the Roman world—to say that they were so easy to assimilate, so attractively written, that handbook science came to substitute for legitimate writing, such as that, for example, of Ptolemy or Galen.

However, handbook writing would seem to have a proper place in a complex society in which scientific activity was going on, as a kind of transmission belt from scientists to the lay public, or even between active scientists in different specialties. What is significant is that no segment of the scholarly world saw fit to continue the kind of original study of nature that is found in classical Greece. It would seem that this kind of activity would even have benefited from a flourishing handbook science, as it does in modern societies. Handbook science itself can not be given as a cause for the disappearance of science in the Roman world. The dominance of the handbook is a symptom, rather than a cause, of the medieval syndrome. Handbook science was a survival of a part of broad Greek science which persisted on its literary and educational merits in the Roman societies. And as time went on, those being educated were more and more interested solely in matters pertaining to social control, including the art of ruling by means of a theological state. Under these conditions, the source of scientific writing dried up, and at the end there were left only the stagnant pools of thirdhand dogmatism.

For European history in general, the fifth century is a major break in continuity. The conquest of the Roman empire by the barbarian invaders changed Europe deeply and irrevocably, and the fifth century is taken as the beginning of the Middle Ages. So far as the history of science is concerned, the division might be made a little differently. With the conquest of Greece by Rome in the second century B.C., scientific activity moved to Alexandria, and in Europe science began to take on its medieval character 600 years before the fall of Rome and the rise of Christianity. And in the Byzantine empire and in the Arabic world, there were no Dark Ages for science, which continued as a slow development, or at least held its own, on the basis laid by the Greeks. When Arab science finally made its way into Europe in the twelfth century, it brought about changes which mark the European Middle Ages into two parts: the earlier Dark Ages, and the Age of Scholasticism.

Before the fall of Rome, the Church had become rich and powerful, and it survived the conquest. Not only that: it was able, without the use of arms, to spread Christianity quickly. Its "ghostly legions" carried the spoken and written Word far into the northern forests. By the eighth century the northern folk sagas were being written in vernaculars based on Latin script. There appeared a consistent written literature in place of the ancient and scanty magical runes, cut into metal or stone, that had filtered north as modifications of ancient Greek and Latin alphabets. Europe thus became Christendom, with a thousand warring factions held together by the tough net of literate Christianity.

A brief recrudescence of Greek science in Italy at the very beginning of the Dark Ages is of interest because it illustrates the nature of the intellectual isolation that in the long run was to reinforce the decline and disappearance of science in medieval Europe. The Visigoth king at Rome, Theodoric, of the sixth century, had been in his youth kept as a political hostage at Constantinople, where he was educated. In the Byzantine empire the Church was subservient to the State, which was primarily a military establishment. In this climate a study of the original classic Greek writings, and even to some extent genuine scientific activity, was kept alive. So that when he came to Rome Theodoric was prepared to appreciate and encourage a remarkable pair of scholars, Boethius and Cassiodorus, in their efforts to translate some of the Greek classics into Latin—or at least he did until the exigencies of practical politics forced him to throw Boethius into prison, where the scholar died young. Boethius had as one of his aims the translation of all the works of Aristotle. He did get through the mathematical and logical texts of Aristotle and certain other Greeks, but the bulk of Aristotle's writings remained lost to Europe for many centuries.

Cassiodorus was cleverer, and lived longer. Apparently he was interested mainly in incorporating what was best in classical learning into religious training, and was disturbed by the shoddiness of Capella's handbook, which had outlined the subjects that were destined to form the basis for priestly education. His superior handling of the seven liberal arts was successful in getting the trivium and quadrivium accepted, but as often happens, the results were not quite what he had hoped, since by giving respectability to the curriculum, he merely established it, and in the long run Capella's handbook was used to teach it. One enduring result of his influence was that some monasteries came to regard copying classical manuscripts as one of their important functions, and it is said that to this is owed the survival of much of the classical Latin literature.

This briefly exerted influence of the Eastern empire was exceptional, and was not to be repeated on any significant scale for many centuries.

On a far border of Western Christendom, political conflict led to a brief excursion into the "scientific" writings of classical Rome, when Bede (637–735) combed the writings of Pliny and other encyclopedists to produce two influential elementary texts, *On the Divisions of Time* and *On the Nature of Things*, the latter a cosmology that provided a theoretical background for the first.

In Great Britain, one of the forms taken by political controversy was conflict over when to celebrate the movable holy feast days. One faction rallied around the observance of Easter on one day, the other naturally choosing a different day. The Venerable Bede's work attempted to give the priesthood an authoritative basis for determining the true dates for such events. But as high as were his intellectual attainments, events had progressed too far for him to reach back into classical Greek science: his writing reflects more the difference between Capella and Pliny than between Pliny and Ptolemy.

As scholars dig deeper into the relics of the early Middle Ages, they find specks of the gold dust of original learning—an herbal or two, for example, that shows evidence of observation of nature—but these only tend to accentuate the prevailing absence of anything like science in the written record of the Dark Ages.

But it must be admitted that in one department of biological science, medieval times were outstanding. The priesthood far outdid A. C. Kinsey in their detailed investigation of the sex life of European males and females. However, we find records of the fear expressed by some priests that perhaps they were putting ideas into the heads of their flock by the techniques of questioning, which might cast doubt on the scientific validity of the investigation, since the method might influence its outcome. These investigations even had their quantitative side, since elaborate tables of fines were set up to correspond to different behavioral situations.

By the tenth and eleventh centuries, European scholars were becoming cosmopolitan enough in their outlook to know that the literary language of science was the language of the Koran. It is an indication of the changing intellectual climate of Europe that scientific enlightenment, at first filtering north through the boundary between the empires by way of occasional *emigrés* from Islam, was by the twelfth century actively sought after by daring adventurers from the north, who sometimes at personal risk went into alien worlds after infidel wisdom, much as a collector might go into the jungle of Borneo after rare and beautiful butterflies.

Although the Christian Crusades of the eleventh through the thirteenth centuries often are cited as the main source of the stimulus given Europe by the culture of Islam, it is likely that they had very little to do with the importation of scientific and other scholarly work into the north. The main pathway of ideas was peaceful traffic with Sicily, which was Moslem until the eleventh century, and above all with the generally tolerant and highly civilized Moslem culture of Spain.

As Charles Singer, in one of his early essays on medieval science visualizes it, the exploration after scientific learning in Spain might have gone something like this. The restless university student, hearing of the scientific and other wonders of exotic Spain, makes his way, probably illegally, across the northern border. He does not know the native language (a kind of hybrid Latin and Arabic) but he might be able to make arrangements to live in one of the Christian settlements whose presence was allowed by the Moslems, where he could find more or less educated priests who knew something of Latin. From these he could eventually learn the vernacular. Now he finds a scholarly Jew, who although he does not know Latin, knows the vernacular, and Arabic; or it may be that the scientific work already had been translated into Hebrew. Thus the translation is laboriously made, first into the vernacular from Arabic or Hebrew, then into Latin.

Thus, during the twelfth century, the works of most of the important classical Greek scientific authors were translated into Latin from the Arabic, or directly from the Greek. They were studied eagerly and began to displace the remnants of Latin handbook science among the more scholarly groups.

It was the impact on the priestly world of these writings, and in particular those of Aristotle, whose scientific, logical, and philosophical works form a uniquely impressive and integrated whole, that produced during the next two or three centuries a flurry of activity that gives to this period the name of the Age of Scholasticism.

It may well be true that the translation and study of the classical Greek literature was an essential preliminary to the true scientific Renaissance of the sixteenth and seventeenth centuries. It is difficult to think of Copernicus without the *Almagest,* or of Vesalius without the sophisticated, if sometimes mistaken, background and tradition provided by Galen. At the same time, the essential spirit of the Age of Scholasticism had little or nothing to do with science. There were stirrings of new scientific observation following the introduction of Arab learning—the original observations on birds in Frederick II's book on falconry, for example—but the results were relatively trivial. Scholasticism was not concerned primarily even with codifying and arranging the newly won ancient knowledge. It was in the main an adaptation to, and a defense against, the swarm of heresies engendered by the brilliance of the pagan learning. It has been said that the writings of the Scholastics, by sharpening verbal tools and logical tricks, were a necessary prelude to the alleged verbal precision of science, but they lack the healthy logic and clarity of classical writing, and the dismal hairsplitting characteristic of them is worse than anything found in modern scientific writing.

Thomas Aquinas, the "Prince of Scholastics," was a thirteenth-century theologian who in a monumental effort met the challenge of Aristotle's writings and bent them to the service of the

Church. In the nineteenth and twentieth centuries the writings of Aquinas, which had been somewhat controversial in the intervening centuries, were given official status by the Roman Church authorities as the best guide to Catholic doctrine. This had the side effect of establishing Aristotle, defenselessly dead for nearly two millennia, as a sort of mascot for the Church.

At the time of Aquinas, when Aristotle's scientific writings were appearing in Latin translation, the prevailing doctrine, owed largely to Augustine, held that all knowledge was revealed knowledge, to be gained by introspection rather than by evaluation of sense experience. Aristotle's writings, although with a large Platonist component, had the trend of making sense experience and reason the main source of knowledge. Aquinas compromised by postulating two compatible and complementary sources, faith and reason, with the latter being provided mainly through the agency of Aristotle, referred to as the "Philosopher." The dangerous aspects of this duality was that it lent justification to a separation of Church and State, but so brilliant was Aquinas' presentation that he won the day. Aquinas mastered the major works of Aristotle, writing detailed and voluminous commentaries on them. With this solid background, in the first part of his famous *Summa Theologica,* concerned with the nature of God, he discusses questions raised in Aristotle's physics along with statements from the Scriptures, achieving a thoroughgoing verbal conciliation of the two texts.

It was during the Scholastic period that the medieval universities flourished, and in them the intricate verbal battles of doctrine, leavened by the infusion of classical wisdom from Islam, reached a very high intensity. These universities furnished the legal talent for the unending political strife of medieval Europe. The long-run significance of the universities was their independence: some were sovereign institutions, governed from within, and subject to no external law. At the height of its power the University of Paris challenged both pope and king; and once when its demands were not met, closed up its establishment and refused all educational services to royalty and priesthood for the better part of a year. Eric Ashby in his *Technology and the Academics* stresses the significance of this independence of universities, which has persisted to the present time, and believes it to be the basis for the long history of the university and a necessity for its continued survival.

Although science was, so far as the written record goes, nearly extinct in medieval times, during this epoch the slow but powerful economic growth of European society provided an essential precondition for the brilliant display of scientific activity that marked the sixteenth-century scientific Renaissance.

The histories of science and of technology do not run parallel. In the Western world there have been periods in which what we call science flourished without any comparable flowering of technology, as in the age of Greek science; and in medieval Europe, science was effectively dead, while, in later medieval times, at any rate, technology was not only maintained at a high level, but made many fundamentally important advances without at all being reflected in a comparable development of science.

It would be well here to point out, or reiterate, two aspects of science that distinguish it from technology. First, science, in the context of a civilized society, is a bookish affair, and if the learned and writing class does not concern itself with technology, then science will not exist. Technology, of the level reached by later medieval times, can be inherited culturally by means of the machines themselves; and the understanding of them can be passed on by oral tradition, by demonstrations from master to apprentice, so that it is not necessarily represented in literature. Second, science is a process of acquiring new knowledge and new

87

understanding. Technology can conceivably exist as a nearly static activity; but science cannot, and reverts to mere bookkeeping, followed by inevitable decay, if it has as its aim merely the recording of known fact and theory. This is not to say that a modern handbook, or a textbook written for specialists, is not a scientific work. It is written in a larger context that does include research into unknown areas, and is thus one of the specialized subdivisions of the whole social enterprise of science. But if there were only such handbooks, copied, summarized, and simplified from generation to generation, science ceases to exist.

The advances in technology made in the last centuries of medieval times profoundly influenced the nature of science when it did reappear. This richly varied technological life of the tenth to fourteenth centuries has long remained hidden, flowing as it did beneath the dominant literary productions of the time, and has required semi-archeological techniques by innumerable scholarly sleuths to reveal what is now known, with much yet to be discovered.

In medieval times, the effective center of Europe shifted away from the Mediterranean into the rainy forests and meadows of the north. Here a vast area was newly brought under cultivation, and these inherently productive lands eventually came to produce the surplus of richly nutritive foods that were to make possible the burgeoning city life of later medieval Europe.

The major technological advances that made possible the highly efficient agriculture of the north appear to have been three: the use of horsepower rather than ox-power; the invention of the heavy plow, which cuts and turns slices of the heavy, rich soil of northern lands; and the consistent application of a crop rotation system involving the use of leguminous plants.

To use horses, which seem overall to be about twice as efficient as oxen, it was necessary to develop adequate harness, and to

equip them with iron shoes. It was not until the time of Charle-
magne that Europe effectively entered the Iron Age. With the
opening of new mines, and the development of water-powered
machinery for bellows and for handling the metal, iron became
abundant enough that its use was no longer restricted to the military. It could be used for the cutting edges of the heavy plows,
which could cut and turn a furrow, instead of merely scratching
the surface, as did the older types used in the Mediterranean region. Its use elsewhere in agriculture (agriculture occupied about
90 percent of the European population) required, it is said, that
every village have a smithy.

The abundance of legumes, including such crops as beans and
peas, assured an abundant supply of protein-rich food, which
handily supplemented the grain crops.

The later centuries of medieval times also saw an unprecedented development of the use of natural mechanical power in
place of man and animal power. Lynn White Jr. says that "The
later Middle Ages, that is roughly from A.D. 1000 to the close of
the fifteenth century, is the period of decisive development in the
history of the effort to use the forces of nature mechanically for
human purposes." Probably in classic times the water wheel was
used for little other than grinding grain; but in medieval Europe
it was put to work in powering iron mills, sawing wood, and so
on. Windmills also came into wide use by the twelfth century, and
by the thirteenth dominate the landscape of the plains of northern Europe. They came to furnish power for all sorts of manufacturing processes—forging iron, minting coins, polishing gems, or
making paper.

To harness this mechanical power a host of mechanical contrivances were needed. Gears, cranes, cranks, connecting rods—all
reached incredible degrees of complexity by the fifteenth century,
even though usually fashioned mainly from wood. White says in

this connection: "Indeed, the four centuries following Leonardo, that is, until electrical energy demanded a subsidiary set of devices, were less technologically engaged in discovering basic principles of transmitting and controlling mechanical energy than in elaborating and refining those established during the four centuries before Leonardo."

In the realm of the military there were engines in abundance on which scientists of the type of Galileo were eventually to develop their analytical powers. The old torsion catapults inherited from Roman times were powered with hair ropes, which offered little possibility for accurate quantitative measurement and prediction. In any event, they did not work well in northern Europe because the hair got wet and lost its elasticity. These catapults were by the thirteenth century largely replaced by trebuchets, or counterweight slings, which used gravity to propel missiles. Modern trials have made a trebuchet with a 50-foot arm and a ten-ton counterweight hurl a stone weighing over 200 pounds for a distance of about 300 yards. This effective and reliable weapon is susceptible to mathematical analysis and prediction in its design and use.

Following the trebuchet was the successful introduction of the cannon, a single-cylinder combustion engine. It became possible to subject the use of artillery to mathematical analysis in routine fashion. The path of the cannon ball in flight became a classic subject for description in the hands of Galileo.

Besides this backlog of technologic advance, which gave impetus to the scientific Renaissance of the sixteenth century, there also preceded it a long period of absorption in medieval universities of the literature of classical Greek science, which had begun to come into Europe, by way of Arab science, in the twelfth century. It is said, with some justice, that modern science not only had its effective beginnings in the sixteenth century, but that it began *de novo,* borrowing little of significance from Greek science. This estimate has some validity in that the content of classical science had little to contribute to modern science. Especially is this true in physics, which had been poorly developed by Aristotle, and which was to be the dominant science in the mechanistic era. But it should be said that the precedent and methods for describing the natural world had been set by classical learning, and it formed the habits of thinking, observing, and writing of the great figures of sixteenth- and seventeenth-century science, who were university men, and who cut their intellectual teeth on the scientific heritage of the Greeks.

We can add to these two predisposing circumstances—a burgeoning technology, and long incubation period with the literary remains of Greek science—a number of explosively sharp incidents that make Renaissance times (roughly 1450–1600) unique, events that would be expected to produce the kind of intellectual ferment in which science would arise and grow with irresistible impetus. Among these developments were the invention of printing by means of movable type, the discovery of the New World, and the disruption of the centuries-old hegemony of the Church by the Reformation. In these circumstances, that most essential characteristic of scientific activity—the unleashing of human curiosity into an exploration of unknown nature—was experienced in extremely vivid form.

$$\Big[\text{C H A P T E R } 6\Big]$$

The Scientific
Renaissance

THE TERM "scientific Renaissance" sometimes is applied to the events connected with the influx of classical Greek scientific writings into Europe in the twelfth century, and has been so named in contrast to the "humanistic Renaissance" of somewhat later times, when special attention was paid to Greek literary works. However, the initial effect of the discovery of Greek scientific writings was to stimulate debate and rote learning rather than the investigation of nature, and science itself did not appear as an important activity until the sixteenth century, which is here taken as the opening of the scientific Renaissance. The scientific Renaissance inaugurated what is usually called modern science. However, the twentieth-century scientist himself is in the middle of a new revolution whose nature and consequences he can see but dimly, but which has likely produced a qualitatively distinct new phase.

This scientific Renaissance roughly coincides with the Reformation, a complex of events mainly political in nature, during which national states were founded, and new classes given political power. Its significance for the rise of science lay mainly in the break-up of the monopoly held by the theologians in literary learning. Although both Protestant and Catholic churches ferociously attacked some of the most insubordinate of the new scientific theories, the very fact of the successful overthrow of papal authority weakened dogmatic control of intellectual life. With the emergence of powerful new economic groups interested in manufacturing and trading, science came to have a strong base in technology, and found its social authorization in classes strong enough to make it independent of theology.

The widening of intellectual horizons by the geographic discoveries of the fifteenth and sixteenth centuries was of great importance for the scientific Renaissance, having much to do with turning thought away from a preoccupation with man's fate to an interest in the world of nature. Among the more concrete results for science was the flood of new plants and animals that collectors brought into Europe during the next 300 years, which inaugurated a kind of activity in biology—naming and classifying animals and plants—that was to dominate the science through the eighteenth century.

It is inconceivable that science could have encompassed the vast range of human experience that opened up in these revolutionary times without the use of printing by movable type as a means of communicating from person to person and from generation to generation. At first printing was merely a method of reproducing the ancient classics already known in manuscript, but within a hundred years, by the middle of the sixteenth century, it was the method for making known and spreading new knowledge, and this under the name of an individual who took the credit and responsibility for it. So that coupled with this device for accumulating and spreading knowledge, for making it social, was the intensely individualistic aspect of authorship. Science was then an essentially individual enterprise, but at the same time individual creative activity was made public on a scale without precedent.

The key date in the scientific Renaissance is 1543, for in that year were published two works which were of fundamental importance in launching the surge of activity that we know as modern science. These were *De Revolutionibus Orbium Coelestium* by Nicolas Copernicus, and *De Fabrica Corporis Humani* by Andreas Vesalius. The first described the structure of the universe, the second the structure of the human body.

Although we are concerned here mainly with the biological sciences, it is necessary, as it has been all along, to consider at least the essentials of the development of the physical sciences. It was the physical sciences, and astronomy in particular, that had during the Renaissance the most powerful influence in the history of ideas, removing man from the center of the stage of the tight medieval drama, and relegating him to a small planet lost in a vast universe. It was not until the time of Charles Darwin that biology was to have as great an influence in the history of ideas.

By the sixteenth century, the best of the classical works in Greek astronomy, among them the highly technical and mathematical *Almagest* of Ptolemy, were being assimilated by the new class of mathematically proficient students that had begun to appear in European universities. Among these students was Copernicus. The chief preoccupation of the Ptolemaic astronomers was adding new refinements to an already incredibly complex system of pathways of the planets to give better agreement with observation.

Copernicus came to the conclusion that the problem never would be solved so long as one held to the fundamental Ptolemaic premise that the sun and the planets revolved about the earth, which was the center of the universe. He therefore changed the premise; and with the earth and other planets revolving about the sun found that the whole scheme of apparent planetary movements as seen from the earth was enormously simplified, from the purely intellectual point of view. But in fact his scheme did not solve the discrepancies between observation and theory that had plagued the Ptolemaic astronomers. In hindsight, we see that the reason for this was that Copernicus clung to one of the old Aristotelian notions that the heavenly bodies had to move in perfect circles, and at constant velocities. In order to reconcile this premise with observations of the apparent motions of the sun and planets, Copernicus had the earth revolving about a center that was not the sun, but was to one side of it. This center was an imaginary point, which itself revolved in a circle about another imaginary point, which in turn revolved about the sun at its center. Even then, the reconciliation of observed fact with theory was incomplete, just as it was with the older earth-centered cosmology, and to get better agreement with observation would have meant the construction of further elaborations, of the same kind that occupied the Ptolemaics.

Copernicus' book was of great professional depth and completeness, and was for this reason valued by his colleagues. They and his immediate successors were, like the Alexandrians, actively making astronomical observations and collecting data. Copernicus is of special interest as providing the kind of link between the revival of Greek learning, as represented by the *Almagest*, and the new observational activity that produced the sixteenth-century scientific Renaissance.

Copernicus himself did not win the acceptance of his revolutionary conception: it was, in any event, not new, but as he pointed out, was a view held by many of the ancient astronomers. The sun-centered planetary system did not constitute a revolution until Galileo and Johannes Kepler, of the next generation of astronomers, marshaled and arranged new observational evidence in such a way as to convince the professional astronomers, and eventually the general public. That it did then constitute not only a scientific but an ideological revolution is shown by the well-known proscription of the theory that the earth moved by the ecclesiastical authorities in the seventeenth century.

Kepler's resolution of the difficulties that Copernicus had in matching observation with theory came from eliminating the Aristotalian conception that planetary movement had to be based on circular motion. Kepler had the advantage of new and more accurate data provided by his younger contemporary Tycho Brahe. Concentrating on the records of the positions of the planet Mars, Kepler eventually found that if he assumed the path to be an ellipse, rather than compound circles, and the speed to be variable, according to a simple mathematical rule, then the predicted movements of the earth and the other planets about the sun closely matched the new data.

The brightest star of the scientific Renaissance was the Italian Galileo Galilei, born in the mid-sixteenth century. As a youth of university age he is said to have had musical and artistic potentialities of the highest order, but early in his university schooling, which was supposed to have trained him for the medical profession, he became passionately interested in mathematics, and devoted himself to its application to mechanical problems so wholeheartedly, and with such virtuosity that by the time he was in his twenties he was lecturing on mathematics at the University of Pisa, although he had failed to obtain a degree.

In Galileo's time Greek scientific literature had become ingrained dogma in the universities. The main obstacle to a student of Galileo's temperament and interests was the great Aristotle, whose feeble physics and vague mathematics were hopelessly inadequate to cope with the flood of new mechanical problems raised by the burgeoning technology of the late Middle Ages. In a collection of notes entitled *De Motu*, apparently gotten together by Galileo about 1590 (when he was twenty-six years old) to use in his teaching at Pisa, one can find comments that illustrate the attitude of the new sixteenth-century physical scientist toward Aristotle. Galileo writes:

> That Aristotle was little versed in geometry is clear in many passages of his philosophical work, but particularly in the passage where he asserts that circular motion does not have any ratio to rectilinear motion because, as he says, a straight line is not in any ratio comparable to a curve. But this falsehood (for it is unworthy of the term "opinion") shows that Aristotle was ignorant not only of the profound and more abstruse discoveries of geometry, but even of the most elementary principles of the science. . . . Aristotle is so rash as to say: "There is no straight line equal to the circumference of a circle." That this is false is proved by the divine Archimedes in his work *On Spirals*.

And, in Galileo's chapter entitled "By what agency projectiles are moved," he begins,

> Aristotle, as in practically everything that he wrote about locomotion, wrote the opposite of the truth on this question too.

Now to the run-of-the-mill university man and theologian, it was Aristotle who was divine, not Archimedes. So that the young Galileo, brilliant in rhetoric and sarcasm, blundered with all sails set into the Establishment. During the second year of his tenure at Pisa, he was publicly hissed at a lecture, whereupon he "found it prudent to resign his lectureship and withdraw to Florence in 1591." He then went to Padua, where he lectured and carried on research for eighteen years, winning the friendship of many influential people, and slowly gathering his forces for another attack on Aristotle. It was during this time that he began his remarkable studies with the telescope, discovering the mountains of the moon, the satellites of Jupiter, and the stars of the Milky Way. Although he had long been a convinced Copernican, in his lectures he held to the accepted earth-centered cosmology. But the spectacular evidence that he was accumulating from his astronomical work, together with the immense strength of his position, and the reputation he had by now made for himself, at last led him to come out in the open on the side of the Copernican sun-centered world view. In a series of publications and letters written between 1610 and 1615, when he had a life appointment that enabled him to devote himself to research, he unfolded a progressively more daring campaign against the astronomy of the Aristotelian school. But he judged incorrectly the political forces of the time. Fighting against the Reformation, the Church had apparently decided to try to outdo the Protestants in their defense of the Scriptures, and Galileo found himself brought before the Inquisition.

This encounter with the authority of the Church was indecisive. Galileo was merely admonished not to "hold, teach, or defend" the doctrine that the earth moved. He did not abandon the conflict; he merely waited for another chance to attack. By 1632, sixteen years later, with a personal friend holding the office of pope, and with a new array of honors, he felt confident that he could go all-out in a final demolition of the official world view with the publication of his *Dialogue of the Two Systems of the World*. This blatant disregard of his earlier promise (at his trial he said he did not have a written copy of the agreement to refer to) moved the Church to decisive action. This time he was punished: he was ordered to recite the seven penitential psalms once a week for three years, was put for life at the disposal of the Inquisition, and was sentenced to a rather lenient house arrest. The book was supressed. During these years of relative solitude he brought together his work on mathematical mechanics in his epoch-making book, *Discourses Concerning Two New Sciences* (1638).

The classic Galilean episode is briefly described here as an example of the kind of event involved in the break-up of the intellectual authority of the Church that occurred during Renaissance times. Nor was this authority captured by the Protestant movement. From the seventeenth century on, science had as its main base of social authorization its close relationship to technology, and the churches lost control of science.

Advances in technology in Europe from the Renaissance on to the nineteenth century concerned mostly the manufacturing arts, which were based on physical and chemical manipulation of non-living substance. The dominant science of this mechanistic era was physical science, and it is not surprising that many consider Galileo the effective founder of modern science.

The relationship of the effective beginning of modern physical science to technology is illustrated by the opening paragraph of Galileo's *Two New Sciences:*

The constant activity which you Venetians display in your famous arsenal suggests to the studious mind a large field for investigation, especially that part of the work which involves mechanics; for in this department all kinds of instruments and machines are constantly being constructed by many artisans, among whom there must be some who, partly by inherited experience and partly by their own observations, have become highly expert and clever in explanations.

Galileo's "two new sciences" were concerned with the strengths of structural materials and with motion. The approach throughout is not descriptive, but is analytic, and abounds in mathematical calculations, usually based on geometry, and in resort to experiment. Probably Galileo could be evaluated as continuing the tradition of Archimedes, insofar as both applied mathematics and experiment successfully to mechanical problems, although Galileo concerned himself with dynamics as well as statics. His analysis of accelerated and projectile motion required a new kind of mathematical thinking that was to lead to the calculus, which was to be one of the significant languages of mechanistic science. His conception that the path of a projectile was a conic section (a parabola) compounded of two motions was destined to extend the principles of mechanics to the astronomical universe. Kepler had already shown the planetary paths to be another conic section, the ellipse (Galileo for unknown reasons ignored this work), and Newton was later to show that the planets were essentially projectiles, given momentum by some initial creative force, and falling eternally through space toward the sun.

The scientific Renaissance of the sixteenth and seventeenth centuries concerned mostly astronomy and physics. As Stephen Toulmin has said of the seventeenth century: "Other sciences, chemistry as much as biology, remained unaffected. True, seventeenth-century scientists were quick to promise radical changes in those other sciences also, but their promises remained effectively unredeemed for a century or more." If we mean by science an emphasis on the experimental method, with its concern with process, which yields the kind of information that is immediately essential for technology, then biology must be said to have remained dormant until well into the nineteenth century. Neither medicine nor agriculture could advance in any fundamental way until after the development of chemistry.

There are, however, two biologists who were prominent in the controversial aspects of Renaissance science: Andreas Vesalius, a human anatomist who helped overthrow the authority of Scholasticism, and William Harvey, who founded the science of experimental physiology some three centuries ahead of its time.

The work of the Belgian Andreas Vesalius has about the same relationship to the classical Greek science of human anatomy as that of the Renaissance astronomers to the *Almagest* of Ptolemy. The "Ptolemy" of human anatomy was Galen, and like Ptolemy, Galen did work of exceptional completeness and merit. However, the scholars of late medieval times gave the writings of Galen an authoritative status, so that when Vesalius began a new and original study of human anatomy, found the inevitable errors in the work written more than a thousand years earlier, and publicized them, he, like Galileo, ran afoul of the Inquisition (the precipitating incident seems to have been that one of the corpses he was dissecting showed signs of life). Vesalius was forced to make a pilgrimage to the Holy Land, and died as a result of a shipwreck on his way back.

Vesalius' work, *The Fabric of the Human Body*, published in 1543, is the first comprehensive treatise on human anatomy that is acceptable by modern standards. One of the most significant features of the work, published when the author was only twenty-eight years old, was the use of extraordinarily fine illustrations. Before the invention of printing such figures could not have been widely distributed, or formed a significant part of scientific activity.

The book of the Englishman William Harvey, *The Motion of the Heart and Blood,* was published in 1628, and like Vesalius' work contradicted many of the teachings received from Galen and other orthodox sources. He says in a preface addressed to his colleagues:

> I have already and repeatedly presented you, my learned friends, with my new views of the motion and function of the heart, in my anatomical lectures; but having now for nine years and more confirmed these views by multiplied demonstrations in your presence, illustrated them by arguments, and freed them from the objections of the most learned and skilled anatomists, I at length yield to the requests, I might say entreaties, of many, and here present them for general consideration in this treatise.

One could select from Harvey's work a few concise arguments which would present the case for the circulation of the blood in irrefutable fashion; but no concise summary has even convinced the majority of the truth of any major new conception. A new position has to be won by endless skirmishes over minor points. The flavor of some of Harvey's intricate argument may be seen in the following quotation:

> . . . and how should the semilunars hinder the regress of spirits from the aorta upon each supervening diastole of the heart? and, above all, how can they say that the spirituous blood is sent from the arteria venalis (pulmonary vein) by the left ventricle in to the lungs without any obstacle to its passage from the mitral valves, when they have previously asserted that the air entered by the same vessel from the lungs into the left ventricle, and have brought forward these

102

same mitral valves as obstacles to its retrogression? Good God! how should the mitral valves prevent regurgitation of air and not blood?

One of Harvey's strengths was his familiarity with the functional anatomy of animals other than man. This experience was of great importance in his discovery, or at least in his demonstration, of the function of the heart, which was not, before his time, known to be a pump. He writes:

Had anatomists only been as conversant with the dissection of the lower animals as they are with that of the human body, the matters that have hitherto kept them in perplexity of doubt would, in my opinion, have met them freed from every kind of difficulty.

And, first, in fishes, in which the heart consists of but a single ventricle, they having no lungs, the thing is sufficiently manifest. Here the sac, which is situated at the base of the heart, and is the part analogous to the auricle in man, plainly throws the blood into the heart, and the heart, in its turn, conspicuously transmits it by a pipe or artery, or vessel analogous to an artery; these are facts which are confirmed by simple ocular inspection, as well as by a division of the vessel, when the blood is seen to be projected by each pulsation of the heart.

Harvey explains why it was that the countless observations made before on the beating heart of a vivisected mammal had yielded so little information:

When I first gave my mind to vivisections, as a means of discovering the motions and uses of the heart, and sought to discover these from actual inspection, and not from the writings of others, I found the task so truly arduous, so full of

103

difficulties, that I was almost tempted to think, with Fracastorius, that the motion of the heart was only to be comprehended by God. For I could neither rightly perceive at first when the diastole took place, nor when and where dilatation and contraction occurred, by reason of the rapidity of the motion, which in many animals is accomplished in the twinkling of an eye, coming and going like a flash of lightning; so that the systole presented itself to me now from this point, now from that; the diastole the same; and then everything was reversed, the motions occurring, as it seemed, variously and confusedly together.

The most famous of Harvey's arguments is his quantitative one, which shows that the amount of blood pumped through the heart is so great that it must circulate, rather than be manufactured as fast as it goes through the heart:

Let us assume either arbitrarily or from experiment, the quantity of blood which the left ventricle of the heart will contain when distended to be, say two ounces, three ounces, one ounce and a half—in the dead body I have found it to contain upwards of two ounces. Let us assume further, how much less the heart will hold in the contracted rather than the dilated state; and how much blood it will project into the aorta upon each contraction;—and all the world allows that with each systole something is always projected, a necessary consequence demonstrated in the third chapter, and obvious from the structure of the valves; and let us suppose as approaching the truth that the fourth, or fifth, or sixth, or even but the eighth part of its charge is thrown into the artery at each contraction; this would give either half an ounce or three drachms, or one drachm of blood as propelled by the heart at each pulse into the aorta; which quantity, by reason

104

of the valves at the root of the vessel, can by no means return into the ventricle. Now in the course of half an hour, the heart will have made more than one thousand beats, in some as many as two, three, and even four thousand. Multiplying the number of drachma propelled by the number of pulses, we shall have either one thousand half-ounces, or one thousand times three drachms, or a like proportional quantity of blood, according to the amount which we assume as propelled with each stroke of the heart, sent from this organ into the artery; a larger quantity in every case than is contained in the whole body!

After Renaissance times, the trend toward specialization that had begun in the ancient science of Alexandria became much intensified, with some specialities quickly producing an amount of literature greater than the totality of ancient science. In the following chapters of this book, certain areas of biology will be followed out in detail, instead of giving a chronological account of the development of biology as a whole. The writings of Andreas Vesalius and William Harvey are here cited as typical examples of work that helped destroy the hold of the authoritarian science of the Scholastics. The writings of other Renaissance biologists and their successors will be taken up in connection with the development of some of the subdivisions of the science of biology. The phase of biology inaugurated by Harvey will be followed up in the chapter "Life as Mechanism."

$$\left[\text{C H A P T E R } 7\right]$$

Mapping the Living World

THE QUANTITATIVE AND EXPERIMENTAL approach of Harvey continued as a minor thread in the development of biology through the next two hundred years, but it was not until the last half of the nineteenth century that the new science of chemistry made this method the most profitable way to approach organic function. During the twentieth century, it has come to dominate biology. The real, or at least the effective, renaissance in biology began in rather obscure fashion with the work of the descriptive botanists, who in the sixteenth century began to produce illustrated descrip-

tions of the plant life of Europe. This descriptive phase represented a genuine innovation in the history of biological science.
Its aim is expressed in the seventeenth-century writings of Francis Bacon, when he envisages an army of biological explorers
roaming the earth for specimens to be brought to great museums,
to be named and classified. An aim such as this is modern, as
compared with Greek science. The vision of a complete and systematic catalogue of the kinds of living things makes Aristotle's
biological writings seem desultory by contrast. He was interested
in variety, but one feels, in reading his *Historia Animalium*, that
the 500 or so kinds of animals he knew something about were, to
him, quite enough.

It was primarily the botanists who founded the science of biological classification, called systematics, or sometimes taxonomy.
The reason for this is that the accurate identification or recognition of kinds or species of plants has always been far more ur-
gent than the identification of animals. Only a relatively few species of larger animals have been of much practical concern. For
plants the situation has been quite different. A moderately large
number of species are used for food, but of more significance
than this is that an indefinitely large number of plant species are
of real or imagined medical importance. In the hill country of the
southeastern United States there still may be found wanderers
who make their living hunting herbs. "They is a yarb," said one,
"could we but know it, for every disease of man!"

This belief in the potency of plants has a real basis in fact.
Plants manufacture in their tissues thousands of kinds of chemical substances that disrupt the metabolism of animals if eaten.
Most of these are poisonous, and probably they function to pro-
tect the plant from attack by insects and other plant eaters.
These substances, many of them belonging to a class of organic
compounds known as alkaloids, are extremely varied in their

effects. Some, like the alkaloids of the root of the poison hemlock, are lethal in small amounts. Others, like the alkaloid caffeine, are cheering and clear the mind when taken in moderation (one estimate puts the lethal dose for man at $2\frac{1}{2}$ grams, the equivalent of some twenty to thirty cups of coffee). They often affect the nervous system profoundly, and in a variety of ways. Sometimes mimicking the effects of disease, and sometimes curing the disease (as the alkaloids of cinchona bark, that destroy the parasites of malaria) or alleviating distress (morphine is an efficient pain-killer), it is not surprising that the thousands of species of plants that contain these physiologically active substances have been associated with medical problems and have been intensively studied, from prehistoric times to the present. Since the compounds, sometimes dangerous, are usually specific to one or a few species of plants, accurate identification of the plant is essential.

There are two kinds of problems involved in biological classification. The first is the classification of individuals into kinds of species. The second is the arrangement of species into groups, or higher categories, such as genera. The first is the more fundamental problem, and concerns even preliterate peoples. The second is a more sophisticated problem that does not become important until the time of Renaissance science.

The significance of the lower category, the species, lies in the fact that every individual of the species is supposed to be like every other individual, at least with respect to essential characteristics. It has to be known in advance that an individual medicinal plant, for example, is going to contain the expected kind of beneficent drug. This is deduced from the fact that other plants that looked just like it—same leaf shape or flower color, for example—are known from previous experience to have the drug. Since there is more or less individual variation, the definition of the species is often a matter of judgment, and its recognition requires a high level of critical ability, judging from recent efforts to set up computer programs to carry out the complex analytic and synthetic operations that are required. However, human beings are born classifiers, and even young children quickly learn to recognize species of plants or animals.

In ancient Greece there was a class of herb-gatherers who sought out medicinal plants, and so large was the number of species reputed to be valuable that these people probably knew a great deal about the names and distribution of the more conspicuous flowering plants. Because Greek doctors were literary men with high social status, this useful folk knowledge could easily become incorporated into the written record.

The Greek medical writer Dioscorides (first century A.D.) described about 600 species of edible or medicinal plants. There are about 3,000 species of higher plants in Greece, and perhaps twice as many in the eastern Mediterranean area that Dioscorides was writing about, so that about 10 percent of the plants were dealt with by the most knowledgeable of the Greek (actually Alexandrian) students of plant classification. The earlier Theophrastus was the greatest botanist of Greek antiquity, but he was an all-round botanist, a student of plant anatomy and development as seen in his botanical garden, and he seems to have lacked a detailed knowledge of the kinds of plants that grew in the wild.

In medieval times some of the Greek medical treatises on the identification and use of plants—herbals, they are called—were recopied, usually deteriorating in accuracy, from one generation of copyists to the next. There also is evidence of some original observation of the medical plants grown in the castle gardens, but in general it can be said that a new cycle of study of plant identification did not begin until the sixteenth century. New observa-

109

tion was necessary, because many of the species of plants growing in northern Europe were different from those known to the
Greeks.

The four Renaissance figures who can be taken as the effective
founders of the descriptive phase of modern biology are the so-
called German Fathers of Botany—Otto Brunfels, Leonard
Fuchs, Hieronymus Tragus, and Valerius Cordus—who worked
in the sixteenth century. They were kin to Vesalius and Harvey
in that, although they were familiar with the Greek scientific heritage, they also studied nature directly. They did not at one bound
exceed the knowledge of the ancients. The botanist Edward Lee
Greene, in an analysis of the early history of botany, came to the
conclusion that Theophrastus a thousand years earlier knew more
botany, from direct observation of plants in his botanical garden
at Athens, than all four German Fathers put together. And it is
true that the Renaissance Germans were relatively crude and un-
informed. Yet they trusted their own eyes above what they were
told on authority.

A significant step taken in the sixteenth century by Brunfels
and Fuchs was to provide illustrations of plants to go along with
the descriptions of Dioscorides; this, of course, had wide significance only after the invention of printing, when woodcuts could
multiply the figures indefinitely. Both Brunfels and Fuchs confined themselves to the medically important plants; and the writings of neither improved upon the written tradition of the ancient Greeks, their descriptions adding little to those of Dioscorides. They did make it possible for semiliterates to identify
some hundreds of medicinal plants. The careful observation
needed to make good drawings called attention to many new features of plants, and the forests and meadows of Europe yielded
many plants not known along the Mediterranean.

Brunfels first trained as a Catholic priest, then deserted to

Lutheranism, where he eventually, at a rather advanced age, made a living by writing popular Protestant texts. He also got a medical degree and practiced medicine. Neither his theological or medical writings seem of any consequence, but his enduring contribution came from the fact that he hired one of the outstanding makers of woodcuts—Hans Weydiz, of Strasbourg—to illustrate his book *Herbarium Vivae Icones,* whose publication in 1530 stands as a landmark in the history of botany.

Brunfel's preoccupation with wild plants is a Renaissance rather than a classic Greek characteristic. German botanists of the northern forests were explorers and pioneers in a wilderness, while the Greeks lived in a sophisticated society in surroundings already altered and tamed by man. Even the Renaissance Italians, facing the beauty of the northern Alps, were affected more by the fresh spirit of the north than by the urban artifacts of the long-buried Roman past.

Leonard Fuchs can be paired with Brunfels as revitalizing botany in the sixteenth century by the production of printed books that were illustrated with woodcuts of flowers both accurate and beautiful. Fuchs was basically an imitator of Brunfels, and his main object was to do a better job of it. Fuchs was able to pay artists (from his earnings as a well-known physician) to prepare 500 large plates which appeared in his *Historia Stirpium,* published twelve years after Brunfels. Later he assembled plates and descriptions of 1,500 species, but could not find a publisher for so massive a work.

It was Tragus and Cordus who produced the first significant original literature (rather than pictures) in botany written in Europe for over a thousand years. Hieronymus Tragus (or Jerome Bock) was a school teacher, a pastor (like the other three Germans, a Lutheran), and doctor who devoted much of his time to the study of plants. The significant features of his work include the fact that he wrote in the vernacular, although his work on plants, the *New Kreuter Buch* (1539), was soon translated into Latin. Also his descriptions are not of the formal kind that make possible direct comparison from species to species, and they include more information than is needed to identify the plant. An example of his style is this description of the common mullein:

> A very notable thing in this plant is the long straight root, of a woody hardness. Its leaves, especially the earlier, lie close to the ground, are rather broad and long, of a whitish aspect and wooly, more so than those of helenium. Not until the second year does it send up its stem, full of a white pith within, like the elder, and sometimes attaining a man's height, clothed with leaves which gradually become smaller and narrower as they approach the summit. The flowers, yellow, wooly, and most sweet smelling are of five distinct leaves, and completely cover the stem from where they begin up to the very apex of it; which falling away are succeeded each by a wooly glove crowded full of seeds not unlike those of a poppy. When the plant is in flower it well resembles a beautiful torch, whence the name King's Torch has been given it.

Tragus did not limit himself to the medical plants, and so began a trend both scientific and Renaissance in spirit. Later editions of his book were illustrated with woodcuts in which the artist strove for both accuracy and beauty. The competition between the artists working on the herbals of this time produced some of the best art of the Renaissance.

The brilliant scientist among the four Germans was Valerius Cordus, who wrote the first European pharmacopoeia, the *Dispensatorium* (1546). He flamed like a meteor through the skies of Renaissance botany, discovering hundreds of new species of plants during explorations that were designed to link up northern botany with that of the Mediterranean coast. He died of fever and exhaustion at the age of twenty-nine in Italy without publishing any of his botanical works, which were left as partly organized manuscripts. Seventeen years later, the naturalist Conrad Gesner assembled some of these notes into the *Historia Plantarum,* in which were described 450 species of plants, many of them previously unknown. Some of the woodcuts of the Tragus *Kreuter Buch* were used to illustrate it, with the editor sometimes associating the wrong figure with the description. Cordus wrote in Latin, and his work represents the first large-scale use of formal, technical descriptions in systematic botany.

The sixteenth-century German Fathers of Botany began the study of European plants. Like the Greeks before them, they dealt with relatively few species, about 500 at the most, so that the problem of classification—the arrangement of species into easily recognized and convenient-sized categories, as a sort of filing system—was not an acute one. It was not until the seventeenth century that explorations overseas brought in so many new species that the problem of classification became paramount, and that the outlines of the botanical part of the map of nature began to be drawn. Also, the science of plant classification was revolutionized by the development of a new technique—that of preserving specimens of plants by pressing and drying them. These collections of plants, now called herbaria, made it possible to compare and describe very large numbers of species in a systematic fashion.

With the work of the Swiss botanist Kaspar Bauhin (1560–1624), the number of species of plants dealt with increases by an order of magnitude. In his *Pinax theatri botanica* he names, describes, and classifies about 6,000 species. He was able to reduce this chaos of diversity to some kind of order because of his ability to recognize natural groupings of species, or genera, which provided a kind of filing system or set of pigeonholes in which clusters of species could be separated off to be studied as problems of manageable size. Bauhin provided a name for each genus, but did not describe it. And although he briefly described each species in the genus, he did not provide a name for the species.

The next large-scale work on the classification of plants was the *Institutiones rei herbariae* (1700) of the French botanist Joseph Pitton de Tournefort, who supplemented Bauhin by describing the genera and naming, but not describing, some 8,000 species.

In England was the third member of the triumverate of great seventeenth-century botanists that preceded Linnaeus: John Ray (1628–1705), a teacher at Cambridge, who had to resign his college post on account of political unorthodoxy. He has been called the "Father of English natural history." He had early acquired a profound knowledge of plants of his country, and his *Catalogous plantorum Angliae* (1670) is the starting point for all British floras. In a three-year tour of the continent he built up a collection of plants that formed the basis for his three-volume *Historia generalis plantorium* (1686–1704) in which over 18,000 species of plants were described.

The Europeans of the eighteenth century were fascinated by the diversity of plants and animals discovered in their overseas possessions, and the nobility and mercantile aristocracy kept elaborate zoological and botanic gardens. Together with the collections of living plants of medicinal importance kept by the universities, there were in Europe over 1,500 botanic gardens by the end of the century. When the young Carl Linnaeus (born 1707), with no assets except an ability to identify plants, went from his native Sweden to Holland to get a degree in medicine so that he could make a living, he found himself besieged by the rich and powerful to study and name their collections. The well-known scientist, teacher, and wealthy physician, Hermann Boerhaave of Leyden, was so impressed with Linnaeus' knowledge of the trees in his private arboretum that he offered to send him for two years to collect on the Cape of Good Hope, and then to America, to return to Holland to a professorship. J. Burman, professor of botany and manager of the Botanic Garden at Amsterdam, wanted him to write on the plants of Ceylon. The wealthy director of the Dutch East India Company, Georg Clifford, owner of a large botanic garden, asked Linnaeus to take over the care and description of the plants and serve as his private physician. Here Linnaeus stayed a year, writing and publishing some of the classics in botanical literature, and living like a prince, with servants and a fine house. In his more mature years, back in Sweden, he continued to find himself in demand as a consultant for influential private collectors. The princess of Sweden bought a fine collection of shells and insects, and asked Linnaeus to describe them. King Adolf Fredrik amassed one of the world's large collections of objects of natural history, and Linnaeus was chosen to write a book on it.

Linnaeus as a schoolboy at Våxjö had learned to name the plants of his region, using the works of Tournefort as a guide. Tournefort took into account some 8,000 species of plants. The classification that made it possible for the user to narrow down his search when identifying an unknown was the weak part of Tournefort's book, as it had been of all the descriptive books before the time of Linnaeus. The diagnostic characters were often difficult for the inexperienced botanist to judge, often being only midpoints in an evenly graded series, instead of sharply defined either-or characters. Linnaeus, early showing his aptitude for recognizing the main chance, saw that the number and structure of the stamens, which had been almost totally ignored in previous classification, could be used as a convenient filing system for the multitude of plant species. This was his secret weapon when he went to Holland. It is said that he amazed even experienced botanists with his ability to solve almost instantly the most refractory problems of identification. He would pop a dried flower into his mouth to moisten it, count the stamens, then pronounce the name of an obscure exotic plant that had defied days of poring through the published classifications.

After completing his university schooling at Uppsala, Linnaeus went to Holland to get the degree of Doctor of Medicine, which he obtained at a well-known diploma mill in a matter of days. But while in Holland, he also went about the serious business of looking up some of the famous botanists of the time, never failing to make a good impression. He had in his baggage the manuscript of a book that he had written as a university student, a work that undertook to classify the whole of nature—mineral, vegetable, and animal—the *Systema Naturae*. The Dutch botanist Gronovius, when he saw this manuscript, was so deeply impressed that he, together with a friend, paid for its immediate publication. It was published in Holland in 1735, when Linnaeus was twenty-eight years old.

This first edition of the *Systema Naturae* was a book wide—measuring about 18 by 20 inches—but thin, amounting to only fourteen pages. The heart of the book consisted of three double-page spreads, one each for the mineral, plant, and animal kingdoms. Here was the Faustian ideal of having the world of nature compressed into print: one admirer said that everyone should have these sheets spread on his walls.

Some idea of the tenor of the work, and an example of Linnaeus' drive to compress everything into brief diagnostic yet colorful phrases, can be presented by this introduction to the last (1788) edition of the *Systema:*

The study of natural history, simple, beautiful, and instructive, consists in the collection, arrangement, and exhibition of the various productions of the earth.

These are divided into the three grand kingdoms of nature, whose boundaries meet together in the Zoophytes.

MINERALS inhabit the interior parts of the earth in rude and shapeless masses, are generated by salts, mixed together promiscuously, and shaped fortuitously.

They are bodies *concrete,* without life or sensation.

VEGETABLES clothe the surface with verdure, imbibe nourishment through bibulous roots, breathe by quivering leaves, celebrate their nuptials in a genial metamorphosis, and continue their kind by the disperson of seed within prescribed limits.

They are bodies *organized,* and have *life* and not sensation.

ANIMALS adorn the exterior parts of the earth, respire, and generate eggs; are impelled to action by hunger, congeneric affections, and pain; and by preying on other animals and vegetables, restrain within proper proportion the numbers of both.

They are bodies *organized,* and have *life, sensation,* and the power of locomotion.

MAN, the last and best of created works, formed after the image of his Maker, endowed with a portion of intellectual divinity, the governor and subjugator of all other beings, is, by his wisdom alone, able to form just conclusions from such things as present themselves to his senses, which can only consist of bodies merely natural. Hence the first step of wisdom is to know these bodies; and to be able, by those marks imprinted on them by nature, to distinguish them from each other, and to affix to every object its proper name.

These are the elements of all science; this is the great alphabet of nature: for if the name be lost, the knowledge of the object is lost also; and without these, the student will seek in vain for the means to investigate the hidden treasures of nature.

The importance of Linnaeus' portrait of nature lay in its originality and creative simplicity. All species of organisms were to be grouped into three levels of higher categories, the genera, orders, and classes, each category to be given one-word names. Previous authors had used a mixture of single words and phrases to designate more or less informal categories. Linnaeus described each category with a very brief diagnostic phrase which was designed to distinguish it from other categories of the same rank, instead of giving the usual relatively aimless description. Coupled with this rigid formality in structure was the poetic precision and fire of Linnaeus' writing, whose aptness persuaded the reader that the author had complete control of his materials.

The double-page spread that, in the first edition of the *Systema,* classified some 750 genera of plants, was blocked off by lines into the orders and classes that served as the master filing system. Twelve of the highest category, the classes, were based on the number of stamens in the flower—Class Monandria (one stamen), Diandria (two stamens), and so on up to twelve. Beyond twelve the number tends to become variable or so large as to be not readily countable, so that the thirteenth class is termed the Polyandria. Where the stamens are not all separate and similar in position and size, the classes are designated according to the degree of fusion (Class Diadelphia, the stamens fused into two groups) or other peculiarities (Class Tetradynamia, two short stamens, four long ones) ; and other classes are designated on the basis of other characteristics. Each of the Classes is then subdivided into smaller groups or Orders on the basis of the number of pistils.

This skeleton outline of the classification of plants was supplemented by two other books that Linnaeus also had written while a student. There were published in quick succession after the *Systema,* while he was still abroad, the *Genera Plantarum* (1737), in which the genera were described in detail, and the *Classes Plantarum* (1738), in which the highest categories were treated. Other works, including the luxuriously illustrated *Hortus Cliffortianus* (1738), which described plants in the huge botanical garden of the director of the Dutch East India Company, were written abroad. When Linnaeus returned to Sweden he had in his trunk the fourteen books he had published while in Holland from 1735 to 1738. These, including a joint work with Peter Artedi on fishes, amounted to over 3,000 pages. Ahead of him, in his mature years, lay the preparation of the flora of the world, the *Species Plantarum,* which made him the leading authority on plants, the "prince of botanists," and which established binomial nomenclature in biological systematics.

But in Sweden there were no scholars in botany of the caliber of his friends on the continent. In Europe he had lived like a prince and was sought after by the wealthy and the learned. Here in Sweden he was an unknown young man with an unused degree in medicine. He did get some notoriety from some bitter criticism of his *Systema Naturae* by a Russian biologist, Siegesbeck.

In describing the classes and orders of plants, Linnaeus called the stamens and pistils husbands and wives, with the result that in some households there were several husbands with one wife, in others various combinations of varying numbers of each. This erotic imagery apparently was in keeping with the taste of the time, and is characteristic of much of Linnnaeus' writing, which abounds with energy and unexpected turns of phrasing. Siegesbeck, writing from a different sort of background in Russia, condemned Linnaeus as too lewd for young students. Siegesbeck was especially incensed by the analysis of the structure of the flowers of the Compositae: "Never would God allow such detestable vice within the vegetable kingdom, that . . . a husband have a mistress so near to his wife." This criticism rankled Linnaeus, for he privately expressed resentment for years. His only public response was to name an insignificant and unpleasant weed *Siegesbeckia.*

Linnaeus had to turn to medicine to be able to marry Sara Lisa and to make a living. In a letter to a friend he complains that he was a laughingstock on account of his botany, and that his friends thought Siegesbeck had annihilated him. But with characteristic competence he in a few years came to the top in the medical profession. According to his own account, he began at the cafes frequented by Stockholm's rakes, where he says, they sat downcast, afraid to drink, "suffering from wounds received in pursuit of Venus." In a letter to a prominent physician he says that gonorrhea has infected nearly all the youth, and begs for formulae to cure it; this would be making him "a gift of a thousand ducats a year." His success in treatment spread to other fields and other illnesses, and soon he could say that he had more patients than all the other doctors in Stockholm put together. But during this period, he was eager to leave medicine should an academic position at the university at Uppsala open up; and when one did, with the death of the professor of botany, he set in motion intrigues, using the help of the Swedish aristrocracy, which within a year gave him the post.

For nearly thirty years Linnaeus was professor of medicine and natural history at Uppsala. He attracted unprecedented numbers of students from abroad, and became highly placed among the politically influential without himself becoming involved in politics. He conducted major scientific explorations of Sweden, as well as colorful local excursions in which hundreds of followers scavenged the countryside for objects of natural history. During all this time he was engaged in what he considered his main life's work, the *Species Plantarum*. As in most of his major works, he had written a preliminary version while a student. After his wide experience with the herbaria and gardens of Europe and England, and correspondence with botanical explorers, he was solidly equipped for the vast project of describing the world's plants, and, working rapidly through a period of ill health, published the work in 1753.

The technical framework for the *Species Plantarum* had already been fashioned by the *Classes and Genera Plantarum*. Every class and genus had been given a one-word name and had been given a brief description. There now remained the task of naming and defining each species.

Linnaeus had in his thinking long ago clearly separated the two functions of naming (or designating) and diagnosis (or description). But he was at first unable to carry out this ultimate simplification of separating names from the description of species. Instead, he set up two systems for naming species—one which both designated and described, the other which only designated. He was rather apologetic about the latter, regarding it only as a kind of handy and shortcut reference system, and lavished his care on what he regarded as the proper name of the species, which was a multiverbal term. In naming the species, he agreed with Humpty Dumpty:

". . . but tell me your name and business."

"My *name* is Alice, but—"

"It's a stupid name enough!" Humpty Dumpty interrupted impatiently. "What does it mean?"

"*Must* a name mean something?" Alice asked doubtfully.

"Of course it must," Humpty Dumpty said with a short laugh: "*my* name means the shape I am . . ."

The "name of the species" was to consist of the name of the genus to which it belonged followed by the "specific name," which was a descriptive phrase-name consisting of two or more words. Thus, a certain species of plant was given the name *Canna foliis utrinque acuminatus nervosis*. "Canna" was the generic name, designating a genus already described in *Genera Plantarum*, and the remaining four words described the leaves in such a way as to differentiate this particular species from all the other species belonging to the genus *Canna*.

In the margin beside each short paragraph devoted to the geographic range and references to what had already been written about the species, Linnaeus put a single "catchword" by which to refer to the species in conveniently brief form. For the species of *Canna* named above, he chose (and rather hastily, since the word did not have to refer to any physical characteristic of the species, but was simply a mnemonic, or indexing, device) the word *indica*. This single word he called the trivial name, or specific epithet.

This nomenclatorial device, introduced only marginally by Linnaeus, was the basis for modern binomial nomenclature, and within twenty-five years after its introduction in the first edition of the *Species Plantarum* (1753), the system was in general use by all biologists. That is, the scientific name of a species was a two-word name consisting of a generic name and a trivial one. Most of this success must in all probability be attributed to the

122

success of the book itself, which was the only workable survey of the world's flora in existence. Linnaeus himself had called it a beginner's handbook, and because of the use of the easily observed stamens and styles as key characters for the major divisions, and the perfectly consistent way of applying names, it was indeed far easier to use than anything that had been published before, even though it lacked pictures.

As Linnaeus saw acceptance of the binomial method grow, and found its usefulness in his own work, his opinion of the importance of the trivial epithet changed, and in one of his autobiographies (he wrote several) he came to regard it as one of the turning points in the history of classification.

As a matter of fact, in finally coming to binomial nomenclature, Linnaeus had simply returned to the almost instinctive way of naming things that is used in everyday language. Thus, in designating different kinds of willow, we might use such names as red willow, black willow, sand willow, narrowleaf willow, etc., with "willow" in each case corresponding to the generic name, and the combination to the binomial. In English the qualifying adjective precedes the noun, but in Latin it follows.

Although the consistent use of the binomial in naming biological species is often said to be Linnaeus' main contribution to systematic biology, this bookkeeping device, although a happily chosen technique, is only a small part of the Linnaean contribution. What he had done was to establish a set of categories, arranged in a hierarchy, each with a standard name and diagnostic description. He did more than suggest this as a system; he applied it to the whole living world, providing a concrete classification which, although as he himself said, was superficial above the generic level, and was destined to be replaced by others, at least provided an unambiguous scheme that could be used as a starting point. Linnaeus had forced the vast expanse of literature on the classification of plants that had accumulated since the sixteenth century through a single narrow organizational channel, and all systematic botany since has been affected by his work.

Another of Linnaeus' contributions was his struggle with a question of highest theoretical significance, that of the difference between artificial and natural classification. Linnaeus thought of himself not as creating an ordered classification of living things, but as discovering and describing an order that already existed in nature. He thought that this order was created by God; as he said, "God created, Linnaeus described." An artificial category was one constructed by the classifier that did not match the order that actully existed in nature. There could be any number of artificial classifications of a group of plants. But since a natural classification was one that matched the order existing in nature, there could be only one natural classification, which thus stood as a goal toward which the classifier came ever closer as he perfected his work. Linnaeus thought that the species he had constructed were natural, and that his genera were natural. However, he admitted failure in constructing natural orders and classes; these, he said, were artificial. He thought that natural orders and classes did exist, but that he did not have the knowledge and ability to define them, and that the task was one for botanists of the future to complete. This was accomplished in some degree later in the eighteenth century, by botanists such as Antoine Laurent de Jussieu and Augustine Pyrame de Candolle. Instead of using Linnaeus' simple scheme of the number and arrangement of stamens for classes, pistils for orders, they were forced to use combinations of a number of characteristics.

The differences between a natural and an artificial classification can be illustrated with the following model. Imagine a sample consisting of a large number of specimens of dogs and cats, of a great variety of sizes and colors. We are asked to sort these specimens out into two categories, based on a single diagnostic, either-or characteristic. There are a multitude of such characteristics to choose from. For example, we could distinguish between those with at least some black fur, and those without any; this would be easy to use, and would make for fast sorting. But even without any specification as to the aim of the classification, we would be dissatisfied with the two groups we had sorted out. If we analyzed the source of our dissatisfaction, we would note that the only distinctive characteristic possessed in common by all the individuals of each category could be the very one that we had used for sorting them out—the color of the fur. The fur color is not correlated with anything else. It has no predictive value: saying that at least some of the fur is black does not make it possible to make other meaningful statements about the category, except perhaps statements about the biochemistry of the black pigment. Such a classification is an artificial one.

In our relatively simple model, we can see almost at a glance that there is a better way of sorting them out. So we bypass (temporarily) the rules of the game, and sort them out into cats and dogs; and then go back to the rules by examining them to look for a single either-or characteristic to distinguish the two. There are many such pairs we could find, for example the structure of the claws—whether the claws are retractile (cats) or nonretractile (dogs). We would find that the single characteristic—retractile claws—is associated with an indefinitely large number of varied features of structure and behavior. It therefore has very high predictive value. Each category has a very large number of characteristics, instead of only one, in common. Such a classification is what is meant by a natural one.

When Linnaeus said that his classes of plants, which were based on the number of stamens, were artificial, he meant that sometimes they contained species that had little or nothing in common except the number of stamens. Also, and as a sort of corollary of this, occasionally a single species of plant would have variable number of stamens, so that different individuals would fall in two or more of the Linnean classes. Linnaeus assumed that people would use common sense when they encountered a situation like this, but at the same time he was unhappy with the logical flaws in the situation.

The principles and techniques established by Linnaeus served to carry systematic biology through the phase of preliminary description or mapping of organic diversity that lasted until modern times. So near at hand are current attempts to reassess the aims and methods of systematic biology that little can be said about them in this general survey; but it can be pointed out that the mapping operation has been carried out in depth in only certain groups of plants and animals, and that a systematic, uniform, and comparative description of the diversity of plants and animals has been only fractionally completed.

The beginning of the international system of nomenclature for naming the species of plants and animals is by general agreement taken to be the works of Linnaeus: for plants, the first edition of *Species Plantarum,* published in 1753 (for fossil plants, and some of the groups of the lower flowerless plants, the work of other and later authors is the starting point); and for animals, the *Systema Naturae,* tenth edition, published in 1758.

After Linnaeus, systematic biology became more and more the concern of the specialists, as ever larger numbers of specimens were brought to Europe. It was not until well into the eighteenth century that geographic exploration of the world could be carried out in well-organized fashion. With the invention of a compensating device that corrected for the effects of changing temperatures it was possible to make good chronometers, and thus determine longitude accurately. A second decisive new technique was the use, towards the end of the century, of fresh fruits or vegeta-

126

bles to cure scurvy, which had always made long voyages a risky affair. Specimens of plants and animals had usually been brought back to Europe as a sort of sideline to buccaneering and commercial activities, but with such voyages as those of the British Captain James Cook (1728–1779) there began an era of strictly scientific explorations that were to make known at least the general outlines of the diversity of living things.

Probably the bulk of the biological exploration even as late as the nineteenth century was, however, carried out by individual enterprise. There were scores of European collectors and adventurers in the tropics gathering the brilliant or grotesque birds and butterflies and beetles desired by wealthy stay-at-home collectors. Some of the best of the field biologists were able to make a living by selling specimens and writing about their adventures in distant lands.

Such a man was Alfred Russel Wallace, born in England in 1823. Without formal schooling, and with no money, he managed to get himself out into the tropics for twelve years. His first expedition—four years in the Amazon basin—yielded little but experience, since nearly all of his large collections of beetles and other things were lost at sea on the way back to England. But back home, and during a walking tour of Europe, he wrote up his adventures into a successful book, *Travels on the Amazon and Rio Negro*. In a little more than a year he was ready to go out again, and on the strength of his now-established reputation as an author and naturalist, was able to get from the British government free transportation to Singapore. Here began a lonely eight-year odyssey through the island mazes of the Malay Archipelago that was to make him one of the leading naturalists of his time.

His account of his explorations—*The Malay Archipelago: the Land of Orang-Utan and the Bird of Paradise*—is one of the classics of travel literature. The richness of experience and observation reminds one of the writings of another amateur, Charles

Darwin, and it is no accident that the two of them made the decisive exploration into the most significant realm of human thought, the concept of evolution.

Wallace does not say anything about such matters in his preface to the first edition of the *Malay Archipelago,* written in 1869, eleven years after a joint statement by Darwin and Wallace of the world-shaking theory of organic evolution, nor anything about the discomforts and dangers of the roving life when he cast his lot with that of adventurous small traders beyond the edge of civilization. With British understatement he says:

As the main object of all my journeys was to obtain specimens of natural history, both for my private collection and supply duplicates to museums and amateurs, I will give a general statement of the number of specimens I collected, and which reached home in good condition. I must premise that I generally employed one or two, and sometimes three Malay servants to assist me, and for three years had the services of a young Englishman, Mr. Charles Allen. I was just eight years away from England, but as I travelled about fourteen thousand miles within the Archipelago, and made sixty or seventy separate journeys, each involving some preparation and loss of time, I do not think that more than six years were really occupied in collecting.

I find that my Eastern collections amounted to:

$$
\begin{array}{rl}
310 & \text{specimens of Mammalia} \\
100 & \text{— — — Reptiles} \\
8,050 & \text{— — — Birds} \\
7,500 & \text{— — — Shells} \\
13,100 & \text{— — — Lepidoptera} \\
83,000 & \text{— — — Coleoptera} \\
13,400 & \text{— — — Other Insects} \\
\hline
125,660 & \text{specimens of natural history}
\end{array}
$$

To this day there has been no worldwide, systematic effort to complete the map of organic diversity envisaged by the biologists of the eighteenth century. The work goes on piecemeal, mostly carried on by more-or-less isolated individuals and with even the most massive efforts—largely supported by the great museums, or other government agencies—devoted to analysis of the biota of limited geographic areas, or to certain groups of organisms of unusual theoretical, economic, or esthetic interest. Preliminary mapping down to the species level has been essentially completed for such groups as the birds and mammals. But so little has been done with most of the groups of insects, for example, that a modern specialist can, in his lifetime, collect by his own efforts more relevant material in his area of interest than has been brought together by all previous work.

The bleak Antarctic, or the Galapagos Islands, where the evolutionary strands uniting the unique animals and plants endemic to the islands have not yet been destroyed by man, or a tropical atoll or desert flat scorched by atomic blasts are of particular interest to modern biologists, and the life of such areas is intensively studied. In the nineteenth century, the most glamorous area of the world that invited scientific exploration was the sea. Especially did the cold black depths of the ocean, which make up the largest environment on the earth, seem to be rich in promise of new and remarkable forms of life.

The Norwegian Michael Sars, pursuing his interest in the crinoids—the sea lilies and feather stars—discovered in the middle of the century that these animals lived at depths of several hundred fathoms (there had been argument as to whether life was possible under the tremendous pressures existing in this environment), and also came to the conclusion that some of the crinoids living in deep water were closely related to extinct species known only as fossils. Later the British naturalist Charles Wyville Thomson got the loan of two government ships to collect from the sea floor of the eastern North Atlantic. He confirmed the existence of a varied fauna at depths below the limit of sunlight, and in 1869 collected near the Bay of Biscay from a depth of 2,435 fathoms a specimen which seemed to show in dramatic fashion that the abyssal depths were indeed the home of primitive life. This specimen was a filmy network resembling egg-white which, under the microscope, gradually altered appearance, and contained foreign bodies, including the skeletons of microorganisms, that changed position. This evidence of slow movement, Thomson thought, showed that "there can be no doubt that it manifests the phenomena of a very simple form of life." The remains of the microorganisms made it reasonable to think that this film of presumed organic matter could assimilate food.

By this time the idea of protoplasm as a substance common to all life was well established, and Ernest Haeckel, a German evolutionist, who was well known for his efforts to reconstruct the evolutionary history of life from a study of contemporary organisms, had found a group of Protozoa that he called Monera, said to consist of protoplasm only, without the nuclei that were embedded in the protoplasm of all other animals. One writer has cynically commented that these "primitive forms of animal life described by Haeckel have been seen by that naturalist alone up to the present," but the slime discovered by Thomson seemed to fit perfectly the concept of the most primitive organisms as visualized by Haeckel. In 1868 Thomas Huxley officially named this material, which he characterized as the simplest known living thing, as *Bathybius haeckelli,* and its importance in the eyes of biologists of that time can be judged by the comment of the American scientist A. S. Packard, writing in 1874: "Bathybius is consequently the most interesting organism (should it be proved to be such) known except man."

Thomson, the discoverer, had been somewhat doubtful that this "formless protoplasm" represented a distinct kind of life, but thought, on account of its different appearance in different localities (he had recovered it from widely separated areas of the sea floor of the Atlantic) that it might represent the growth and decay of several different kinds of organisms. When, a few years later, he headed the staff of biologists of the famous *Challenger* expedition, the question of *Bathybius* was kept in mind. One of the results of this expedition was the discovery that *Bathybius* was not organic at all, but was merely a precipitate of gypsum (calcium sulfate) produced by adding alcohol to the samples.

In general, the hopes of finding spectacular "missing links" among the animals of the sea floor were not realized. The fantastic small fishes that live in the depths are remarkably adapted to this realm of darkness and sparse food, with light-producing organs, wide jaws and prehensile teeth, and hugely distensible bellies, but they are specialized derivatives of groups of fishes well known elsewhere. However, the samples of life taken from these relatively inaccessible depths are meager, and much doubtless remains to be learned. It may turn out that the most interesting aspect of the deep sea environment is the biology and chemistry of the ooze that covers the sea floor.

Although slight in comparison with the nineteenth-century marine military campaigns of the Ruler of the Seas, the biological exploration carried out with the 2,300 ton British wooden steamship *Challenger* was one of the momentous developments of the science of that century. Voyaging over the world's seas for three and a half years, the six naturalists aboard gathered vast collections from the ocean and isolated islands. These collections were eventually written up in a set of fifty thick volumes, the famous "Reports of the *Challenger* Expedition."

Such nineteenth-century explorations established the general outlines of the biological economy of the sea. That of the land is fairly obvious, with the luxuriant green blanket of vegetation providing food for the varied animal life. But except for the seaweed of the coasts, and occasional masses of floating weed in areas like the Sargasso, the crystal clear blue waters of the open ocean seem, at a glance, to be barren of plant life. It was found that by towing very fine-meshed nets through the water, a great variety of microscopic single-celled plants could be collected. Most important of these were the diatoms, which have shells of the glasslike silicon dioxide, sometimes intricately and beautifully sculptured. The explosive growth of knowledge of the diatoms at this time is shown by the fact that only about fifty species were known when the group was first monographed in 1824, while about 4,000 species were known when the *Challenger* set out in 1872. Diatoms are so important as food for marine animals that they have been called the "grasses of the sea," and although they are often rather sparsely scattered through the water, so vast is the ocean, and so deep the illuminated layer of water in which they live, that they and related plants create more food from sunlight and carbon dioxide than all terrestrial vegetation combined.

Because plants were of great medical importance, the detailed study of their classification is older than animal classification. It was an eighteenth-century botanist, Linnaeus, who in working out a systematic and uniform method for mapping the diversity of plants, established the taxonomic procedures that came to be used for all living things, and as the founder of modern biological classification. Although it was the first to mature, systematic botany suffered from a defect which allowed animal rather than plant classification to become, in the following century, the center of developments which led to the formulation of the theory of evolution. This defect was that the functional and adaptive significance of the structural features used in the classification of plants was not understood.

Very little is known of the life of plants in nature, so that the meaning of structural differences between genera or families or orders is difficult to evaluate, and only in the twentieth century has the question been given effective attention. It may be that some of the major features of plant structure—the numbers of petals of some symmetrical flowers, or other rigidly geometric features—are not significant in relation to the environment, but rather are related to the internal problems of embryonic development or growth, since plants differ from animals in that the cells cannot move about during development so as to produce the final structure, but remain fixed in position. Whatever the reasons, the relationship between structure (as used to classify) and the life of the plant in its natural environment tends to be obscure.

Animal structure, by contrast, easily lends itself to functional analysis. Thus, although animal classification at first more or less followed the relatively sterile pattern of the older plant science, the obviously adaptive nature of the structures used in classification led the more discerning biologists to look on animal diversity as a diversity of function and a diversity of adaptation, rather than one of abstract structural patterns. This is an attitude that is basic to a theory of natural selection as a cause of organic diversity, hence to a theory of evolution. It is not necessary here to follow out in detail the advance in the classification of animals that came after the time of Linnaeus. The theoretical significance of this work will be dealt with in the chapter on Darwinian evolution.

CHAPTER 8

The Evolutionary Outlook

PRIMITIVE MAN, LIKE THE MODERN SCIENTIST, does not believe that the earth has always existed. His mythologies tell of the creation of the earth and its inhabitants. In the more primitive cultures the creators are wise and omnipotent animals, but by civilized times, the creators or Creator come to have human qualities. It was the ancient Greek Ionian philosophers who brought speculations concerning the origin of the world into the realm of science by relieving the gods of responsibility for creating the world. Such philosophers as Thales and Anaximander believed that matter itself could interact so as to produce creative change. Layers of earth, water, and mist, acted upon by an envelope of fire, Anaximander thought, could produce the earth and the heavens; and as for man, he evolved from fish that came out upon the new dry land. During the later development of Greek thought, scientific cosmogonies (theories of the origin of the world) became complex and diverse, and persisted into early Roman times, as in the writings of Lucretius, but were eventually blotted out by the Dark Ages.

The official cosmogony of Christian Europe was a descendent of those that existed in the Near East before Greek times, subsequently modified by the Platonic rather that the Ionian elements of Greek philosophy. A cosmogony, like that of medieval Europe, that specifies creation by a supernatural Being is not a scientific theory because it is not possible to formulate deductions from it that are capable of disproof by observation or experiment. But if such a cosmogony specifies details as to how or for what purposes supernatural intervention is carried out, as was done in the Christian Mosaic account, these details often can be used as scientific theories or hypotheses. The theory of the Deluge, for example, can be and was so used, but the fact that this particular theory was effectively disproved during the nineteenth century meant, for practical purposes, only that the authority of a particular church that preached it as dogma was undermined. The disproof could not have any logical relevance to the basic theological assertion of the Mosaic account, an assertion which is scientifically meaningless.

With the scientific Renaissance of the sixteenth century, an interest in scientific cosmogonies was renewed. A scientific cosmogony is necessarily evolutionary: a formulation that says the universe is eternal and unchanging, is, although a scientific formulation, not a cosmogony, by definition. The evolution of the universe, of the earth, and of living things was widely discussed (if not always believed in) from the sixteenth century on by such major philosophers as Francis Bacon, Descartes, Pascal, and Kant. With the accumulation of factual information beyond that recovered in the Greek writings, specialists as well as philosophers began to be deeply concerned with the evolutionary approach to their disciplines. In biology this tendency culminated in the work of Charles Darwin. Even though Darwin was responsible for one of the great revolutions in the history of thought, his theory, that the evolution of living things took place by natural selection, was only one episode in a wide stream of evolutionary thought that concerned the evolution of the universe, of the earth, of life, and of human culture. It is some aspects of evolutionary thought in general that are the subject of the present chapter.

Isaac Newton had in the seventeenth century successfully described the solar system as a machine in which the planets eternally orbited about the sun, a view which is the antithesis of the evolutionary outlook. It was known, however, that there were certain small irregularities in planetary movements that were not explained by the Newtonian analysis. These opened up the question as to whether the solar system was really a stable, self-correcting system. Pierre Simon de Laplace, the French astronomer, examined this question carefully and was able to show that these irregularities were in fact, like all other features of planetary motion, repetitive, even though the cycle in one instance was as long as 900 years. This, then, tended to confirm the nonevolutionary view that the solar system was not changing in any sustained, progressive way ("progressive" as used here has no connotation of "improvement" or progress to a "higher level," but refers to long-term irreversible change in which each new state is the result of a preceding state; progressive change is thus an exact synonym for evolutionary change).

Laplace, however, on the basis of other evidence believed that the solar system had come into existence by gradual evolutionary processes and was, over very long periods of time, still changing in some respects. He stated this belief in a footnote in his important book, written for the general reader, titled *Essay on the Systems of the World* (1796). The chief fact leading him to an evolutionary outlook was that the orbits of the planets all moved in the same direction. At this time, powerful telescopes had revealed a large number of nebulae, vast rotating discs of glowing gas lying far out in the universe. It is an obvious step to postulate that the solar system had arisen by condensation of a rotating nebula into a central sun surrounded by a family of planets, if one has a personal bias toward requiring that natural objects have evolutionary origins.

Astronomers also took into account certain one-way processes that demanded that one think in terms of evolution. It could be shown that the sun radiated heat in enormous amounts. Even if made of "pure coal," as one astronomer put it, a burning sun would not have lasted more than a few thousand years. Laplace's nebular hypothesis predicted a source for the heat of the sun that could have fueled it for millions of years: as a nebula contracts, the law of conservation of energy requires that the central mass radiate heat, and the sun could still be contracting at a rate high enough to account for the heat it radiates. However, this could not go on indefinitely. This loss of energy from the sun and other celestial objects by radiation—a one-way, irreversible process summarized by the famous second law of thermodynamics— necessarily brings an evolutionary slant to cosmological thinking.

In 1786 William Jones, British lawyer and orientalist, who had taken up the study of Sanskrit to document his codification of Hindu and Moslem laws while a judge in India, wrote that "The

Sanskrit language, whatever may be its antiquity, is of wonderful structure; more perfect than the Greek, more copious than the Latin, and more exquisitely refined than either, yet bearing to both of them a stronger affinity, both in the roots of verbs and in the forms of grammar, than could have been produced by accident; so strong that no philosopher could examine the three without believing them to have sprung from some common source which, perhaps, no longer exists."

This was at a time when the story of the tower of Babel was a widely accepted theory accounting for the diversity of languages, and when scholars were trying to derive European languages from the Hebrew. Sanskrit proved, with the work of the German scholars Franz Bopp (1816) and Jacob Grimm (1819), to be the key for understanding the origin of the Indo-European languages. This evolutionary view of the gradual origin and differentiation of a group of languages, all traceable in a general way to a common ancestor, had much to do with establishing a favorable intellectual climate for evolutionary concepts in other areas of knowledge.

Also influential was the so-called higher criticism, or the study of the origin of the Bible, as carried out by critical studies of the literary consistency of different sections, and of the relation of biblical texts to other ancient manuscripts. This could hardly fail to corrode the status of a given version of the Bible as final and revealed knowledge, a matter mostly peripheral to scientific theory, but one that was in practice very important in helping naive and unphilosophical scientists to become independent of the pressure exerted by ecclesiastical authority.

As the science that deals with the rocky framework of the surface of the earth, geology furnishes direct evidence as to the nature of the changes that have taken place during earth history. Yet it has played a strangely ambiguous role in the development of evolutionary thought. It began to emerge as a science in Darwin's youth, and formed an indispensable part of the background that led him to his theory of organic evolution; but at this time the outlook of its founders was firmly anti-evolutionary.

After the Renaissance, there was a line of thinking that led from Descartes through Gottfried Leibniz to Georges Buffon that treated the history of the earth as a purely physical problem. These speculations had the defect, so far as early nineteenth-century geology was concerned, of being too general and too little based on fact to be of much use in detailed interpretation of the history of the earth's crust. The origin and history of the earth on the scale that concerned these older writers was primarily a problem in astronomy, and it was not until the twentieth century that this problem was again taken up, using a great deal of new information about the chemistry of stars and planets, in such a way as to be useful to geology.

The other line of speculation had close connections with nonscientific problems involved in scriptural authority, producing books with titles like *The Sacred Theory of the Earth,* in which sensational accounts of imaginary catastrophes made geology popular with the general reading public as well as with political authorities. This trend was especially well developed in eighteenth- and nineteenth-century England, and persisted in the United States in the writings of such influential scientists as Louis Agassiz until well past the middle of the nineteenth century.

The French naturalist Buffon in his *Theory of the Earth* (1749) described six stages in the history of the earth as it cooled from an incandescent mass, a history destined for a frozen conclusion 60,000 years in the future. Basing his calculations on experiments with heated iron globes, he allowed about 3,000 years for the earth to condense to a solid sphere, another 30,000 years before it got cool enough to touch, to support life. Animals appeared on the land 30,000 years later, about 15,000 years before the present. The earth is already too cold, Buffon thought, for its internal heat to produce volcanoes. He thought volcanic heat came from burning coal beds, so that volcanoes appeared only after there had been time for the remains of forests to accumulate and to be buried.

The first of the important men in modern geology, the Scotsman James Hutton, could find little use for such a broad outline in his *Theory of the Earth, with Proofs and Illustrations,* published in 1795. Hutton was one of those self-motivated amateurs who were important in nineteenth-century science. After getting a medical degree that was never used, he took up agriculture on a small inherited farm, developed it to a high degree of efficiency, then leased it for enough income to be able to devote an uneventful life in Edinburgh to scholarship. His high reputation rests mainly on his geological work, and this only by the chance that his difficult and obscure writing on this subject was rendered into plain English by his friend John Playfair, who in 1802 spread Hutton's doctrines with his *Illustrations of the Huttonian Theory of the Earth.*

Hutton thought that questions of origins were beyond the scope of geology, and that it should confine itself to the study of rocks and of the wind and water and other agents that altered and produced them. With every rain, sand and mud are carried from the hillsides downstream, and out the river mouths, where sediments continually accumulate and spread out into layered deltas. It could be observed in deep mines that there was a source of subterranean heat; if river sediments were deeply buried, the pressure and high temperature could change the silts and sands into stone. Hutton thought that the heat caused relatively slow heaving and buckling of the earth's crust, as manifested in earthquakes, which over long periods of time produced mountain ranges and the tilted strata of sedimentary rocks that could be seen on their flanks.

The French biologist Lamarck, who had been led into geology mainly by his work on living and extinct shells, like Hutton spoke out for a science of earth history based on observation of processes that can actually be seen in operation. In his *Hydrogeologie*, published in 1802, he said that erosion alone was responsible for shaping the earth's surface. He had the idea that the ocean basins gradually cut their way around the world, the waves eating at the eastern margins of the continents, and piling up the eroded rock on their western sides, this mainly from the influence of the moon.

The opposing school of the catastrophists had some observational evidence to support it in the work of the French scientist Cuvier, whose remarkable researches on the bones in the rocks of the Paris basin founded the science of paleontology. What Cuvier found were beds of vast numbers of fossil bones, like huge graveyards, and that in a given layer were remains of animals of species different from those either above or below. This evidence, together with the small amount of information available from other parts of the world, was used in the influential *Essay on the Revolutions of the Surface of the Earth*, which was an introduction to his massive four-volume work on fossil bones of extinct animals, published in 1811. Soon after, the essay was translated into English under the title *Essay on the Theory of the Earth*, and in Great Britain this and other writings of Cuvier became a scientific bulwark for the school of sensational geological writing.

Evidence for the latest of the worldwide cataclysms described in his *Essay* was provided by the remains of such now-tropical animals as elephants and rhinos found frozen in ice in Siberia. These tropical animals had been killed and frozen in an instant by a widespread catastrophe, Cuvier thought. They were so well-preserved that even their long shaggy fur could be seen, and a later critic of Cuvier ironically observed that these animals must have had such long and dense fur "to keep them warm in the tropics." Elsewhere, according to Cuvier, there were great floods that covered all countries inhabited by men and other animals, with only a few individuals escaping to repopulate the dry land exposed when the waters receded.

The founder of modern geology was the Englishman Charles Lyell, who, although he came after Cuvier, was in thought the successor of Hutton. He studied on a worldwide scale the literature of geology and brought it together in his detailed and judicious *Principles of Geology*, a textbook in three volumes that came out over a period of three years, from 1830 to 1833. The first two volumes were revised even before the third had appeared, and in subsequent revision through eleven editions this authoritative textbook exerted a guiding influence in the rapidly maturing science.

Lyell, like Hutton, believed that physically the earth was the same in the past as now. There had been minor cycles of uplift and erosion, but through time without beginning, there had been no long-range progressive change. Cuvier, on the other hand, believed that sudden catastrophes, more violent and widespread than anything experienced by man since the Deluge, were important in earth history. But, paradoxically, Cuvier agreed with the uniformitarians in saying that living things had always been pretty much the same, the apparent changes after each catastrophe resulting merely from sudden migrations of animals from unknown regions to replace those exterminated. Lamarck, who founded the science of invertebrate paleontology, believed that the progression apparent in the record of the rocks was real, that evolution had taken place. Lyell carefully considered Lamarck's theory, but rejected it in favor of an interpretation similar to

Cuvier's. In 1830, Lyell felt confident in denying progressive change in life. Geologists had only made a few pinprick samples on the earth's surface. It was too soon to generalize on the basis of this limited evidence. Maybe mammals would yet be found in the oldest rocks. The older the strata, the more they would have been subject to erosion and other destructive forces, so one could expect their record to be most incomplete. The sudden catastrophic extinctions described by Cuvier were illusions caused by incomplete sequences of rock layers. The sudden appearance of new forms of life was likewise an illusion. During the slow, rhymic, local changes of climate that were characteristic of earth history, whole floras and faunas might become locally extinct, but they could be replaced by immigrations from other areas, and in an incomplete fossil record this could give the illusion of sudden extinction.

The only exception that Lyell made to his theory that life had always been about as it is now was for man. He admitted that if human works as big as the Egyptian pyramids and temples or the Roman roads had been in existence during the time the rocks of the geological record were deposited, they could not fail to have been discovered by geologists. Man, he thought, must have been created by some supernatural agency at a very recent time in earth history.

Also Lyell was forced to admit from the evidence of fossils, and the fact that the living world was by now fairly completely explored, that species do become extinct and that new ones appear. He made this conform to his uniformitarian doctrine by assuming that new species appeared about as often as species became extinct, and that the new species differed only in minor detail from already existing ones. He even calculated an average rate at which new species came into existence, reaching the conclusion that the formation of a new species was such a rare event that it could even in his own time be happening, say in the forests of Britain, with a good chance of the event going unnoticed. He conceived, then, of species dropping out of existence, and of their being replaced inconspicuously by some unknown process that did not create any real novelties.

It would be a mistake to think that Lyell's approach is scientific because he said that only the geological forces in action now were in action in the past, and that Cuvier's was unscientific because he postulated catastrophes of far greater violence than anything known to man. What happened was that in the long run the new facts of geology, that kept pouring in at an ever-increasing rate, were explained better by uniformitarian than by catastrophist views. The deep, flood-deposited gravels, for example, were usually found to be more or less local and of different ages, instead of being worldwide and contemporaneous, as had been postulated by the theory of the universal deluge.

Lyell's view meant that if mountains were lifted up by the inch-by-inch, or sometimes yard-by-yard movement of earthquakes, then the earth is very old indeed, while with Cuvier's view earth history did not necessarily extend very far into the past. Similarly, the gradual deposition of sediments by normal stream action meant that the lowest of the miles-thick layers of sedimentary rocks were very ancient.

The modern verdict on the major contribution of Lyellian geology to the evolution theory is that it allowed enough time in earth history for organic evolution to take place—it gave Darwin the "gift of time," as Loren Eiseley puts it. Also by interpreting the geologic past in terms of known processes it gave biologists confidence that it was possible to interpret the history of life in scientific fashion.

The first of the biologists to use evolution theory in a large-scale and systematic fashion to explain the facts of biology was the French naturalist Jean Baptiste Lamarck, whose *Philosophie Zoologique*, published in 1809, is in large part devoted to a discussion of the causes and results of organic evolution. The role of Lamarck in the development of evolution theory is not easy to evaluate. It has been said that Lamarck's writings served mainly to discredit evolution as a worthwhile biological theory. However, even though his evolutionary writings were ridiculed during his lifetime, and not even mentioned in Darwin's *Origin of Species* of 1859, he did bring the idea of evolution forcefully to the attention of biologists (even though they thought it unscientific), and Darwin himself, as he published successive revisions of his book to meet criticism of his own theory of evolution by natural selection, had to rely more and more on one of the factors that Lamarck had thought an important cause of evolution: the inheritance of acquired characters. To the present day important biologists have termed themselves Lamarckians, but they represent a minority opinion, and although evolution itself is taken as fact, the causes of evolution postulated by Lamarck cannot be shown to exist by experiment or observation.

Lamarck can be regarded as an intellectual descendent of the materialistic philosophers of the French Age of Reason. One of the most influential of these in the field of popular science writing was Georges Buffon. Buffon did some experimental work in physics, and translated one of Newton's books on mathematics into French, but early in life he began (1749) his vast *Histoire Naturelle, générale et particulaire,* which by 1804 extended into forty-four volumes of detailed descriptions of man and other vertebrate animals and such nonbiological subjects as mineralogy. They were written for the general reader, and proved to be immensely popular. In these volumes were his essay on the history of the earth (discussed here previously) and hints of an evolutionary origin of animals and man. His heretic views brought condemnation from the Church, and Buffon yielded gracefully by writing, in a later volume, that he believed everything written in the Scriptures about Creation, and hereby abandoned anything he had said that contradicted Moses.

Lamarck died in 1829 at the age of eighty-five, with his writings, except for those on the classification of plants and animals, discredited by influential opinion of his time. Until the age of fifty, Lamarck had been a well-known botanist—the author of a successful *Flore Française*, which went through several editions—and a member of the French Academy of Science. He contributed an important "Dictionaire de Botanique" to the great *Encyclopédie Méthodique*. He was a protégé of Buffon's and in company with Buffon's son made a collecting trip through Europe gathering materials for the Royal Garden. As a result of administrative changes at the time of the French Revolution, Lamarck's position as herbarium keeper was abolished, and he was appointed to a post as a zoologist in the Museum of Natural History, although he had not done any work with animals. Going into a new field at the age of fifty, Lamarck entered a phase of intense creative activity which produced writing on meteorology, geology, general works on biology, and a seven-volume work on invertebrate animals. Had he confined his efforts to this last work, his reputation as a biologist would have been secure, for he made many important innovations in classification, successfully untangling problems that had baffled Linnaeus and Cuvier.

Lamarck's writing on meteorology was particularly disastrous, attracting the attention even of Napoleon. It is related that on being presented to Napoleon, he handed the Emperor a copy of his well-known book *Zoological Philosophy*. Without glancing at it, Napoleon remarked, "Is it your absurd *Meteorologie* with which you are disgracing your old age?" Lamarck, it is said, burst into tears.

Lamarck included his theory of organic evolution in *Recherches sur l'organization des corps vivants*, which was published in 1802. This work is little known. After its publication, Lamarck began to assemble his general views in a more ambitious work which was to be titled *Biologie*. Lamarck's *Biologie* was never published, its place being taken by the *Philosophie Zoologique*, which has been widely translated and has been the most influential of Lamarck's speculative writings. The *Philosophie*, Lamarck said, was essentially an enlarged revision of the *Recherches*.

The word "biology" apppears to have been invented independently by Lamarck and by the German biologist Gottfried Treviranus in the latter's *Biologie; oder die Philosophie der lebenden Natur* (1802–1822). Like Lamarck, Treviranus described a theory of organic evolution. The term "biology" gained general usage in the English language in the writings of Thomas Huxley and Herbert Spencer in the middle of the century. Lamarck's concept of a science that could be called biology is justified in the *Philosophie*. He thought that the old Linnaean classification of nature into three kingdoms—plant, animal, and mineral—should be replaced by a division into two major entities—organic (plants and animals) and inorganic, and notes the great difference between these realms:

. . . between crude or inorganic bodies and living bodies there exists an immense difference, a great hiatus, in short, a radical distinction such that no inorganic body whatever can even be approached by the simplest of living bodies. Life and its constituents in a body make the fundamental difference that distinguishes this body from all those that are without it.

How great then is the error of those who try to find a connection or sort of gradation between certain living bodies and inorganic bodies!

Lamarck also invented the related term and concept, "biosphere" to designate the living part of the world.

Although he thus sees a great gulf between the living and non-living worlds, Lamarck also thought that the simplest plants and animals were constantly arising from inorganic matter by spontaneous generation. Minute algae and protozoans quickly appear and flourish in the smallest natural body of water, and Lamarck assumed that when their habitat dried up, these fragile organisms had no way to survive, and thus perishing had to be replaced, when circumstances again became favorable, by spontaneous generation.

Lamarck considered life to consist of matter, of the right kind and arranged in the proper way, together with an inciting cause that produced the movement and other phenomena of life. This inciting cause, he explained was not a "vital principle" peculiar to life, but one or two of the "subtle fluids" of the physical science of his time—caloric (or heat) and electricity. It was also the interaction of these with matter that produced spontaneous generation.

Once the simple organisms arise by spontaneous generation they can evolve, thought Lamarck, in the course of succeeding generations into more complex organisms. In a brief statement on the origin and evolution of life, Lamarck says:

> Thus as soon as nature has endowed a body with life, the mere existence of life in that body, however simple its organization may be, gives birth to the three faculties named above [assimilation, reproduction, and death]; and its subsequent stay in this same body slowly works its inevitable destruction.

But we shall see that life, especially in favourable conditions, tends by its very nature to a higher organization, to
the creation of special organs, to the isolation of these
organs and their functions, and to the division and multipli-
cation of its own centres of activity. Now since reproduction
permanently preserves all that has been acquired, there have
come from this fertile source in course of time the various
living bodies that we observe; lastly, from the remains left
by each of these bodies after death, have sprung the various minerals known to us. This is how all natural bodies are
really productions of nature, although she has directly given
existence to the simplest living bodies only.

Lamarck, then, gives as the main cause of evolution an innate
tendency for living things to increase the complexity of their organization and function; or more simply, evolution takes place
because organisms have a tendency to evolve. This is merely a
restatement, it is not a scientific theory that can be tested by experiment or observation. Just as a dictionary definition of a word
must involve terms different in operational significance from the
word being defined, so a scientific theory or hypothesis must be
framed as to involve operations different from the process that is
being explained.
    The observation that led Lamarck to the theory that such a ten-
dency toward progression exists was that the main groups of animals could be arranged as a more-or-less evenly graded series
leading from the infusorians (including protozoans) through
such groups as the insects, annelid worms, and fishes, to the
mammals; but Lamarck would have stated his conclusion in more
scientific form if he had said merely that this observation (to the
extent that it is true) indicates that evolution has taken place, not
that it says by what mechanisms evolution has taken place. La-

149

marck did not say that all species of animals could be arranged in a "single chain of being," from lowest to highest; all he said was that the main groups could be so arranged:

> . . . nature, by giving existence in the course of long periods of time to all the animals and plants, has really formed a true scale in each of these kingdoms as regards the increasing complexity of organisation, but that the gradations in this scale which we are bound to recognise when we deal with objects according to their natural affinities, are only perceptible in the main groups of the general series, and not in the species or even in the genera. This fact arises from the extreme diversity of conditions in which the various races of animals and plants exist; for these conditions have no relation to the increasing complexity of organisation, as I shall show; but they produce anomalies or deviations in the external shape and characters which could not have been brought about solely by the growing complexity of organisation.

The classification proposed by Lamarck bears out very well his assertion that there did exist a graded series of stages in organization from lowest to highest:

First stage. No nerves; no vessels; no specialized internal organ except for digestion (infusorians and polyps).

Second stage. No ganglionic longitudinal cord; no vessels for circulation; a few internal organs in addition to those of digestion (radiarians and worms).

Third stage. Nerves terminating in a ganglionic longitudinal cord; respiration by air-carrying tracheae; circulation absent or imperfect (insects and arachnids).

150

Fourth stage. Nerves terminating in a brain or a ganglionic longitudinal cord; respiration by gills; arteries and veins for circulation (crustaceans, annelids, and molluscs).

Fifth stage. Nerves terminating in a brain which is far from filling the cranial cavity; heart with one ventricle, and the blood cold (fishes and reptiles).

Sixth stage. Nerves terminating in a brain which fills the cranial cavity; heart with two ventricles, and the blood warm (birds and mammals).

Lamarck does not assert that the groups within each stage can be arranged end-to-end to take their place in a single graded series of animals; indeed, he says they cannot.

To the main cause of evolution (the innate tendency of life toward increasing complexity) Lamarck added a second, which is responsible for the deviations that animals show from a single graded evolutionary series, and which accounts for the characteristic adaptive features that one sees in animals. This second factor involves the influence of the environment, and Lamarck speculated that this influence was realized through the operation of two laws. The first law states that if an organ is used, it tends to increase in size and strength; and that if it is disused, it deteriorates and finally disappears. The second law is that these effects of use or disuse are inherited.

An example of the effects of the use of an organ, and of the consequences of the inheritance of these effects, which has provoked the ridicule of generations of biologists, is provided by his famous explanation for the long neck of the giraffe:

It is interesting to observe the result of habit in the peculiar shape and size of the giraffe (Camelo-pardalis) : this animal, the largest of the mammals, is known to live in the interior of Africa in places where the soil is nearly always arid and barren, so that it is obliged to browse on the leaves of trees and to make constant efforts to reach them. From this habit long maintained in all its race, it has resulted that the animal's fore-legs have become longer than its hind legs, and that its neck is lengthened to such a degree that the giraffe, without standing up on its hind legs, attains a height of six metres.

The effects of disuse (although nothing is said of possible evolutionary consequences) are described in this example:

M. Tenon, a member of the Institute, has notified to the class of sciences, that he had examined the intestinal canal of several men who had been great drinkers for a large part of their lives, and in every case he had found it shortened to an extraordinary degree, as compared with the same organ in all those who had not adopted the like habit.

It is known that great drinkers, or those who are addicted to drunkenness, take very little solid food, and eat hardly anything; since the drink which they consume so copiously and frequently is sufficient to feed them.

Now since fluid foods, especially spirits, do not long remain either in the stomach or intestine, the stomach and the rest of the intestinal canal lose among drinkers the habit of being distended, just as among sedentary persons, who are continually engaged on mental work and are accustomed to take very little food; for in their case also the stomach slowly shrinks and the intestine shortens.

Taken by and large, Lamarck's evolution theory is a failure, making at best a minor contribution to the development of biology. He provided no explanation for the progressive feature of evolution—the appearance of more complex from simpler types —and his professed explanation for what he took to be only the detailed and even deviant features of evolution—the individual adaptations of organisms—was based on a premise (the inheritance of acquired characters) which could rather easily be proved false.

Compared with the successful theoretical work of Charles Darwin, that of Lamarck is more diffuse, being merely a part of a much more extensive philosophical work on zoology. Lamarck's effort, so far as evolution theory is concerned, is thin and scant compared to the massive performance of Darwin. Lamarck's work also suffered from the fact that, at least in zoology, he was a cabinet naturalist rather than a field naturalist. It would take a man with a profound knowledge and understanding of the lives of animals and plants in nature to formulate an effective theory of organic evolution.

Evolution
by Natural Selection

THE THEORY OF ORGANIC EVOLUTION by means of natural selection was made a part of the general theoretical structure of science by Charles Darwin's *On the Origin of Species by Means of Natural Selection, or the Preservation of Favoured Races in the Struggle for Life,* published in 1859. This theory occupies a central position in modern biology, organizing diverse data that range from observational natural history on the one hand to biochemistry on the other. It for the first time brought the apparent teleology or purpose of the living world into the realm of scientific explanation, thus creating a revolution in thought comparable in magnitude to those of Newton, Marx, or Freud.

As was pointed out in the preceding chapter, along with the growth of science during and after the sixteenth and seventeenth centuries there was progressive development of evolutionary thinking, at first among the philosophers, then among the popular writers, and finally among the specialists in the various scientific disciplines.

Up to the time of Darwin, Lamarck was the only biologist to develop a theory of organic evolution in extensive fashion. Its failure as a scientific theory was discussed in the preceding chapter. The writings that will be taken up here as a background to the development of Darwin's theory will be those of such popularizers as Erasmus Darwin and Robert Chambers, whose work was read by Darwin. He apparently knew nothing of the development of evolutionary theory by the philosophers.

There were scattered through the technical biological literature of the first forty years of the nineteenth century nearly all of the main ideas that appeared in the *Origin*. In the third edition of the *Origin* (1861), Darwin, in response to criticism, inserted a brief "Historical sketch of the progress of opinion on the origin of species, previously to the publication of the first edition of this work," in which he lists, besides the well-known general writers, some thirteen references in the technical literature to evolution or to natural selection, and historians continually find more. Darwin, however, had undoubtedly never seen most of these references when he wrote his book. As in Darwin's other books, the fabric of the *Origin* is woven from primary facts of natural history, gathered from his own observations and those of others, not from ideas expressed by others. He always seems to be completely uninterested in tracing out the historical development of a line of thought.

Nevertheless, Darwin inherited a part of the cultural heritage of evolutionary thinking as surely as he inherited the wealth from his father that made him independent for life. When he entered the world of science by being proposed for the post of naturalist on the *H.M.S. Beagle*, he was introduced as the "grandson of the eminent philosopher, Erasmus Darwin." And when Charles Darwin, just returned from the voyage of the *Beagle*, opened his notebook on "transmutation" that was to lead, decades later, to the *Origin*, his first entry was a reference to his grandfather's book *Zoonomia*, a book which contained an account of the evolution of living things.

Erasmus Darwin was a scientist and poet who made his living as a highly successful physician. The best known of his three books of poetry was the *Botanic Garden*, something of a textbook of botany, said to be enthusiastic and filled with a love of nature, but entirely lacking in other poetic qualities. His theory of evolution was propounded in his prose treatise on medicine entitled *Zoonomia*, a well-known work that was translated into several languages. Here Erasmus points out that such facts as the structural similarities of warm-blooded animals—including man—and the fact that man has by artificial selection produced widely different breeds of dogs, would lead one to conclude that the great diversity of living things has been produced from a common ancestor, from "one living filament, which the great First Cause endowed with animality." Some of Erasmus' ideas as to the causes of evolution were remarkably like the later ones of Lamarck, and Charles Darwin wrote that his grandfather "anticipated the views and erroneous grounds of opinions of Lamarck." Very likely it was the influence of his grandfather's work that helped prepare in his unconscious mind the seed bed from which there emerged his conviction that evolution had taken place.

Charles Darwin had at the age of twenty-seven completed a

five-year voyage around the world as naturalist on a British exploring vessel; at thirty had produced what has been called one of the best travel books ever written; by middle age had an unsurpassed command of the immensely wide field of natural history and at the age of fifty published the *Origin;* and by the end of his life had written twenty books and over eighty technical papers. With little visible effort he increased the fortune left by his father to the point that he was a millionaire. All this was accomplished with a humorous and quiet modesty unparalleled in the lives of the great men of science.

Darwin's gifts of energy, of a true democratic spirit, of simplicity, and of courage were resolutely deployed to give him complete mastery of the field of natural history, to communicate to the broadest audience possible for one his interests and background, and to fight for his beliefs without envy or rancor. He wrote in one of the most effective and unassuming styles ever used by a scientific writer, never rising above the level of understanding of the naturally quick-witted common man. He directed from behind the scenes a remarkably astute campaign that won worldwide acceptance of the theory of organic evolution. His lieutenants and close friends were among the most competent and influential naturalists of the nineteenth century: Joseph Hooker (a widely traveled botanist), Asa Gray (the founder of American botany), Charles Lyell (the founder of modern geology), and Thomas Huxley (zoologist and fearless propagandist).

A most significant fact of Darwin's career is that he was always a free agent. When he was sent to the University of Edinburgh to get a degree in medicine, he had learned, he says candidly in his "Autobiography" (written for his children, not for publication), that he would inherit enough from his father, a successful physician, to live comfortably, which "was sufficient to check my efforts to learn medicine." At Edinburgh the valuable part of his education was his voluntary association with a few young naturalists, and the free and easy life of a young sportsman. He was an avid and apparently expert huntsman. While there he heard Audubon talk on North American birds; and a "negro lived in Edinburgh, who had travelled with Waterton, and gained his livelihood by stuffing birds, which he did excellently: he gave me lessons for payment, and I used often to sit with him for he was a very pleasant and intelligent man." Darwin developed such a horror of lectures at Edinburgh that later at Cambridge he refused to go even when they promised to be of value.

Hearing of Darwin's aversion to a medical career, after two years at Edinburgh, Darwin's father ("very properly vehement against my turning into an idle sporting man, which seemed then a very probable destination") decided to send him to Cambridge to be a clergyman. Again it was really the son who decided his destiny, for "at Cambridge my time was wasted as far as academical studies were concerned, as completely as at Edinburgh and as at school." In other words, he did pretty much as inclination led him. He nostalgically recalls that "I got into a sporting set, including some dissipated low-minded young men. We used often to dine together in the evening, though these dinners often included men of a higher stamp, and we sometimes drank too much, with jolly singing and cards afterwards."

He knew several young naturalists, and became friends with the botanist, Professor Henslow. More pleasurable than shooting and riding he found to be the sport of collecting beetles. He writes, in his old age, of the innate photographic memory of the hunter: "I am surprised what an indelible impression many of the beetles which I caught at Cambridge have left on my mind. I can remember the exact apppearance of certain posts, old trees and banks where I made a good capture . . . I had never seen in those old days *Licinus* alive, which to an uneducated eye hardly differs from many of the black Carabidous beetles: but my sons found here at Down a specimen, and I instantly recognized that it was new to me; yet I had not looked at a British beetle for the last twenty years."

In order to get his B. A. after three years at Cambridge, Darwin had to

> get up Paley's *Evidences of Christianity* and his *Moral Philosophy.* This was done in a thorough manner, and I am convinced that I could have written out the whole of the *Evidences* with perfect correctness, but not of course in the clear language of Paley. The logic of this book and, as I may add, of his *Natural Theology* [which was essentially a textbook on biological adaptation], gave me as much delight as did Euclid. The careful study of these works, without attempting to learn any part by rote, was the only part of the academical course which, as I then felt and as I still believe was of the least use to me in the education of my mind. I did not at that time trouble myself about Paley's premises; and taking these on trust, I was charmed and convinced by the long line of argumentation.

Often it is said that Darwin's appointment to the history-making voyage of the *Beagle* was purely a matter of chance, and this is true, but the inference that he might not have therefore become a widely traveled naturalist in his young manhood may not be a sound one. While at Cambridge he was profoundly interested in Humboldt's *Personal Narrative,* copying out long passages on Teneriffe to try to work up enthusiasm among his friends for an expedition there, and he says that he seriously planned a trip to the island. When the *Beagle* was two years out, in Valparaiso, the captain, R. Fitz-Roy, was invalided and temporarily relinquished his command. It was thought that the voyage would have to be abandoned, and the ship return to England. In a letter to his sister Catherine Darwin he wrote of a plan to leave the ship and explore South America on his own: "One whole night I tried to think over the pleasure of seeing Shrewsbury again, but the barren plains of Peru gained the day. I made the following scheme (I know you will abuse me, and perhaps if I had put it in execution, my father would have sent a mandamus after me); it was to examine the Cordilleras of Chili during this summer, and in winter to go from port to port on the coast of Peru to Lima, returning this time next year to Valparaiso, cross the Cordilleras to Buenos Ayres, and take ship to England."

The five-year odyssey with the *Beagle* was to end Darwin's wanderings. By the time of his marriage, three years after his return, his health had begun to deteriorate, and it seemed to him clear that he would spend the rest of his life as a semi-invalid. One of the most important consequences of his malady—which has never been identified—was that he had to live more or less as a recluse. After a few years in London, he and his wife took a house in the country, at Down, where he lived for the rest of his life, and he summarized the period there from 1842 to 1876 (when his "Autobiography" was written), in this way:

Few persons can have lived a more retired life than we have done. Besides short visits to the house of relations, and occasionally to the seaside or elsewhere, we have gone no-where. During the first part of our residence we went a little into society, and received a few friends here; but my health almost always suffered from the excitement, violent shivering and vomiting attacks thus being brought on. . . . From the same cause I have been able to invite here very few scientific acquaintances.

My chief enjoyment and sole employment throughout life

has been scientific work; and the excitement from such work makes me for the time forget, or dims quite away, my daily discomfort. I have therefore nothing to record during the rest of my life, except the publication of my several books.

During his long semi-isolation at Down, he kept up a warm and vigorous correspondence with friends and other scientists, some of which may be found in the two-volume *Life and Letters of Charles Darwin*, edited by his son Francis. Although quiet and peaceful, the house at Down functioned, in an unobtrusive way, as a kind of staff headquarters where the strategy for the victory of the theory of evolution was developed and carried out under the direction of Darwin, largely through letters to select and powerful friends, but especially after the publication of the *Origin* in 1859, to an ever-widening circle of correspondents reaching into Europe and the United States. The mature Darwin was a skillful general, knowing when to bide his time and when to strike, and how to marshall and use the forces represented by the key people who were his contacts with the outside world. Darwin never appeared on a lecture platform during these years, and only once publicly defended himself from a newspaper attack, which action he regretted.

Darwin's scientific life is divided into two periods, approximately by the event of his moving to Down. The first period is that of the voyage and his triumphant return to England with specimens and notes, winning immediate fame in scientific circles. During this time he published his account of the voyage (*Journal of Researches into the Geology and Natural History of the Various Countries Visited by H.M.S. Beagle*), which made him known over the world long before the publication of the *Origin of Species*. He superintended, as editor, the preparation of five volumes on the vertebrate animals (including fossil mammals) collected by himself during the expedition. There also was a work, written by himself, entitled *The Structure and Distribution of Coral Reefs,* that was based on his own observations, and which turned out to be an enduring contribution to geology. This period, which ended when Darwin was thirty-nine years old, was the time of the hidden incubation of the theory of evolution.

The second period in Darwin's scientific life, which lasted for forty years, ended with his death at Down in 1882. This was the time of the *Origin:* of its slow growth, its publication near the middle of the period, and its subsequent revisions and defense in a series of editions which terminated in 1872. While the *Origin* was the main axis of Darwin's life after the period of the voyage, he usually worked on several projects at once, which nearly all came to fruition in the numerous books and technical papers that came out of the quiet home at Down, with its gardens and greenhouse. Darwin was more an investigator than a writer, and other then the great syntheses of the *Origin* and the *Descent of Man,* his writing was based in large part on detailed study of specimens, as in his work on the classification of barnacles, or upon painstaking experiments and observations carried out over long stretches of time, as in his *Variation of Animals and Plants under Domestication* (1868), *Insectivorous Plants* (1875), *The Effects of Cross and Self Fertilization in the Vegetable Kingdom* (1876), or *The Formation of Vegetable Mould, through the Action of Worms, with Observations on Their Habits* (1881).

It was during the voyage, while studying the natural history of South America—comparing the fossils of huge, extinct armadillo-like animals with their small modern descendents that live in the same area, noting the geographic range of the two kinds of large ostrich-like birds that live in South America, and observing the mosaic patterns of distribution of the giant turtles and of the birds of the Galapagos—that Darwin became convinced that evolution had taken place by the transmutation of species. In a sense he had to discover evolution for himself. By this is meant only that the writings of Erasmus Darwin, or of Lamarck, had not convinced him that evolution had occurred, and that other unrecorded readings, or conversations on the topic, which he would have inevitably encountered by this time, had made little impression on him. By this is meant that it must have dawned upon him at one time or another during these years of wandering, in his late twenties, that these evolutionists were right, after all. But Darwin's method of work was not the historical method. He did not work with other people's words. He set about putting together his theory not by assembling what other people said about evolution, but by assembling facts about distribution, embryology, survival, geology, and other relevant topics. He wrote the first edition of his *Origin* as if he were the first person in the world to write about evolution by natural selection. And indeed it was "his" theory, if by this he meant that most of the professional naturalists of his time believed in "special creation," as he had himself before the voyage. And certainly it was "his" theory, if he also meant by this not only that evolution had taken place, but that it had taken place by natural selection, a theory that he for the first time documented with abundant evidence from diverse areas of natural history.

In July of 1837, ten months after landing at Falmouth, he began his series of notebooks on the transmutation of species. Like others before him, he saw at the beginning that the key analogy to evolution in nature was the kind of evolution that man had produced by selecting varieties of domestic animals and plants. What process in nature was operating that could produce the same results? In his notebooks, Darwin had, within a little more than a year after starting on the project, written down the idea that species vary in nature, just as they do in the garden and farmyard, and that those variants better adapted to their environment would tend to survive and leave offspring, those poorly adapted would be eliminated. Thus there was a "natural selection" completely analogous to artificial selection. In his "Autobiography" this idea is credited to reading Malthus, which is erroneous, according to the chronology of his own notebooks. At any rate, he did read Malthus (who, in his *Essay on Population,* wrote about excess people being eliminated by the struggle for survival) shortly afterward, and this stage in the evolution of his ideas may not have been clear in his own mind, in retrospect. Probably what he did owe to Malthus was an appreciation of the enormous population growth even in slow-breeding organisms, if causes of mortality are checked.

By 1842 Darwin could write out his theory in nearly complete form. The manuscript of this sketch, discovered after his death, has since been published for its historical interest. This work, known as "Charles Darwin's sketch of 1842," amounts to about fifty printed pages. As this title indicates, it is a sketch, with sentences incomplete, and many of the phrases only references to matters which were to be looked up. However, the material was well organized, and was arranged in chapter headings which were retained in the enlarged essay written two years later, and which blocked out the organization used in the *Origin.*

Two years later, in the summer of 1844, Darwin expanded the sketch into a book-length manuscript, which was published after his death as a companion piece to his sketch of 1842. Titled the *Essay of 1844,* it comes to about 160 printed pages. It is as cogent as the *Origin,* published fifteen years later, and might well have been as effective had it been published in its place. Whether it would have been as effective in 1844 is another matter.

Some months before he finished the 1844 draft Darwin had informed Joseph Hooker about his theory that species were not immutable in an often-quoted letter written in January of 1844:

> Besides a general interest about the southern lands, I have now ever since my return engaged in a very presumptous work, and I know no one individual who would not say a very foolish one. I was so struck with the distribution of the Galapagos organisms, etc., etc., and with the character of the American fossil mammifers, etc., etc., that I determined to collect blindly every sort of fact, which could bear in any way on what are species. I have read heaps of agricultural and horticultural books, and have never ceased collecting facts. At last gleams of light have come, and I am almost convinced (quite contrary to the opinion that I started with) that species are not (it is like confessing a murder) immutable. Heaven forfend me from Lamarck nonsense of a "tendency to progression," "adaptations from the slow willing of animals," etc.,! But the conclusions I am led to are not widely different from his; though the means of change are wholly so. I think I have found (here's presumption!) the simple way by which species become exquisitely adapted to various ends. You will now groan, and think to yourself, "on what a man have I been wasting my time and writing to." I should, nine years ago, have thought so.

Otherwise, Darwin said little or nothing to his friends about his "species work" as he called it. In the second edition of his *Journal of Researches,* published in 1845, he revised the section on the Galapagos Islands, and inserted two statements which hint at his new views on evolution. In describing the now-famous Galapagos ground-finches ("Darwin's finches") he says, in 1845 "Seeing this gradation and diversity of structure in one small, intimately related group of birds, one might really fancy that from an original paucity of birds in this archipelago, one species has been taken and modified for different ends." And, of the fossils of the pampas of South America: "This wonderful relationship on the same continent between the dead and the living will, I do not doubt hereafter throw more light on the appearance of organic beings on our earth, and their disappearance from it, than any other class of facts." The alterations in this edition of the *Journal* appear to be his only public statements that bear on his opinions about evolution, the apppearance of new species by natural processes, until 1858.

The fact that Darwin kept such a considerable work as the 1844 essay so nearly a secret requires some explanation, although Darwin himself does not have much to say about it. It is obvious, however, that if he circulated it privately, the ideas would leak out and be appropriated wherever useful. In a letter to the American botanist Asa Gray written much later, in 1857, he briefly outlines his theory, and says, "You will, perhaps, think it paltry in me, when I ask you not to mention my doctrine, the reason is, if any one, like the author of the *Vestiges*, were to hear of them, he might easily work them in, and then I should have to quote from a work perhaps despised by naturalists, and this would greatly injure any chance of my views being received by those alone whose opinion I value."

It would seem in character for Darwin to feel that the 1844 effort was too slight to warrant publication, but that this was not the main consideration for not publishing it is shown by the fact that he did not go ahead and expand it. Instead, he dropped the project rather completely for a period of several years.

Perhaps what decided him to forget it until better times was the publication of a popular book on evolution called *Vestiges of the History of Creation*, which appeared anonymously in 1844.

This, it later became known, was written by Robert Chambers, who was a geologist, an authority on the antiquities of Scotland, and a publisher interested in getting good but cheap informative books to the general public. Chambers said that such facts as the similarities within groups of organisms, the progression from lower to higher vertebrates in the fossil record, and the resemblances between embryos of animals that are widely different when mature could only be explained by evolution.

Biological evolution was only part of the theme of the *Vestiges*. The author describes the whole sweep of cosmic evolution, in the style of the authors of the eighteenth century, and treats organic evolution only as one aspect of a general Law of Development that governs the history of the universe. In living things, Chambers thought, there was a driving force towards improvement like the one that drove an embryo towards development to the adult. He made the relationship between embryonic and evolutionary development closer than analogy. He thought, for example, that a fish and a man followed the same course of embryological development, but that some influence made the fish stop at the point characteristic of its species, and go off at a tangent to become a fish, while at the same point the human embryo would have continued on to its destiny. In the production of a new species, a tendency to go on past the normal stopping point manifests itself. Countering the objection that the idea of man's origin from lower animals is degrading, Chambers uses arguments of a theological kind:

It has pleased Providence to arrange that one species should give birth to another, until the second highest, give birth to man, who is the very highest: be it so, it is our part to admire and submit. The very faintest notion of there being anything ridiculous or degrading in the theory—how absurd does it appear, when we remember that every individual among us actually passes through the characters of the insect, the fish, and reptile (to speak nothing of others) before he is permitted to breathe the breath of life. But such notions are the mere emanations of false pride and ignorant prejudice. He who conceives them, little reflects that they, in reality, involve the principle of a contempt for the works and ways of God.

The *Vestiges* was saturated with errors of biological fact and interpretation, ranging from the trivial to the fantastically absurd, and was savagely attacked by many biologists, with a lack of mercy that did no credit to the professionals. They showed their obtuseness in failing to appreciate the scope and aim of the author who, obviously, claimed no standing as a professional biologist.

This ungracious attitude toward the book was, however, by no means universal among the scientific profession. In the very influential *American Journal of Science* there appeared in 1845 this editorial review of the *Vestiges:*

This work commences with a spirited sketch of the astronomical system according to the Nebular theory. The author then proceeds to give an outline of the structure of the earth and the various steps in the progress of its formation, both as regards the origin of its rock strata and the successive changes in animal and vegetable life. Discussion with regard to the origin and development of animals, the early history of mankind, the mental constitution of animals, and the general condition of the animated creation, constitute a large part of the work; and the whole is presented in a novel and interesting light, with many bold conceptions and startling opinions. Although we cannot subscribe to all of our author's views, we would strongly recommend the work to our readers.

Apparently Adam Sedgewick, professor at Cambridge, and a leading geologist, did appreciate its scope, and feared its influence, for in 1850 he added an enormous Preface to his slender volume on "A Discourse on the Studies at the University of Cambridge" of which 200 pages or so were specifically a refutation of the *Vestiges*. Elsewhere, in a review, he writes:

> The world cannot bear to be turned upside down. . . . If our glorious maidens and matrons may not soil their fingers with the dirty knife of the anatomist, neither may they   poison the springs of joyous thought and modest feelings, by listening to the seductions of this author; who comes before them with . . . the serpent coils of a false philosophy. If the philosophy of the *Vestiges* be accepted by the multitude as true What then will follow? The reader can judge for himself: I can see nothing but ruin and confusion in such a creed. . . . If current in society it will undermine the whole moral and social fabric, and inevitably will bring discord and deadly mischief in its train; and on this account . . . I believe it utterly untrue.

Chambers' book was a popular success, being the kind of work that would delight the intelligent liberal with wide reading interests. It sold nearly 25,000 copies in England before the publication of the *Origin*, going through many editions, and was frequently reprinted in the United States. It was one of Abraham Lincoln's favorite books, and he became a warm advocate of the "new doctrine" of evolution.

Darwin read the *Vestiges* carefully. In an undated letter (probably 1844) to Hooker he wrote, "I have also read the *Vestiges*, but have been somewhat less amused at it than you appear to have been: the writing and arrangement are certainly admirable, but his geology strikes me as bad, and his zoology far worse." And in February of 1845 he wrote to William Darwin Fox, a cousin, "Have you read that strange, unphilosophical, but capitally-written book, the *Vestiges:* it has made more talk than any work of late, and has been attributed by some to me—at which I ought to be much flattered and unflattered." In October, 1845, Darwin wrote to Lyell about Sedgewick's review of the *Vestiges:* "I have been much interested with Sedgewick's review; though I find far from popular with our scientific readers. I think some few passages savour of the dogmatism of the pulpit rather than of the philosophy of the Professor's Chair . . . . Nevertheless, it is a grand piece of argument against mutability of species, and I read it with fear and trembling, but was well pleased to find that I had not overlooked any of the arguments, though I had put them to myself as feebly as milk and water."

It may be that the reception of the *Vestiges* showed Darwin that it was an extremely bad time to come out with another book on evolution. Quite likely his work would have been misinterpreted and lost in the maelstrom of criticism that was swallowing up the scientific reputation of the author of the *Vestiges.* Also Darwin may not have been too certain of his own reputation as a biologist at the time, since he speaks in his letters of the desirability of doing some work on classification himself if he were going to write about the species question, and he was encouraged to take up work in this direction by Hooker.

In July of 1844 Darwin established a safety point in his work on evolution with a letter to his wife requesting that in event of his death she take steps to publish his 1844 essay:

> I have just finished my sketch of the species theory. If, as I believe, my theory in time be accepted even by one competent judge, it will be a considerable step in science.

I therefore write this in case of my sudden death, as my most solemn and last request, which I am sure you will consider the same as if legally entered in my will, that you will devote £400 to its publication . . . I wish that my sketch be given to some competent person, with this sum to induce him to take trouble in its improvement and enlargement.

And the businessman Darwin adds: "Should one other hundred pounds make the difference in procuring a good editor, request earnestly that you will raise £500." He preferred that Lyell be the editor, but also suggests Hooker and others as possibilities.

This step was evidently taken only because he had just finished the essay, and could have had nothing to do with the *Vestiges*, which did not come out until October of the same year.

The situation was, then, that by 1842 Darwin had worked out in nearly complete form his theory of evolution, five years after beginning work on the subject. Within another two years he had written it up in essentially publishable form. The outline of the theory was the same in 1842 as it was in 1859, except for the principle of divergence, which he added in the early 1850s to explain how it came about that species not only changed, but did so in such a way as to steadily become more different from each other, in the course of adapting to different modes of life. Except for this one development, the theory lay dormant for the next eight years, while Darwin turned to the description and classification of some 200 species of barnacles, a chore so long-drawn-out and laborious that Darwin's son once asked a little friend, where does *your* father do his barnacles?

Darwin has said that this long diversion into purely descriptive work on dead specimens made a trained naturalist of him. It may be that this reflects an underestimation of the work he had already done as a naturalist on the *Beagle*, but anyway, his two-volume monograph of the barnacles was the kind of thing that the world of "professional" biologists looked on as the proper kind of work for a naturalist. Darwin performed with the same kind of competence he had shown on the voyage. Starting with a single remarkable barnacle he had found on the coast of Chile, he obtained use of the large collection at the British Museum, and by correspondence got large amounts of material from collectors in Britain, the United States, and Europe, so that in all he had about 10,000 specimens to work with. Previous work on the classification of the group was superficial, and Darwin had to do real pioneering work, discovering new characters for classifying them by doing laborious dissections. He was more than a pioneer, though, because his work is still, a hundred years later, the standard reference.

Darwin's treatise on the barnacles is far more generous than the usual systematic work. What would for most systematists of his time pass for a complete classification of the barnacles is in Darwin's treatment a synopsis crowded into a little over thirty pages of fine print at the end of the second volume. He goes at the problem as a biologist, not as a systematist, and most of the text is devoted to anatomy, natural history, variation, and distribution. Darwin at one point refused to have his name go after the new species he described—he thought that this vanity was responsible for much of the shoddy species describing that had been done—but he gave in (the only way he could have made good his threat was to refuse to publish the books), and his name stands as that of the discoverer and original describer of some eighty or ninety new species of fossil and living barnacles, about 45 percent of all the species known in the mid-nineteenth century.

The volumes on the barnacles (*Monograph of the Cirripedia*) came out in 1854. Shortly after this, Darwin began raising pigeons, as part of his work on the origin of species. His opening argument in developing the theory of evolution was to be that man could change the form and habits of domestic animals by selection, and he wanted to have firsthand experience with the results. The pigeons were a good choice because there were numerous varieties which were much different in structure and behavior, and it seemed fairly certain that all had been produced by human selection from a single wild species, the Rock dove, which was still in existence. Also, they were conveniently small, with a short generation-time. As always with Darwin, he had here a good appreciation of the ingenuity, competence, and devotion of the amateur. One of his favorite illustrations of the unswerving enthusiasm of the British hobbyist he found in a treatise on "Pigeons" by a Mr. J. Eaton, who wrote:

> If it was possible for noblemen and gentlemen to know the amazing amount of solace and pleasure derived from the Almond Tumbler, when they begin to understand their properties, I should think that scarce any nobleman or gentleman would be without their aviaries of Almond Tumblers.

During this early period of renewed effort in his evolution project, Darwin also did experimental work on methods whereby seeds and small animals might be carried to islands. He soaked seeds (and wanted to soak lizard eggs) in salt water, and raised seedlings from mud that could as well have been fastened to a duck's foot.

He also pursued other projects in rather leisurely and high-spirited fashion. He wrote to Hooker in 1855 that "Miss Thorley [a governess in the family] and I are doing *a little Botanical work*! for our amusement, and it does amuse me very much . . . I have just made out [identified] my first grass, hurrah! hurrah! I must confess that fortune favours the bold, for, as luck would have it, it was the easy *Anthoxanthum adoratum*; nevertheless it is a great discovery; I never expected to make out a grass in all

173

my life, so hurrah! It has done my stomach surprising good."

In 1856, Darwin, in the middle of what could have been an endless series of experiments, was jogged by Lyell to write up his theory in publishable form: someone else might come up with the same idea. Darwin replied with: "I do not know what to think; I rather hate the idea of writing for priority, yet I certainly should be vexed if anyone were to publish my doctrines before me." But he did begin in 1856 to write up, not the brief sketch suggested by Lyell, but what he intended as a work of some thousand pages or more, which was to have the title *Natural Selection*.

By 1856, at least Lyell, Hooker, and Fox, in England, had been let in on the project, and in the same year Darwin wrote Asa Gray in America to say that he had been working for the past nineteen years on the proposition that species were not created, but were descended from parent species: "species are only strongly defined varieties." In May of 1857 Darwin wrote to Alfred Russel Wallace, then in the Malay Archipelago, concerning a paper of Wallace's that had been published in a British journal, which set out some of the same kind of evidence that Darwin had used to come to his conclusion that species had evolved. Here Darwin was not at all as frank as he had been with Gray; he tells Wallace that he had been working for twenty years "on the question how and in what way do species and varieties differ from each other."

Wallace eventually turned out to be the catalyst for the fast-moving events of 1858–59 that for the first time brought the question of evolution before the scientific world with compelling force. In 1858 Wallace, still in the Archipelago, wrote out in a few hours a sketch of a theory of evolution by natural selection, and sent it to Darwin, with the request that it be forwarded to Lyell. Darwin wrote to Lyell, June, 1858:

He [Wallace] has to-day sent me the enclosed, and asked me to forward it to you. It seems to me well worth reading. Your words have come home with a vengeance—that I should be forestalled. You said this, when I explained to you here very briefly my views of "Natural Selection" depending on the struggle for existence. I never saw a more striking coincidence; if Wallace had my MS. sketch written out in 1842, he could not have better made a short abstract! Even his terms now stand as heads of my chapters. Please return me the MS., which he does not say he wishes me to publish, but I shall of course, at once write and offer to send to any journal. So all my originality, whatever it may amount to, will be smashed, though my book, if it will even have any value, will not be deteriorated, as all the labour consists in the application of the theory.

In other correspondence Darwin appealed frantically to both Lyell and Hooker for help in deciding what to do. His friends quickly and astutely worked out a plan of action which was put into effect in a month: In July there was read before the Linnaean Society a five-page précis of Darwin's theory (prepared by him for this purpose), an abstract of Darwin's letter to Gray in the previous year (which showed that Darwin had not borrowed from Wallace), and Wallace's paper, entitled "On the Tendency of Varieties to Depart Indefinitely from the Original Type," which came to twelve pages.

The first that Wallace, in the Malay Archipelago, knew of this was when he got two kind letters from Darwin and Hooker, after it was all over, and proof sheets of his paper as it was to be published. It was not until January of the next year that Wallace's comments got to England, and Darwin writes to Lyell: "I enclose letters to you and me from Wallace. I admire extremely the spirit in which they were written. I never felt very sure what he would say. He must be an amiable man."

It would of course be interesting to know if the papers of Darwin and Wallace would themselves have brought about the revolution in thinking that took place in biology within the next decade, but history is not an experimental science. Darwin at once abandoned work on the huge, diffuse "Natural Selection," and started on what he called an abstract of only 400 or 500 pages, with the design of getting it published within a year.

So far as known, no one rushed into print with the pronouncement that Darwin and Wallace had just made a great contribution to science. Darwin did see a comment by a Rev. S. Haughton made in an address to the Geological Society, Dublin, and conveyed it to Hooker: "This speculation of Messrs. Darwin and Wallace would not be worthy of notice were it not for the weight of authority of the names (i.e., Lyell's and yours) under whose auspices it has been brought forward. If it means what it says, it is a truism; if it means anything more, it is contrary to fact."

Working about three hours a day, and during a time of unusually poor health, Darwin struggled through the composition of his "Abstract" (to the last he wanted to call the book an *Abstract of an Essay on the Origin of Species. . . .* !), sometimes wasting hours in checking, in a heap of twenty years' accumulation of notes, the accuracy of a minor point, sometimes reluctantly abandoning a line of discussion that would have led him too far afield if pursued to the end. He was more than halfway through by the end of 1858, sending Hooker, and sometimes Lyell, pieces of the manuscript for comment as he proceeded. The book was published late in November, 1859, under the title *On the Origin of Species by Means of Natural Selection; or, the Preservation of Favoured*

Races in the Struggle for Life. The 1,250 copies of the first printing were bought by booksellers on the first day.

The book did what the brief Darwin–Wallace paper did not do—it convinced people. The brief papers sound too hypothetical at first reading; they do not engage the interest of the reader, nor start him thinking actively. There is enough detail in the *Origin* to get the reader—especially the trained biologist—involved from the beginning, in the manner of a good detective story. Doubtless the Darwin–Wallace papers by themselves would have started some other biologist on the road to turning out a book comparable to the *Origin* in a few years, but Darwin had already been traveling that road for a long time.

The way that Darwin approaches evolution in the *Origin* is the same way that he apprehended the problem twenty years before: just as man, beginning with a few wild species, could produce by conscious selection the immense variety of domestic plants and animals, so nature, acting by unconscious selection in the unending slaughter of the young, can produce change and variety from preexisting species, from as far back in time as the beginnings of life. Since natural selection preserves, until the age of reproduction the individuals better adapted for the circumstances in which the species lives, it can produce the adaptiveness, the apparent design, that is the most impressive attribute of living nature. This is the core of Darwin's theory of evolution by natural selection, and its discussion takes up more than half his book. He then shifts to a more or less deductive phase in which, having already shown that evolution has taken place, or at least could have taken place, he shows that the facts of geologic succession, of geographic distribution, morphological similarity within the natural groups of the systematist, resemblances of embryos, and rudimentary organs could readily be explained by a theory of descent, whether or not modification had taken place by means of natural selection. Of course the argument can also be turned around, and made an inductive one, with these facts leading to the theory that evolution has taken place, as Darwin says near the end of the book: "Finally, the several classes of facts which have been considered in this chapter [which has the title "Mutual Affinities of Organic Beings: Morphology: Embryology: Rudimentary Organs"] seem to me to proclaim so plainly that the innumerable species, genera, and families of organic beings, with which the world is peopled, have all descended, each within its own class or group, from common parents and have all been modified in the course of descent that I should without hesitation adopt this view, even if it were unsupported by other facts or arguments." He thus acknowledges the weight of arguments that had been used by others before them, like the author of *Vestiges*, to show that evolution had taken place. Darwin's synthesis in addition had given a reasonable explanation as to how evolution took place, with the overwhelming advantage that this explanation at the same time cleared up that greatest of all mysteries, the adaptiveness, the purposiveness, of organic nature.

The theory of evolution by natural selection also explained the existence of the plan of Nature, the intellectually exhilarating order found by the students of classification from Linnaeus on, who saw, with the animal and plant species of the entire world spread before them, that variety was not the projection of a meaningless kaleidoscope, but that there were a relatively few major patterns of organization, repeated with minor variations to produce the hundreds of thousands of species of organisms that make up the living world. Darwin pointed out that the species of a higher category are alike because they have a common ancestry. Modern neo-Darwinians, applying the principle of natural selection more widely than did Darwin, see another factor added. Species that give rise to new categories are those that have achieved an adaptation, or invention, that proves to be of general significance, thus founding a dynasty of species that exploit this major evolutionary advance in various minor ways, retaining the major adaptation that gives the category unity. They acknowledge that several species more or less related might happen upon the adaptation, producing a higher category that does not spring strictly from a single ancestory, and thus adding a complication to the study of evolutionary lineages.

There have been many attempts to sort Darwin's long argument out into a neatly logical pattern, but his book is an inextricable tangle of induction and deduction. He argues like a skilled lawyer, with appeals to fixed minor beliefs that will lead the reader to accept the major thesis, with subtly designed straw men that he demolishes with the reader's approval, with blurred conceptions that allow the reader to take the alternative that best pleases him. Darwin knew how to slide over the difficulties that could not be explained with facts then available. This is not meant in a derogatory sense; it probably was by far the best way to deal with such a diffuse topic as evolution. He had at his command a knowledge of natural history so vast that he could choose an appealing and seemingly leisurely pathway to his conclusion through a jungle of facts, and describe the journey in language of such high technical accuracy that it was beyond professional reproach. He was a man well fitted in his time to write the book that convinced the scholars and academicians that the operation of natural law had produced the varied living world. It may be that the most enlightened part of the general public was already ahead of the scientific world in this respect, but the victory of evolution could not be lasting or effective until it had become an integral, functional part of scientific theory.

Within about a decade after the publication of the *Origin,* the majority opinion among the scientific community was that organic evolution had taken place, which represented a change in intellectual climate owed entirely to Darwin's work. Although it was Darwin's skillful use of the theory of natural selection to explain how evolution and adaptation had come about that brought about the acceptance of evolution, it was the theory of natural selection itself that came increasingly under attack in the decades following the publication of the *Origin*.

There has been ever since the time of Darwin a number of warring camps among students of evolution as to the cause, or causes, or the most important cause of evolutionary change. This confusion can be found to some extent within the *Origin* itself, and in later editions of the book, Darwin gave increasing weight to factors other than natural selection as being involved in evolution without, however, abandoning natural selection as the chief cause. Even in the first edition, he allows that Lamarckian use and disuse (he does not mention that author by name in this connection) accounts for the evolution of certain structures. In discussing the fact that wingless beetles are characteristic of oceanic islands, Darwin points out that natural selection could account for the loss of wings, since the individuals that had a tendency to fly would be blown out to sea, but he does not make this the sole factor: ". . . the wingless condition of so many Madeira beetles is mainly due to the action of natural selection, but combined probably with disuse." Elsewhere he again speaks of the combined effects of use and disuse, and in discussing the degenerate eyes of animals living in caves, he says that "disuse by itself seems to have done its work."

When the critics of natural selection gained in strength during the 1860s and 1870s, Darwin merely had to shift emphasis to the nonselectional causes of evolution that he had already postulated. This never took on the character of a rout; the bulk of the *Origin* remained unchanged in successive editions, through the sixth and last published in 1782, even though additions and alterations tended to contradict the older parts of the work. He never came much nearer to panic than could be inferred from statements such as the following reply to his critics, taken from *The Descent of Man and Selection in Relation to Sex* (1871) :

> I may be permitted to say, as some excuse that I had two distinct objects in view; firstly, to shew that species had not been separately created, and secondly, that natural selection had been the chief agent of change, though largely aided by the inherited effects of habit, and slightly by the direct action of the surrounding conditions. . . . Some of those who admit the principle of evolution but reject selection, seem to forget, when criticizing my book, that I had the above two objects in view; hence if I have erred in giving to natural selection great power, which I am very far from admitting, or in having exaggerated its power, which is in itself probable, I have at least, as I hope, done good service in aiding to overthrow the dogma of separate creations.

The diversity of opinion as to the causes of evolution continues among biologists of today, but the majority of these now give to natural selection an even more important role than that assigned it by Darwin in his first version of the *Origin*.

In Darwin's time, the development in science that most affected evolution theory was the application of physics to the geological problem of the age of the earth. In the 1860's, William Thompson (later Lord Kelvin), one of the leading physicists of the day, carefully analyzed the problem on the basis of such considerations as the friction of the tides, loss of heat from the sun by radiation, and loss of internal heat from the earth by radiation, coming to the conclusion that the age of the earth was very much less than geologists had supposed, to be measured in tens of millions instead of hundreds of millions of years. He was very much aware of the implications for evolution theory, stating that his demonstration of a limited age of the earth made it absolutely necessary to reject the Darwinian theory of evolution by natural selection, which Darwin had said to be a slow and gradual process.

Although some physicists and geologists were skeptical of Thompson's methods and conclusions, it became more or less fashionable among the geologists to go along with the dominant physicists and scout the older conception of vast stretches of geological time. This continued until the turn of the century, when the discovery that radioactive minerals produced heat threw Thompson's theory onto the trash heap.

Darwin was deeply concerned about the implications of Thompson's work, and mentions it in the last edition of the *Origin*. But, characteristically, he does not make it a central point nor find it necessary to make a major revision of the book. Its discussion concerns only a few paragraphs, and the flavor of these is interesting in showing Darwin's soft polemic methods. He prefaces the section on the duration of geological time with this remark, retained from the first edition: "He who can read Sir Charles Lyell's grand work on the *Principles of Geology*, which the future historian will recognise as having produced a revolution in natural science, and yet does not admit how vast have been the past periods of time, may at once close this volume." He then adds that, after all, even a million years is a very long time: ". . . take a narrow strip of paper, 83 feet 4 inches in length, and stretch it along the wall of a large hall; then mark off at one end the tenth of an inch. This tenth of an inch will represent one hundred years, and the entire strip a million years."

The very little change that animals have undergone in the hundreds of thousands of years since the Ice Age made Darwin think that the time needed from the evolution of life before the oldest but quite complex animals known in the fossil record appear must be very long indeed, but "Here we encounter a formidable objection; for it seems doubtful whether the earth, in a fit state for the habitation of living creatures, has lasted long enough. Sir W. Thompson concludes that the consolidation of the crust can hardly have occurred less than 20 or more than 400 million years ago, but probably not less than 98 or more than 200 million years. These very wide limits show how doubtful the data are; and other elements may hereafter to be introduced into the problem." Then, even if Thompson is right, "It is, however, probable, as Sir William Thompson insists, that the world at a very early period was subjected to more rapid and violent changes in its physical conditions than those now occurring; and such changes would have tended to induce changes at a corresponding rate in the organisms which then existed."

Another critic who attracted Darwin's attention was the engineer Fleeming Jenkin, who wrote a critical review of the *Origin* that was published in 1867. Darwin's son found among his father's effects a marked copy of the review on which Charles had indicated a passage as a "good sneer." Jenkin had said that the advocate of evolution by natural selection

can invent trains of ancestors of whose existence there is no evidence; he can marshal hosts of equally imaginary foes; he can call up continents, floods, and peculiar atmospheres; he can cry up oceans, split islands, and parcel out eternity at will; surely with these advantages he must be a dull fellow if he cannot scheme some series of animals and circumstances explaining our assumed difficulty quite naturally. Feeling the difficulty of dealing with adversaries who command so huge a domain of fancy, we will abandon these arguments, and trust to those which at least cannot be assailed by mere efforts of imagination.

Jenkin then goes on to the serious business of refuting natural selection.

Darwin refers to this review in the sixth edition of the *Origin,* without mentioning the author's name. As with the criticisms from the physicists of Thompson's type, Darwin puts on a minor patch or two by way of acknowledgment, but does not yield in any fundamental way to Jenkin's objection that any favorable variation would be quickly swamped out of existence by crossing with normal animals, so that such variations could not be involved in natural selection. Jenkin's assumption that marked variations show blending inheritance was in fact wrong, and Darwin himself cites examples in *The Variation of Animals and Plants under Domestication,* of such marked variants as the short-legged Ancon sheep, where the offspring of crosses between the variant and normals are not intermediate, but take after one parent or the other.

A. W. Bennett was a contemporary of Darwin whose criticism of natural selection, delivered in an address to the British Association for the Advancement of Science (1879), was prefaced by some remarks that give good documentation for the revolutionary nature of Darwin's work:

The fascinating hypothesis of Darwinism has, within the last few years, so completely taken hold of the scientific mind, both in this country and in Germany, that almost the whole of our rising men of science may be classed as belonging to this school of thought. Probably since the time of Newton no man has had so great an influence over the development of scientific thought as Mr. Darwin.

Bennett goes on to criticize the theory of natural selection as a cause of evolution, using what he calls a mathematical approach, as indicated by the title of his paper, "The Theory of Natural Selection Taken from a Mathematical Point of View." He takes as an example of evolution to be explained one of the remarkable butterflies that resembles in color pattern a species of butterfly that is inedible. Itself edible, the mimic butterfly has diverged by evolutionary processes from its near relatives to look like its model. Bennett points out that if the variation acted on by natural selection is a large one that produces the mimicry at a single bound, then it will be lost by blending inheritance in subsequent generations. But if it takes place by the slow stages that Darwin postulates to be usually involved in evolution, then he thinks it safe to say that as many as a thousand single steps must be involved. Bennett imagines that these steps are too small to be noticed by a predator, and makes the assumption that twenty of them must take place, one after another, and purely by chance, to accumulate to the point where the change will become evident to the predator and become effective in natural selection. Using some elementary arithmetic, he is able to show that the chances of this happening are only one out of ten billion, so that he feels he has demonstrated that gradual evolution by natural selection is impossible. So naive and arbitrary are the assumptions that the criticism seems trivial, yet this sort of analysis was standard anti-Darwinism for decades.

Objections of this kind were not answered until well into the twentieth century, when geneticists like R. A. Fisher, using the fact that variations, small or large, could have a permanent genetic basis that made it impossible for them to be lost by blending inheritance, were able to demonstrate by mathematical means that even a very small fractional advantage in survival and leaving offspring would cause the useful hereditary traits gradually to become widespread in the population.

Although the twentieth-century science of genetics was responsible, toward the middle of the century, for the revival of Darwinism that is now in full swing, curiously enough the first effect of the new science was to submerge the theory of evolution by natural selection. The phrase "Darwinism is dead" was a product of the biology of the early twentieth century, so that this development is outside the scope of this book, but it can be described briefly. The deadliest blow to Darwinism was the discovery by Hugo de Vries, near the turn of the century, that a species of evening primrose occasionally gave rise to individuals that were much different from their parents, different enough that they could be called new species, and this without any intermediate stages. Evidently species arose at a single step, by some inner derangement of the hereditary apparatus, so that Darwin's natural selection was not involved in producing new species. The De Vries theory of the origin of species by mutation took the biological world by storm, as had Darwin's theory a half century before, chiefly because of the influence of laboratory biologists who had little conception of the diversity and adaptive character of the world of nature. As it eventually turned out, De Vries' primrose proved to be a hybrid that, for complex genetical reasons, was spontaneously breaking down into partial reversions towards the parental types, and represented a very exceptional rather than a normal situation, so that this form of the "mutation" theory of evolution had to be abandoned.

Without going into the complex but fascinating developments in mid–twentieth-century biology that brought about the revival of the theory of evolution by natural selection, it can be said that the modern conception is that genetic mutations take place, so far as their ultimate morphological and physiological expression is concerned, without direction, and merely supply the randomly varying building bricks from which natural selection fashions new species or preserves old ones in a creative fashion. This was the essence of Darwin's original position, and is the one he reiterates as late as 1868, in concluding the *Variations:*

> . . . if an architect were to rear a noble and commodious edifice, without the use of cut stone, by selecting from the fragments at the base of a precipice wedge-formed stones for his arches, elongated stones for his lintels, and flat stones for his roof, we should admire his skill and regard him as the paramount power. Now, the fragments of stone, though indispensable to the architect, bear to the edifice built by him the same relation which the fluctuating variations of organic beings bear to the varied and admirable structures ultimately acquired by their modified descendants.

It was in *The Variation of Animals and Plants under Domestication* that Darwin published a complete theory of heredity. This massive two-volume work contained the material that he had originally intended to include in the *Origin,* but which was condensed into the first chapter of that work when it was prepared for speedy publication in 1858–59. In retrospect, it seems fortunate that this material was eliminated for, although it is relevant to evolution, it actually is concerned more with heredity as such, and would have detracted from the effectiveness of Darwin's argument for evolution.

Darwin's theory of heredity, which he called pangenesis, was a sort of appendix to the *Variation.* It was constructed, he says, to account for such facts as the regeneration of amputated limbs, embryonic development, graft hybrids, and the facts of inheritance, including the inherited effects of use and disuse. It often is said that he was driven to this theory to meet the objections to natural selection set out by Thompson, Jenkin, and others, since it provides a theoretical basis for Lamarckian inheritance of acquired characters which can speed up evolution enough to fit into Thompson's abbreviated earth history, or can produce evolution by means other than natural selection. However, Darwin's presentation of the theory does not at all give this impression, since he is concerned with explaining many phenomena other than inheritance of the effects of use and disuse. In a letter to Lyell written in 1867 he says that the theory of pangenesis was twenty-six or twenty-seven years old, so that he had been thinking about it for about as long as he had been concerned with evolution itself.

The essence of pangenesis is that all the cells of the body give off characteristic self-reproducing units called gemmules that assemble in the germ cells (eggs and sperm) and are thus the units of heredity. If a part of the body is affected by the environment, or by use and disuse, the gemmules are correspondingly affected. The theory is much like many of the theories of heredity that had been propounded from the time of Hippocrates onward (characteristically, Darwin was ignorant of these, even of a well-known one written by Buffon) through the end of the nineteenth century. Like all of these theories, Darwin's pangenesis was a complete failure. The enormously diverse and complexly interrelated facts of inheritance proved extremely refractory to any sort of theoretical organization until Mendel's brilliant suggestion, made in the mid-nineteenth century, was recovered by the scientific world in 1900 and opened the pathway that led to the modern science of genetics.

The history of scientific theories shows that all theories have a limited life span, the successful ones surviving only as special cases of more comprehensive theories, in the way that Newtonian mechanics survives as a special case of relativity theory. Neo-Darwinism, which represents a fusion of classical Darwinism (modification by natural selection) and modern genetics (in which particulate heredity is transmitted by the nuclear apparatus), also will be engulfed in more inclusive theory as our experience with biological materials is widened. Of course, the form of the new theory can not be predicted. However, new discoveries as to the nature of viruses and of various cell particulates seem to require that evolution theory would have to concern itself more with flexible, symbiotic associations of self-reproducing entities than it has in the past.

[CHAPTER 10]

The Units of

Life

ONE OF THE MAIN ACCOMPLISHMENTS of nineteenth-century biology was to create a workable conception of an integrative level intermediate between the particles of chemistry (atoms, molecules) and the whole organism. This development, the creation of the cell theory, was made possible by the microscope. What the scientist will do is determined to a large extent by what is available in the way of novel tools to work with. The tool *par excellence* of nineteenth-century biology was the light microscope, and it was the use of the microscope that shaped the development of the theory of the cell as the basic unit of life.

So far as high magnification and a sharp image was concerned, the seventeenth-century microscopes made by the Dutchman Antony van Leeuwenhoek were not equaled until the nineteenth cenury. His microscopes were single minute lenses, nearly spherical in shape. It is possible to make such a lens rather easily by allowing the surface tension on a drop of melted glass to round it up into a sphere. Leeuwenhoek (1632–1723) was a secretive worker and it is not known exactly how he made or used his remarkably fine lenses, but it is known that he ground them instead of making them by the fusion process. It is said that he could even grind a lens out of a grain of sand. Possibly he delicately ground his lenses into a shape not quite a sphere (which gives a better image than a spherical lens), using some optical means to check the progress of his work. At any rate, his detailed drawings of objects (spermatozoa, for example) drawn at magnifications of 2,000 diameters were astonishingly accurate. No one else ever raised the art of making and using the single-lens microscope to such a high level.

To use the single-lens microscope, the eye, lens, and object all had to be kept within the space of a fraction of an inch, which made manipulations of the object quite difficult, so that the style of microscope generally used was the compound microscope, which had two or more lenses in series, with a comfortable working distance between eye and object of several inches. In these the spherical and chromatic abberations of each lens are multiplied to the point where the image was impossibly distorted unless the magnification is kept low and the aperture kept small, which made for dim light. Two famous British contemporaries of Leeuwenhoek, Robert Hooke (1635–1703) and Nehemiah Grew (1641–1712), who made important observations on the microstructure of organisms, used compound microscopes of about 30 diameters magnification.

Chromatic aberration, which produces a fuzzy color fringe in the image, is caused by the fact that different wavelengths of light are bent unequally by glass, and Newton had shown on theoretical grounds that nothing could be done about it. However, lenses made of components of different kinds of glass with different refractive indexes are without this refractive error. By the first two decades of the nineteenth century, achromatic compound microscopes that were effective up to about 200 diameters were in use. The British microscopist Joseph Jackson Lister discovered a method of spacing the lenses in such a way as to reduce spherical aberration, which greatly improved the performance of the compound microscope, and in 1827 contributed to a paper in which for the first time the microscopic structure of animal tissue was made out with reasonable accuracy.

By 1830, commercially made achromatic microscopes had about the same resolution as the microscopes made nearly two centuries earlier by Leeuwenhoek. By 1870, as a result in gradual improvement in making lenses, microscopes were available that could resolve points about one-third of a micron apart (the human red blood cell averages seven or eight microns in diameter). About ten years later, the new principle of oil immersion, which eliminates the air gap between lens and object, gave the final advance in resolving power of the light microscope, which now became limited by the wavelength of visible light. In the twentieth century, this barrier was broken by the electron microscope, which has increased magnification by three orders of magnitude.

At the high magnifications reached by these late nineteenth-century microscopes, somewhat over 1,000 diameters, it was necessary to have the materials that were studied cut into very thin transparent slices, to transmit light, and to stain them delicately with a variety of specific stains which threw into contrast different components of the tissues. The solutions of these mechanical and technical problems developed to a very high degree of perfection parallel with the evolution of the light microscope.

It was against this technical background that the cell theory developed. Many of the components of the cell that made the theory meaningful—the nucleus, and certain details of nuclear structure, for example—were on the order of a micron or so in diameter, which required the best light microscopy to see and interpret.

The typical cell, as described in a textbook, is a minute, approximately spherical structure enclosed in a membrane and housing a central body called a nucleus; and the cell theory, in minimum form, states that the cell is the basic unit of structure of plants and animals. Now even the most cursory examination of living plant or animal tissue under a microscope, without the benefit of selective stains, should convince the thoughtful student that the cell theory is largely a product of the imagination.

Most of the vertebrate body is made up of the muscles used in locomotion. If one looks at a fresh bit of this tissue under the microscope, he will see nothing even vaguely resembling the typical cell. A thin slice prepared from the massive bony skeleton will not demonstrate, without the most derivative kind of interpretation, that the animal body is constructed of cells. Laboratory teaching of cell theory usually begins with selected relatively uncommon examples of the so-called typical cell, stained with dyes known to color the nucleus selectively, so as to distinguish it from a variety of other objects found inside the cell. It must have taken as much thinking as observation to construct the theory; and in fact, the theory in complete form is the product of a swirling confusion of observation and polemic that lasted through much of the nineteenth century.

The cell theory can be traced back to the seventeenth-century observations of Robert Hooke on wood, cork, and the pith of several kinds of larger plants stems. His first published observations were included in a book on trees by John Evelyn (1644) ; here he describes the microscopic porous structure of a polished section of petrified wood, and compares it with the similar structure of wood from living trees. A year later, in his famous *Micrographia*, he figures and describes cork, with its multitude of empty "pores or cells" that give it resiliency and lightness. He saw that pith also was made up entirely of such cells, but with thinner walls. In terms of modern cell theory, cork is made of the dead walls laid down by living substance that once occupied the "pores," so that Hooke was observing the results of cellular activity, rather than the cells themselves; but nevertheless, the structure of wood, cork, or pith faithfully represents the basically cellular composition of those plant tissues.

Like some other developments in seventeenth-century biology, the observations of Hooke were about a century ahead of their time, and microscopy remained essentially quiescent until the nineteenth century.

Probably the earliest effective emphasis on the living part of the biological unit of structure was provided by Robert Brown in his study (1833) on orchids and the milkweed family, where he points out that a nucleus is a regular component of plant cells. This was the emphasis that was to lead to the Schleiden–Schwann theory, as the cell theory of the mid-nineteenth century was called. Both these workers began with the nucleus as the essential unity, stating that each cell was derived from a nucleus. Before Schleiden and Schwann, cells, or cellular structure had been observed in both plants and animals, but this is a long way from the statement that living things are composed entirely of cells or their products.

The botanist M. J. Schleiden was an ex-lawyer with doctorates in medicine and philosophy. As a botanist, he was influential in directing the interest of younger men toward the microscopic study of the development of plants, chiefly through a controversial textbook entitled *Principles of Scientific Botany*, published in 1842. His celebrated formulation of the cell theory for plants was presented in a paper entitled "Phytogenesis" (which means plant development) published in 1838. Here he says,

> As the constant presence of this areola [the nucleus of Robert Brown's work] in the cells of very young embryos and in the newly-formed albumen could not fail to strike me in my extensive investigations into the development of the embryo, it was very natural that the consideration of the various modes of its occurrence should lead to the thought, that this nucleus of the cell must hold some close relation to the development of the cell itself. I consequently directed my attention particularly to this point, and was fortunate enough to see my endeavours crowned with success.

Schleiden believed that the nucleus, which he called the cytoblast, arose *de novo* from undifferentiated fluids and granules in the plant tissues. It then produces the rest of the cell and the cell walls, and finally disappears, leaving the cell walls behind. In 1838 he not only did not apply the cell theory to animals, but specifically excluded it from the animal kingdom:

> . . . manifold have been the endeavours to establish the analogies between the two great divisions of the plant and animal kingdoms. But eminent as the men have been who have devoted their attention to this subject, it cannot be denied that all attempts which have hitherto been made with this view have been entirely unsuccessful . . . The cause of this . . . is, that idea of individual, in the sense in which it occurs in animal nature, cannot in any way be applied to the

vegetable world. It is only in the very lowest orders of plants, in some *Algae* and *Fungi* for instance, which consist only of a single cell, that we can speak of an individual in this sense. But every plant developed in any higher degree, is an aggregate of fully individualized, independent, separate beings, even the cells themselves.

Schleiden then describes plant growth in terms of his cell theory:

1. The plant grows, that is, it produces the number of cells allotted to it.

2. The plant unfolds itself by expansion and development of the cells already formed. It is this phenomenon especially, one altogether peculiar to plants, which, because it depends upon the fact of their being composed of cells, can never occur in any, not even the most remote form in crystals or animals.

3. The walls of the fully-developed cells become thickened by the deposition of new matter in layers.

Theodor Schwann, usually thought of as the co-author of the cell theory, owes this position to the stimulus he gained from conversations with Schleiden before the publication of the latter's *Phytogenesis*. Schleiden was enthusiastic about the importance of nuclei, which had generally been neglected, except by Brown, and Schwann was reminded of similar structures he had seen in the notochords of young frogs and fishes. He quickly found that nuclei were as characteristic of animal tissues as of plant tissues, and extended Schleiden's theory to the animal kingdom. Schwann says, in the English version (1847) of his *Microscopical Researches*, published in German in 1839, by way of historical introduction to the subject, that:

As soon as the microscope was applied to the investigation of the structure of plants, the great simplicity of their structure, as compared with that of animals, necessarily attracted attention. Whilst plants appeared to be composed entirely of cells, the elementary particles of animals exhibited the greatest variety, and for the most part presented nothing at all in common with cells. This, harmonized with the opinion long since current, that the growth of animals, whose tissues are furnished with vessels, differed essentially from that of vegetables. An independent vitality was ascribed to the elementary particles of vegetables growing without vessels, they were regarded to a certain extent as individuals, which composed the entire plant; whilst, on the other hand, no such a view was taken of the elementary parts of animals.

After a lengthy discussion of the mode of development of animal cells, in which he followed the views of Schleiden on the role of the nucleus, he summarized his (actually, their) cell theory as applied to both plants and animals.

> . . . there is one universal principle of development for the elementary parts of organisms, however different, and that this principle is the formation of cells.

and,

> . . . the fundamental phenomenon attending the exertion of productive power in organic nature is accordingly as follows: a *structureless* substance is presented in the first instance, which lies either around or in the interior of cells already existing, and cells are formed in it in accordance with certain laws, which cells become developed in various ways into the elementary parts of organisms.

It would seem that Schwann was responsible for getting this version of the cell theory accepted. His book of 1839, somewhat revised by the author, was translated within a decade in England, with Schleiden's paper of about thirty pages appended as a supplement. Schwann neatly organized and made comprehensible the subject of animal histology by classifying all tissues into a few main types based on their mode of cellular formation, which made his work indispensable in a variety of disciplines, including medicine.

Yet, seen from the standpoint of modern cell theory, the writings of both Schleiden and Schwann have a murky quality, which results mostly from their aim of forcing a mechanistic interpretation upon their observations. They wanted to demonstrate that life could be interpreted in terms of mathematics and chemistry and, in the rational spirit of the century, this was often associated with the idea of spontaneous generation of life from nonliving matter. In Schwann's special, limited version of spontaneous generation, nuclei and eventually cells formed themselves out of structureless substance. This gives their theory an entirely different weight and import from modern cell theory, which states that nuclei come only from preexisting nuclei, cells only from preexisting cells. Modern theory is much closer to the outlook of Pasteur, which implies that the ultimate living units are of such complexity that new ones are formed only by growth and division of preexisting units.

The Schleiden–Schwann cell theory had immediate repercussions in medicine. The German pathologist, anthropologist, and politician Rudolph Virchow conceived of illness as the sickness of individual cells, and in fact the microscopic examination of tissues added valuable new tools for diagnosis, with certain cell abnormalities being associated with specific diseases. His ideas and observations were brought together in the influential *Die Cellular Pathologie* in 1858, which was within two years published in translation in England.

This book was mainly concerned with establishing microscopy as a branch of medicine, but is known in biology for its theory that all cells come from preexisting cells. The doctrine *omnis cellula e cellula* was eventually accepted, and accounted for a subtle shift of emphasis away from the idea that the whole organism directly controlled the minutest details of body functioning, including the controlled emergence of cells from diffuse materials, and toward the concept that there was an intermediate level of organization between the chemical and the whole-organism level, in which more or less autonomous cells were the significant unit. Virchow's theoretical grasp of cellular pathology was weakened by the fact that the germ theory of disease was not yet developed, and the mode of cell and nuclear division was not yet known, but his work nevertheless was a well-placed steppingstone in both the history of medicine and of the cell theory.

An important contribution to understanding the structure of animal tissues was made by Lionel S. Beale, who like Virchow busied himself with making microscopy a part of medical investigation. He emphasized the difference between nonliving cell products—which may make up the bulk of such tissues as bone or cartilage, or even all of such structures as hair or fingernails— and the living cell itself.

As a result of such advances, by the last third of the nineteenth century, attention was focused on minute bits of living matter, each capable of reproducing itself, and each with an obviously important internal structure, the nucleus.

By about 1860, microscopists had learned how to treat dead and sliced tissues with reagents that gave characteristic colors to different parts of the cell. As it turned out, the nucleus was so much different in its chemical makeup from the rest of the cell that it could be strongly stained by a variety of methods. Also, during the process of cell division, the relatively diffuse stain of the nucleus became concentrated into deeply colored objects in the nucleus so that with the improvement of both staining techniques and the light microscope, it became apparent towards the end of the century that the nucleus itself was a complicated structure whose components behaved in a definite fashion during cell division.

The spermatozoan was interpreted as a single cell made up mostly of nucleus, and it was observed in 1875 by Oscar Hertwig that the fertilized egg of a sea urchin had two nuclei—one already there, belonging to the egg cell, and one brought in by the sperm cell. These two nuclei fused, and the resulting fusion nucleus divided to form the nuclei of the first two cells of the developing sea urchin embryo. Subsequent cell nuclei could all trace their ancestry back to the original fusion nucleus of the fertilized egg. In 1882 the doctrine of all cells from cells was thus supplemented by the dictum (owed to W. Flemming) that all nuclei came from preexisting nuclei.

The study of the structure and behavior of the nucleus was one of the big breakthrough areas in late nineteenth-century biology. The same thing was happening to the exploitation of the germ theory of disease, but cytology (ostensibly the study of entire cells, actually at that time mainly concerned with the behavior of the nuclear components) is pure, nonapplied science, so that its sudden growth gave us the first example of the kind of research biology that has come to dominate twentieth-century science: many workers, largely supported by the state, active in a limited area and producing results that follow thick and fast, so that it becomes increasingly difficult to associate a single line of theoretical development with a single scientist.

To the microscopists of this time the beauty and precision of nuclear events, seen with fine microscopes that pushed magnification to the limits of light, and colored with subtly chosen arrays of esoteric dyes, seemed indicative of a new world of order that would reveal some of the deepest secrets of life. It had become certain that every individual in sexually reproducing organisms began life as a single cell formed by the union of two single cells, one from each patient. Because of the fact that the cell from the male, the spermatozoan, consisted mostly of nucleus, the conviction spread that the nucleus was the carrier of heredity. Ernst Haeckel, the imaginative champion of Darwinism in Germany, has been credited with first (1866) stating the idea explicitly. The elaborate mechanism of nuclear division, it was assumed, must have something to do with the process of inheritance.

In hindsight, it seems conceivable that the essentials of Mendelian genetic theory could have been worked out solely by microscopic examination of the nuclear events in cell fusion (in the fertilization of the egg), during ordinary cell division, and during the specialized kind of cell division seen in the production of sperms and eggs. Actually, the genetic theory was worked out independently of cytological investigations, and intersected the development of cytology (in 1900) just a year or two before the final observations were made on the nuclear components that would have made the theory obvious. But no doubt the genetic evidence itself guided the way to these last few cytological discoveries.

In the cycle of cell division and growth, it could be seen that the nuclear membrane disappeared, and that the diffuse stain that distinguished the nucleus first became strongly concentrated into a tangled, colored thread, the chromatin, which then seemed to break up into a number of short, very deeply stained rods which W. Waldeyer in 1888 called the chromosomes. Different organisms displayed the formation of the chromosomes with different degrees of clarity, and there was much microscopic exploration in many out of the way places: ovules of orchids; staminal hairs of *Tradescantia*; the gonads of grasshoppers, flatworms, roundworms, sea urchins, and rabbits.

August Weismann had decided that the chromosomes must be the carriers of heredity, and that since the sperm and egg contributed equal amounts of chromosomal material, then there must be a time, at the formation of new germ cells (sperms and eggs), when the number of chromosomes must be halved, in order to prevent the number from doubling in each generation. This predicted reduction division was four years later observed in a species of insect, and eventually was found to be general.

The missing observations that would have been needed to set up a Mendelian-type theory solely from observations on chromosomes are these: That the number of chromosomes in the body cells is constant for a species, and that there are half as many *kinds* of chromosomes as there are chromosomes (or in other words, the chromosomes exist in pairs). It could have been deduced from this that a sperm or egg would have one of each kind of chromosome (or half the total number of chromosomes).

Given a particulate theory of inheritance—and the pre-Mendelian theory of Weismann, for example, was particulate—the fact that each kind of chromosome was represented, and represented only once in a sperm or egg cell would be taken to mean that each chromosome had its own kinds of particles, and that therefore each particle was represented only once in the germ cell. In the fertilized egg, and in all the body cells divided from it, each particle would be represented twice, one particle having come from the male, the other the female.

This is also the essence of Mendelian genetic theory which remained hidden from the scientific world until 1900: that a given characteristic is represented by two particles of heredity, one from each parent, and that in a germ cell it is represented by only one particle.

Weismann had by 1893 worked out in elaborate detail a theory of heredity, but it had to be discarded with the rediscovery of

Mendel seven years later. He supposed the ultimate particles of heredity, which he called determinants, to be located on the chromosomes, just as in modern theory. The main difference, and one that led the theory into oblivion, was that Weismann thought there should be many, possibly hundreds of complete sets of particles in a germ cell, and that a single chromosome had several sets in it. He thought this was necessary because he had the idea that ancestors for many generations back had to be represented by actual complete sets of particles, in order to explain a reversion of type to some ancestor other than the parent.

By supposing each particle to be represented in the organism an indefinitely large number of times, Weismann destroyed the possibility of the simple mathematical relationships in heredity that made Mendel's theory successful. Weismann's elaborately verbal theory had little to offer in the way of suggesting definite genetic experiments, and thus offered no serious competition to Mendelian theory. As will be pointed out elsewhere, Weismann's theory concerned itself as much with development (how does the complex adult organism develop from the fertile egg cell?) as with heredity, and was perhaps a more useful guide for investigating embryology than heredity.

Another way of studying heredity was initiated by the English anthropologist Francis Galton (1822–1911), known also for his work on fingerprints as a method of identification and his work on meteorology. With help from a mathematician, he developed a method for expressing degrees of similarity between parents and offspring in mathematical terms. As summarized in his book *Natural Inheritance* (1894), Galton was able to show that, for large populations at least, about one-fourth of the total inheritance came from each parent, and the remainder from grandparents and more remote ancestors. Galton's statistical approach, which has been continually refined and expanded, is especially useful in describing the inheritance of characteristics of the graded type rather than the either-or type studied so successfully by Mendel. However, it did not concern itself much with the mechanism of inheritance nor did the theory suggest useful ways to get at the problem of how inheritance was accomplished.

Towards the end of the century, several students of heredity, notably W. Bateson, came to the conclusion that it would be better to try to follow out the inheritance of characteristics that were of the simple either-or type, instead of the continuously variable characters such as human beauty, intelligence, weight, or height that had absorbed the attention of earlier workers like Galton. If it is possible to divide individuals into two definite types—say red or white, tall or dwarf—without any intermediates, then, he said, select this for study, even if it is an exceptional kind of variation. Also only one characteristic at a time should be investigated. This made it possible to cut the experimental situation down to bare-bone simplicity.

By 1900, three workers had ready for publication results of studies of inheritance that dealt with just such characteristics: H. de Vries, C. Correns, and E. von Tschermak. Now Gregor Mendel had carried out such a program thirty-four years before, without attracting attention from students of heredity. His work had been mentioned only four times, and then without any understanding; but one of the citations stated that Mendel had found constant numerical relationships among hereditary types, and this is apparently what caught the eye of at least two of these three, probably not before 1899. De Vries sent off for publication three papers, probably written within a few days of each other, in March of 1900, describing the same kinds of results (but in different plants) that had been reported by Mendel. One of these papers did not mention Mendel at all. One did mention him as an afterthought, and the third did so in some detail and in such a way as to credit him with the discovery. Correns had mentioned Mendel in a paper published in January of 1900, and later in the year published an account of his own extensive experiments with peas that confirmed the work of Mendel. Von Tschermak published two papers in 1900 on inheritance, one of them written after he had seen the Correns and De Vries papers; his observations were based on only two years' work with peas.

A three-page paper by Hugo de Vries published in the Parisian *Comptes Rendus* was the first of the flurry of the six papers that appeared in 1900 on Mendelian genetics. In it he lists examples of crosses between eleven pairs of different species of plants in which there were differences of the either-or kind that Mendel had worked with, and listed for each pair the percentages of the resulting hybrids that showed about 25 percent of one (the "recessive" character), 75 percent of the other (the "dominant" character), just as Mendel had found in hybrids between varieties of the garden pea. He makes no mention of Mendel, and concludes the paper by saying, "the totality of these experiments establishes the law of segregation of hybrids and confirms the principles that I have expressed concerning the specific characters considered as being distinct units." Here he is referring to his own book, *Intracellular Pangenesis*, published in 1889, which does little more than state that heredity is particulate, which was the dominant theory of the last quarter of the century. However, he there stated that each particle is associated with a single characteristic of the organism, which represents a step in the direction of Mendel.

His colleague Carl Correns seems to have regarded the *Comptes Rendus* note as an attempt to establish priority for the discovery of the fundamentally important 3:1 ratio. In his own contribution to the birth, or rebirth, of genetics, published in the *Berichte der Deutsche Botanische Gesellschaft*, he says:

The latest publication of Hugo de Vries . . . which through the courtesy of the author reached me yesterday, prompts me to make the following statement:

In my hybridization experiments with varieties of maize and peas, I have come to the same results as de Vries, who experiments with varieties of many different kinds of plants, among them two varieties of maize. When I discovered the regularity of the phenomena, and the explanation thereof— to which I shall return presently—the same thing happened to me which seems to be happening to de Vries: I thought that I had found *something new. But then I convinced myself that the Abbot Gregor Mendel in Brunn had, during the sixties, not only obtained the same result through extensive experiments with peas, which lasted for many years, as did de Vries and I, but had also given exactly the same explanation, as far as that was possible in 1886.*

And,

At the time I did not consider it necessary to establish my priority for this "rediscovery" by a preliminary note, but rather decided to continue the experiment further.

He then fixes the priority which gave to the modern science of heredity its name, "Mendelian genetics":

This I call Mendel's law. It includes the "loi de disjunction" of de Vries, also.

And, finally, in a postscript added in proof:

In the meantime de Vries has published in these proceedings [the *Berichte*] . . . some more details concerning these experiments. There he refers to Mendel's investigations, which were *not even mentioned in the "Comptes Rendus."*

206

E. Tschermak's important paper also appeared in the *Berichte*. In an explanation of the background of his work, he writes:

Stimulated by the experiments of Darwin on the effects of cross- and self-fertilization in the plant kingdom, I began, in the year 1898, to make hybridization experiments with *Pisum sativum*. The group to which *Pisum sativum* belongs was especially interesting to me because in it are found exceptional results from the generally accepted principle of the advantageous effect of crossing different individuals and different varities in contrast to self-fertilization.

Tschermak noted that some of his results, which were not related to the problem he had set out to solve, were in agreement with Mendel's work on *Pisum*. And he adds to his paper a postscript:

Correns has just published experiments which also deal with artificial hybridization of different varieties of *Pisum sativum* and observations of the hybrids left to self-fertilization through several generations. They confirm, just as my own, Mendel's teachings. The simultaneous "discovery" of Mendel by Correns, de Vries, and myself appears to me especially gratifying. Even in the second year of experimentation, I too still believed that I had found something new.

It is impossible to determine from these three documents just how much Mendel actually contributed to clearing up the thinking of the authors. The speculative writings of Darwin and Weismann on the mechanism of inheritance had led the geneticists of the last quarter of the century quite deeply into a muddle which was only gradually being resolved by microscopic observations on chromosomes; and one would imagine that Mendel's thinking would seem startingly clear to a geneticist of the year 1900.

Gregor Mendel (1822–1884), born into a peasant family, escaped poverty and insecurity by entering, at the age of twenty-one, a monastery at Brünn, and was later ordained a priest. In the course of unsuccessful efforts to get a teaching certificate in science, he attended the University of Vienna for two years, where he came in contact with some excellent teachers in mathematics and science, who were themselves productive research workers. This experience probably was decisive in determining the simplicity and precision with which he formulated and carried out a series of experiments lasting eight years on inheritance in the garden pea, *Pisum sativum*. Although self-fertilization is the rule in this plant, crosses are easily made experimentally, which makes it a good subject for genetic studies.

Mendel's *Experiments in Plant Hybridization* begins with the observation that there had already been published an enormous amount of work on the subject, but Mendel goes on to say:

> Those who survey the work in this department will arrive at the conviction that among the numerous experiments made, not one has been carried out to such an extent and in such a way as to make it possible to determine the number of different forms under which the offspring of hybrids appear, or to arrange these forms with certainty according to their separate generations, or definitely to ascertain their statistical relations.

It may be that an orderly mind and a good grasp of the proper experimental approach to a subject which was, or at least should have been, a quantitative one, accounts for the economy and precision of his eight-year-long program of experimentation. A careful analysis of his work made by the theoretical geneticist R. A. Fisher indicates that Mendel's paper describes an actual sequence of experiments, and not a selection of data from a mass of poorly organized experiments that was made with the advantage of hindsight. The explanation that Fisher leans to is that Mendel knew what he was going to get before he started; that is, he had the advantage of foresight. Simple observations in two or three instances of the fact that crosses between hybrids whose parents differed in the either-or kind of characteristics that Mendel was interested in yielded a population in which the two kinds were present in an approximate 3:1 ratio would give enough for him to work out the whole hypothesis. The work that followed would then merely demonstrate it to be true to a reasonably well-informed scientific public (which it did some thirty-four years later). Fisher is even of the opinion that the knowledge of the process of inheritance in Mendel's time was such that the theory could have been worked out with no new observations at all.

Mendel had available several varieties of garden peas, supplied by commercial seedsmen, which differed from each other in such characteristics as height, flower color, texture of seed coat, and so on. These were true-breeding, remaining constant for these characteristics for generation after generation. When two such varieties were crossed, the offspring were not intermediate between the parents, but were all like one parent; thus, all the offspring from a cross between tall plants and short ones were tall. At least this was true for certain characteristics, and Mendel limited himself to these. But when the tall hybrid plants are crossed with each other, both parental types reappear: in one experiment that Mendel records, out of 1,064 such progeny, 277 were short, 787 were tall. The significant thing about Mendel's approach was that he interpreted this not as just the bald figures, but as a 3:1 ratio, and that the actual ratio, 2.84:1, was only a chance, therefore meaningless deviation.

A 3:1 ratio could be explained (or predicted) by assuming that each tall hybrid plant contained a pair of hereditary factors governing height, one for tall, one for short. The simplest assumption would of course be that it got one from each of its parents by way of the pair of germ cells that gave rise to it. The factor for tall overrides (is dominant over) the factor for short, resulting in a tall individual. When germ cells are produced, these cells have only one or the other factor, and germ cells of the two kinds are produced in equal numbers. Chance combination of these gametes will produce one-fourth of the time a plant with two factors for short, two-fourths of the time a plant with one factor of each kind, and one-fourth of the time with two factors for tall. Since tall is dominant, the last two categories both give tall plants, and a 3:1 ratio results. Mendel could either have created this simple theory of heredity (two factors for each character in the parent, one in the germ cell) and predicted the 3:1 ratio, or seen the 3:1 ratio and deduced the theory. The last seems more unlikely: one does not generally "see" a ratio—a ratio is an abstraction. Or Mendel may have had the instantaneous flash of intuition that seems to fuse two such approaches.

One of the curious things about Mendel's work, which was brought out by Fisher's analysis, is that the data given by Mendel are too close to the expected result. Taking all of Mendel's experiments, Fisher shows statistically that the chances of getting as good a fit to prediction as Mendel reported are about 1 out of 14,000. Especially damaging is the evidence from some experiments in which Mendel made the wrong prediction, overlooking the statistical effects of small samples. Here the results are very close to the wrong prediction, and the reported data agree with the corrected predictions so poorly that such results could be expected to happen only once out of about 2,000 trials. Since all the assumptions that Fisher made in this last example are not completely verified, his conclusions may not be corrrect in detail, but the overall verdict seems to be that Mendel's data are biased in favor of predicted results. However, the varied experiments have been repeated again and again, with Mendel's general conclusions always being verified.

Mendel, although working in isolation, was careful to establish contact with the outstanding authority in plant heredity, Karl Nägeli, a professor of botany at Munich who wrote much on a wide range of problems in cytology and heredity. But in a reply to Mendel concerning the paper of 1866 (*Experiments in Plant Hybridization*), which Mendel had sent him, he conveyed his opinion that Mendel's work was only a trivial beginning, that the observations on the simple either-or characters were merely incidents, and that Mendel would do better to work with the plants that he, Nägeli, wanted to know more about. Mendel dutifully, for some years, made his way into the maze in which Nägeli and other students of heredity had been so deeply lost. The hawkweed, *Hieraceum*, one of their favorite experimental subjects, had the ability to produce offspring, with no visible warning, by asexual rather than sexual reproduction; since this was not known at the time, so-called hybridizing experiments gave complete nonsense as far as a theory of inheritance was concerned. He also did some equally unrewarding work on honeybees (which also have an anomalous reproductive pattern). He later became deeply involved in administrative work as abbott of the monastery and did no further scientific work.

When Nägeli in 1844 published his own now-forgotten work of more than 800 pages on inheritance, he made no mention of Mendel or of his theory. He had disapproved of Mendel's work when he first heard of it, and never had occasion to change his mind. One of the old Marxist leaders is credited with the saying that "One should never underestimate the intelligence of the masses." The behavior of Nägeli, and many others like him, reminds one that to make sense out of intellectual history there needs to be a corollary, to the effect that one should also never overestimate the intelligence of the professional and bureaucratic classes.

Genetics, although a major subscience of biology, is essentially a twentieth-century science that begins with the rediscovery of Mendel. The hereditary particles of Mendel, the "Merkmal," become the genes, situated on chromosomes, composed of a definite chemical substance (polynucleotides), and relating structure to function in that each, by its complex molecular structure, guides the manufacture of a certain kind of protein enzyme. It often is said that the genes of the fertilized egg carry all the information needed for the development of the organism, but this is an oversimplification. No organism starts out as a collection of genes—these are always embedded in the relatively enormous cytoplasm of the egg. And also there is yet no certainty that all the essential biochemical reactions are enzyme-controlled.

One of the reasons that August Weismann did not contribute to establishing a workable theory of heredity was that he tried to solve two problems at once: that of heredity, and that of development. Mendel and the geneticists of the early twentieth century contented themselves with letting a gene or hereditary particle stand for a characteristic of the organism, without troubling themselves about the chain of events connecting gene and character.

Weismann is best known for his concept of the germ plasm, which carries heredity from generation to generation, and stands in contrast to the body, or soma, which is a sort of excrescence that houses and nourishes the germ plasm, and sees to it that germ plasms are properly mixed by sexual reproduction. This concept was specifically developed to counter Darwin's theory of pangenesis, which held that hereditary particles gathered from all parts of the body to form the germ cells, and that the particles faithfully represented the parts of the body that they came from.

Weismann matched his conception of the completeness and permanence of the germ plasm with a theory of the progressive decay and deterioration of its hereditary material in the formation of the soma, as it developed from the fertilized egg by repeated cell divisions.

As was said before, Weismann attached no significance to the morphology and numbers of the chromosomes, which he called "idants." These idants were bearers of the ids, several or many to a chromosome, and probably equivalent to the small spherical dark structure sometimes seen on the chromosmoes. The id was an important unit in that it carried the hereditary information necessary to produce an individual; that is, it could theoretically guide the development of the egg to an adult organism. The many ids represented the heredities of the parents and of many ancestors besides, as actual aggregates of heredity, rather than in the potential recombinations of modern genetic theory. The ids were in turn made up of very large numbers of the basic particles of heredity, the determinants. Finally, in the cells of the body, the determinants released equivalent particles called biophores, which went out of the nucleus and exerted their influence in the cytoplasm. As the cells divided during development of the embryo, the ids gradually broke down, the number of determinants steadily decreasing, until finally there was only one kind of determinant (but existing in many varieties), and these determined the kind of cell that was produced. In the cell there took place a battle of the determinants, in which was decided which variety of the kind of determinant—each variety from a different id—that could become effective. In modern terminology, the id would be the equivalent of the whole chromosome complement, the determinant would be the gene, and the biophore the "messenger RNA."

Embryology, until toward the end of the nineteenth century, was a descriptive rather than an experimental science. With the aid of the microscope and highly developed staining and sectioning techniques it had been learned that the individual begins its life as a single cell, the fertilized egg, which by repeated cell division gives rise to the mature organism, composed of very large numbers of different kinds of cells. After 1859 the main theoretical formulation used to guide or interpret research in embryology was the theory of recapitulation, whose strongest advocate was Ernst Haeckel. This theory stated that during embryonic development an organism repeats its evolutionary history; that is, ontogony repeats phylogeny. The similarity, often superficial, between embryos of animals so diverse as fish and man was taken as one of the kinds of evidence that evolution had taken place. The deduction that a study of embryos would make it possible to work out the actual lines of evolutionary descent of organisms led to the careful study of thousands of species of many groups of animals, to produce a highly developed science of comparative embryology. The presence of clefts in the wall of the pharynx (the "gill slits") of the embryos of both fish and man is explained by the descent of mammals (through reptiles and amphibians) from the fishes. In the fishes, the clefts become part of the breathing apparatus; in man, most are suppressed as the embryo grows older, one pair remaining as the Eustachian tubes. The circulatory system of the human embryo also has some similarities to that of both embryonic and adult fishes.

However, there are many embryonic structures that do not appear in the adult of any animal, and clearly cannot represent a part of an evolutionary sequence. At best, the structure of embryos gives only scattered and often obscure clues as to evolutionary relationships. In no instance is an embryo a replica of the mature form of any ancestor. The changes that an embryo goes through cannot be more than partially explained by recapitulation. Instead of representing adaptation to an external environment, the changing structures of the embryo represent the solution of internal problems of development, within the embryo. The embryo has to produce the structures that in the mature animal cope with the problems of the external world. Embryonic development is concerned with efficient ways of achieving the end point of development, and this usually means suppression or profound modification of structures that were of adaptive significance in the free-living stages of ancestral forms. The problem of the causes of embryonic development remains one of the outstanding mysteries of modern biology.

With the failure of the recapitulation theory as an explanation of the facts of embryology (and in any event, such a theory could not provide explanation at a chemical or physical level), attention was turned to experimental methods, in which the normal course of embryonic development was interfered with in precise and reproducible ways. The founder of experimental embryology is usually taken to be Wilhelm Roux, who in 1888 described the results of injuring one of the two cells that resulted from the first division of a fertilized frog's egg. He found that usually this resulted in only a half-embryo being formed, and when, as sometimes happened, the injured half belatedly developed in spite of the injury, Roux interpreted it as the result of the immigration of "differentiating influences" from the developing half-embryo on the normal side. From such experiments he concluded that each cell developed independently of its neighbor and that total development was the sum of partial mosaic developments. That is, the embryo is not an integrated, self-regulating system but one that can be fragmented, with each fragment going its own way. Roux, however, did not think that this principle explained all of embryology, since he says that the interaction of neighboring parts influences the final shape of such structures as the liver and lungs or the patterns of blood vessels.

The later work of Hans Driesch led to an opposite conclusion. Driesch (1894) separated completely the first two cells of the embryo of a sea urchin and found that each developed into a complete although dwarf sea urchin larva. He suggested that perhaps Roux would have found the same thing had he been able to separate completely the two cells of the developing frog egg, but says: "I have tried in vain to isolate amphibian blastomeres; let those who are more skillful than I try their luck." Later work has shown that neither Roux nor Driesch were correct in trying to extend their conclusions to the whole animal kingdom: different organisms show different degrees of pre-patterning or determination in the cytoplasm of the egg cell.

Driesch in later life deserted science to become a professor of philosophy, and is one of the most-quoted of writers who favor the concept of vitalism. Among much other evidence that he thought supported this doctrine, he believed that the self-determining properties of the half-embryo of the sea urchin, which regulated itself to produce an entire embryo, showed that there was some vital principle in addition to the forces of physics and chemistry that governed biological phenomena.

$$\left[\text{C H A P T E R } 11\right]$$

Life

As Mechanism

SOMEONE ONCE ASKED AN EXPERT on computers if it would ever
be possible to make a computer that could function like the human brain. The answer—"You tell me what the brain does, in objective terms, and we'll make a computer that will do it"—lies
near the heart of the so-called mechanist–vitalist controversy in
biology. If the vitalist should ask, "but could you make a machine
that is afraid?" the mechanist could, in answer, propose a machine that would turn and roll away at the approach of a cat, or
perhaps devise a system that would release the neurohormones

identified in animals that have been presented with fear stimuli, or even have his machine say "I am afraid" as it fled. It would be the essence of the mechanist position to say that anything a living organism does is based on some arrangement of the kinds of matter and energy known to physics. That the actual arrangement of matter found in living systems may be at present beyond his capacity to duplicate (although he might be able to make a working imitation) is, he would say, simply a technical matter, without deep theoretical implication. A little reflection will show that the definition of the mechanist position implied here is somewhat circular. When the mechanist asks what it is that an organism does, expressed in objective terms, he is really asking for a description in operational—hence mechanical—terms, so that even by being able to describe a biological process, one admits to mechanism.

Like a storage battery, or an electric lamp, or a gasoline engine, a living plant or animal is a mechanism, if by mechanism is meant an assemblage of matter and energy that functions in characteristic ways. The crux of this assertion is that only the kinds of matter and energy of ordinary physics are present in living matter, that their only unique characteristic is their organization or pattern. And since Darwin showed that the structural and functional pattern of the most complex organisms can arise by means of natural selection, which is itself a mechanism—self-reproducing entities with a degree of variance, competing for limited resources—the mechanist sees no justification for the insistence of the vitalist that some yet unknown organizing force is needed to produce biological phenomena.

Driesch said of his experiments with sea urchin embryos, in which a divided embryo gave rise to two complete embryos, that since it was impossible to conceive of a machine that could be cut in half, then regenerate itself, then an embryo could not be regarded as a mechanism. Therefore, some supra-physical vital force must be involved. It is obvious, however, that this statement has no more force than a challenge to the ingenuity of a designer of machines.

If we look at the vitalist and mechanist positions from the levels-of-organization approach, we see that there are some subtleties involved which make the controversy not quite so clear cut as implied by the foregoing discussion. The emergent levels produce patterns that interact in new ways; that is, atoms interact in different ways than do their constituent protons, electrons, and neutrons. Thus chemistry, in a sense, involves new principles an laws, so that chemistry is not equivalent to physics. Nor is biology equivalent to chemistry. Now one could say that the "vital force" of the vitalist doctrine is merely emergent force that comes into existence when the enormously complex patterns of living material come into existence. But this would be a fatal retreat into the mechanist position. It would mean, for example, giving to chemical "forces" a privileged status in relation to physical forces that the vitalist would like to reserve for the relationship between living substance and all of the rest of nature. It is clear that the result would not be the one originally intended by the vitalist, who wants the world of life set apart from the rest of nature because it expresses the influence of a supernatural, all-pervading intelligence in the universe. In the emergent-level concept, it would be just as reasonable to say that chemical forces are "supernatural."

The mechanist can justly point out that if emergent "forces," chemical or biological, are merely the result of new or higher patterns, then he can bring these so-called forces into existence merely by assembling the patterns. He can create the simpler organic molecules found in living things that were, at the beginning of the nineteenth century, thought to be in principle beyond the possibility of laboratory synthesis. A stumbling block to the synthesis of the large molecules, such macromolecules as the protein enzymes, has been that only in the mid-twentieth century has it been possible to describe in detail what it is that has to be put together—an acceptable apology for failure to synthesize them. Now that their structure is known, the synthesis of enzymes seems to be, even at the present level of chemical technology, quite feasible. As the situation stands at present, it would seem that the vitalist position is one that lies outside the realm of science, and attempts to apply it in science merely take, in essence, the form of saying that "it's no use trying" to understand this or that biological phenomenon.

Describing life as mechanism means describing it in terms of physics and chemistry. An organism is more of a chemical than a physical machine, chemical reactions being of more general interest and significance in biology than the movement of parts, which is concerned mostly with such specialized problems as locomotion or circulation. Although not as important as chemistry in biology, physics is historically interesting because it is the older science, taking form in the seventeenth century in the hands of Galileo. The first effective mechanical analyses were based on physics, as the demonstration by Harvey (1628) that the heart is a pump that forces blood through a closed circuit. Harvey had studied medicine at Padua, so was at least indirectly influenced by Galileo's thinking. The philosopher René Descartes was profoundly impressed by Harvey's work, and did much to win general acceptance of his theory of circulation of the blood. Descartes tried to analyze completely the human body as a machine, which led him into absurd speculations of the function of various organs. Subhuman animals, he thought were nothing but machines, while man differed in possessing consciousness (or soul) which could not be explained on mechanical principles, and represented an addition to his machinelike body.

The mechanical analysis of body function was extended by the work of the influential Italian scientist Giovanni Borelli, who studied at the University of Pisa while Galileo was a resident of the city, and who worked for several years in a Galilean scientific academy. He wrote on astronomy and physics, but his best known book is *De motu animalium* (1680). In describing the motion of animals, he begins with the basic assumption that it is the "flesh" (muscles) of animals that provide force for movement, and that they do so by forcibly shortening. He diagrams arrangements of muscle and bone as so many systems of levers, in a quite modern fashion. Running and walking, swimming of both mammals and fishes, flying, and even the walking of insects are discussed by Borelli. Modern studies of such aspects of biological mechanism, although much more sophisticated, involve no fundamentally new principles beyond those applied by these early disciples of Galileo.

The science of chemistry was born of the use of fire. Man-made charcoal from the caves of Peking man is over a quarter of a million years old; glazed pottery, glass, and metals from smelted ores are a few thousand years old; and experiments with fire became intensive and varied with the work of the medieval alchemists. Chemistry, then, has a background nearly as venerable as that of biology, but chemistry is usually considered not to have emerged as a science until near the end of the eighteenth century, when in France it was given a quantitative aspect by the consistent use of the balance and a new operational concept of a chemical element.

In Greek science, observations on burning, on smelting ores, on the behavior of weather and of living things had led to the concept of the four elements, which persisted as a major organizing principle or theory in pre-chemistry up into the eighteenth century.

When Linnaeus classified the things of the world, he begins with:

Fire; lucid, resilient, warm, evolant, vivifying.
Air; transparent, elastic, dry, incircling, generating.
Water; diaphanous, fluid, moist, gliding, conceiving.
Earth; opaque, fixed, cold, quiescent, sterile.

And phlogiston, a somewhat sophisticated version of the element "fire," reigned briefly as one of the main organizing theories of eighteenth-century chemistry.

The conception of four elements is surprisingly flexible and powerful. Terrestrial objects were considered to be mixtures of all four of the Aristotelian elements, in characteristic proportion. The fire in wood became apparent when one burned it; earthy ash remained; water condensed on cold objects held near the flame; one knew that wood contained light, invisible air because it floated on water, or perhaps emitted bubbles when immersed. One could pour fire into a dull, earthy ore and convert it into a shining metal, rich in fire. Or in the days of phlogiston theory, charcoal, which was rich in phlogiston, could be made to transfer it into the ore to make the bright metal. Lamarck, the nineteenth-century biologist, knew phlogiston existed because he could see it, a shimmering layer on rooftops heated in the Paris sun.

Chemistry effectively became a science with the work of the Frenchman Antoine Laurent Lavoisier (1743–1794) and his collaborators. The essential characteristic of his work was that he insisted on a quantitative, numerical framework on which the qualitative observations of chemistry could be organized, a framework constructed by the systematic use of the balance, by the use of weight as the fundamental property of matter. In practice, this had to be supplemented by the use of more-or-less elaborate devices to collect and weigh any gases given off during a chemical reaction, or to hold them if they had to be supplied for the reaction.

During the time when Lavoisier was active, the phlogiston theory was proving itself to be effective in making sense out of the mass of qualitative observations that was accumulating, and for a while made rapid headway. But it did not explain the quantitative observations of the kind that Lavoisier and others were beginning to make; or at least it did not explain them unless one made *ad hoc* assumptions about its weight—that sometimes phlogiston had positive, sometimes negative, weight, or sometimes no weight at all. Lavoisier, although at first he used the phlogiston theory, found that by discarding it and the hypothesis of its variable weight he could much simplify his interpretation of chemical reactions. Although the phlogiston theory lingered for some time after the work of Lavoisier, it gradually gave way to his more straightforward concepts.

Instead of a few Arisotelian elements or alchemistic "principles" which blended together and could never be purified and weighed, Lavoisier and other prominent French scientists worked out a list of about thirty elements. The first two elements, heat and light, differed from the rest in being weightless. The other elements included oxygen, nitrogen, and a series of solids and liquids that, for the time being, at least, could not be broken down any further. It was assumed that each element could be obtained in pure form, and could be recovered from a compound into which it had seemingly disappeared. Probably one of the more important results of Lavoisier's work was the demonstration that water, the venerable Aristotelian element, could be produced by the combination of hydrogen and oxygen, with the weight of the product equaling the weight of the reactants.

However, it turned out that the whole tangle that centered around the problems of phlogiston, oxygen, combustion, and respiration could not be straightened out on purely chemical grounds. What was needed was the same sort of clarification that had been given physics by the concept of force; this was provided by the work of Benjamin Thompson Rumford and others who were able to define heat as a form of energy rather than a chemical substance. With this conception, the problems connected with the chemistry of respiration and combustion began to sort themselves out rapidly, and could be approached by a rich variety of experimental methods.

A decisive step towards the fusion of chemistry and biology was made by the concept that respiration and combustion were equivalent. Lavoisier and Pierre Simon de Laplace, the astronomer and mathematician, in 1783 were able to describe this in terms of the newly discovered element oxygen. Not only was mercury converted into its red, earthy "calx" by combining with oxygen (instead of by losing phlogiston, according to the older theory), but the red color of arterial blood, they thought, also resulted from combination of oxygen with substances in the blood. Animal heat, just like the heat of combustion, came from the union of oxygen from the air with combustible substances in the body.

The idea that burning and animal respiration were more or less equivalent had been around for some time, but the discovery that plants could carry out a process that was in a sense the reverse of combustion was a startling new fact, one of major importance in ordering the grand lines of our conception of the world of life. Joseph Priestly (1733–1804), a British minister, was a prolific author of more than twenty volumes, mostly on theology, but including some important although rather chaotic descriptions of his varied experiments in chemistry. Priestly had observed that a candle burning in a closed container rendered the air unfit for sustaining animal life, and also that an animal kept in a container until it showed signs of suffocation made the air unfit for supporting combustion. But if in a vessel of such unwholesome air he put a "sprig of mint," in eight or nine days the air was restored, so that either an animal or flame could exist in it. Priestly extended this to a large view of nature (1774):

> The injury which is continually done to the atmosphere by the respiration of such a number of animals, and the putrefaction of such masses of both vegetable and animal matter, is in part at least repaired by the vegetable creation. And not withstanding the prodigious mass of air that is corrupted daily by the above mentioned causes, yet, if we consider the immense profusion of vegetables upon the face of the earth . . . it can hardly be thought but that it may be a sufficient counterbalance to it and that the remedy is adequate to the evil.

This conception of interaction between the plant and animal kingdoms is a basic theory of ecology—the science of the relationship between organisms and their environment. Priestly spoke of "dephlogisticated air" instead of oxygen, but Lavoisier described this characteristic activity of plants—photosynthesis— in terms of his element, oxygen. In the process, he says, both water and carbon dioxide decompose; "the hydrogen leaves the oxygen to combine with the carbon so as to form the oils, the resins, and the plant body, at the same time the oxygen of the water and of the carbonic acid is set free in abundance."

In the first half of the nineteenth century the advance of chemistry into biology mainly took the form of analyzing the composition of living—or at least just-killed—substance. It was soon established that all organisms contain carbon, and that no elements were found in them that were not found in minerals. Life activity, whatever it was, could not produce distinctive elements. However, when it came to finding out what chemical compounds made up plants and animals, the situation turned out to be quite different. The differences were such that for many years chemists thought that forces other than those brought into play in the laboratory must be operating in living things. The two branches of chemistry—organic and inorganic—were therefore held to be fundamentally distinct. This implied that organic chemistry must be observational and descriptive, in contrast to inorganic chemistry, where compounds could be freely synthesized.

One of the chemical differences observed was that the compounds in living things did not seem to obey the law of combination by weight in definite proportion, a law that was the cornerstone for the atomic theory of matter. In the inorganic kingdom, elements combined with each other in definite proportion by weight or simple multiples of these ratios, which could be explained by supposing that chemical combination was an atom-by-atom affair. An atom could combine with one, two, three, or rarely four atoms of another element; and since all atoms of a given element are of identical weight, and cannot be split, then combination by definite and multiple proportions by weight will follow. But from living things there can be recovered compounds in which carbon and oxygen, for example, are mixed in all proportions, as if the elements carbon and oxygen were homogeneous substances that blended together.

This difficulty was eventually cleared up by the conception that carbon was a unique element in being able to combine with other carbon atoms to build up indefinitely long chains, or linked rings, with atoms of other elements such as hydrogen and oxygen attached at the sides. The molecules of most organic compounds thus differed from those of the inorganic compounds by having a large number of atoms in which the combining weights in a compound with, say, 8 carbon atoms for every 15 atoms of oxygen, would not be distinguished, except by very precise methods, from those in a compound with, for example, 9 carbon for every 17 oxygen atoms.

Organic chemistry, dealing with complex molecules, had to develop a specialized symbolism in which "structural" formulae of the atoms were represented by diagrams. Astonishingly elaborate and diversified laboratory techniques were gradually developed in which the chemist, often guided by intuition, produced one or another organic compound to correspond to one or another complex diagram on paper, moving atoms from one position to another at will.

Perhaps not surprisingly, it was at first thought that the synthesis of organic compounds was beyond the reach of laboratory procedures, and was in the domain of "life force" thought to reside in living tissues. The first penetration into this domain was made by Friedrich Wöhler in 1828 with his announcement of the creation of the organic compound urea from the inorganic compound ammonium cyanate. There was, however, some opportunity for quibbling, because of the lingering doubt that ammonium cyanate was really inorganic. Also, the formation of urea was not strictly a synthesis, being merely an alteration in molecular structure (both compounds have the same empirical formula, CH_4N_2O). These objections, however, did not stand up in the face of later successes. By 1845 Wöhler's student Adolph Kolbe had synthesized acetic acid from its constituent elements carbon, hydrogen, and oxygen. It has been pointed out that none of these syntheses are independent of life because they are carried out by laboratory workers. The reader can be left with this problem (if it is a problem).

The first organic chemists were concerned mainly with the analysis of the composition of organic materials. There is another field of chemistry, however, which is concerned with the chemical reactions that go on within living things, with the ways in which the compounds are synthesized and broken down in organisms and, ultimately, with the functional significance of these biochemical changes. In a way analagous to that in which inorganic chemistry became divided into physical chemistry and inorganic chemistry, organic chemistry became divided into organic chemistry (that dealing with carbon compounds) and biochemistry, or the chemistry of life. Joseph Priestly, who studied photosynthesis, was therefore perhaps an early biochemist, but the subject first took on its modern form in the hands of the French scienist Louis Pasteur (1822–1895).

The great amount of information that had been gathered about the structure of animals during the eighteenth and nineteenth centuries was being interpreted in terms of function, but this function was largely seen as a matter of mechanical engineering. When Lavoisier and Priestly described respiration and photosyntheses, they made a beginning in the study of what might be called chemical engineering in plants and animals, but this understanding of the adaptive significance of biochemical processes was one of the last of the main areas of biology to develop. Pasteur was the first consistently to see the chemistry of organisms as another facet of the adaptiveness of nature, and was even a good deal ahead of his time, since functional biochemistry at the intracellular level did not really gain momentum until well into the twentieth century.

The circumstance that made Pasteur a pioneer biochemist was that he worked with microorganisms—yeasts and bacteria—

which, even under the best microscopes, are almost structureless. They are not "mechanical engineers"; instead, they are adept at the chemical manipulation of their environment. Pasteur understood this, and also that these chemical processes were present, too, in the more familiar higher plants and animals, where they were largely masked and hidden by the complex organization of the animal body and were relatively inaccessible for study. The microbes have turned out again and again to offer the key approaches to the study of the chemistry of life.

The titles of the chief published works of Louis Pasteur give no hint that he was one of the greatest theoretical scientists of all time. They are: *Studies on Wine* (1866), *Studies on Vinegar* (1868), *Studies on the Disease of Silkworms* (1870), and *Studies on Beer* (1876). Pasteur's career seemed dominated by circumstance; he served in one scientific campaign after another, as dictated by the needs of industry or public health, and René Dubos has entitled a biography *Louis Pasteur: Free Lance of Science.* At the start of his career Pasteur was deeply interested in problems of the most theoretical and abstract kind, and as it turned out, his lifetime commitment to practical, applied science did not betray this early interest. The best road to a goal may be the long and roundabout one, and during an eventful and busy life Pasteur arrived at the solution of biological problems of the most profound theoretical importance, discovering them in the midst of practical problems.

Pasteur made his name in science during the first ten years of his professional life, which he devoted to studying crystals. By the early nineteenth century it had been discovered that certain transparent crystals when placed one behind the other in a certain way blocked light. This astonishing behavior could be explained by assuming that a crystal could sort out waves of light into parallel planes. If one crystal was oriented so that its ordered (polarized) light was in planes perpendicular to those of the other, no light at all could get through. Also, some crystals could, upon receiving polarized light, twist the planes either to the right or left, as revealed by the appropriate detector. It had been discovered that crystals of the mineral quartz were of two kinds, one that could twist polarized light to the left, the other to the right. This was correlated with different arrangements of the crystal faces of the natural mineral, some quartz crystals being right-, others left-handed. More surprising than this behavior of crystals was the fact that the solutions, in which individual molecules are dispersed, of certain chemical compounds also rotated polarized light. These "optically active" compounds were the ones that interested Pasteur.

One mystery that drew his attention was the behavior of tartaric acid, which was found in vats of fermenting wine grapes. It existed in two kinds: one that could rotate polarized light, the other not. It was said that these two were identical in every respect, including the shape of crystals obtained from solution. Pasteur, reasoning from the analogy of the quartz crystals, felt that there must be some difference in the crystals, so he set about looking for the difference, preparing crystals of many different salts of the tartaric acid. He found the difference in a tiny facet on one side of the crystal somehow overlooked by previous investigators. The optically active form had the facet, always turned to the right. He then examined the inactive form, expecting to find no facets, or one on each side. Instead he obtained two kinds of crystals from the solution of the inactive kind, one with facets turned to the right, the other to the left. The two kinds together in solution must mutually cancel optical activity, a hypothesis Pasteur proved correct by sorting out with tweezers the two kinds of crystals, then dissolving them. One solution rotated polarized light to the right, but the other was a new kind of tartrate—it twisted the light to the left. This experiment, which Pasteur could demonstrate before the eyes of his colleagues, with its unique opportunities for the display of patience, manual skill, and intelligence, immediately established his scientific reputation. His subsequent work on these optical isomeres laid the foundation for a whole branch of organic chemistry.

What particularly impressed Pasteur was the fact that all the organic compounds that were optically active in solution were derived from living things. To this day it has proved impossible in the laboratory to synthesize an asymmetric organic molecule without at the same time producing equal quantities of molecules with the opposite symmetry; or to synthesize one without the initial presence of some other kind of asymmetric molecules. Living things regularly produce asymmetric molecules of either right or left properties, instead of a mixture of both kinds (Pasteur's original inactive tartrate came from two different kinds of organisms in the same fermenting vat, as he found by exploring Europe, looking into wine vats).

Although Pasteur was, during the great vitalist–materialist controversy that dominated nineteenth-century science, called a vitalist, he sought a materialistic explanation for this puzzling characteristic of life. He pointed out that the earth is in itself asymmetrical, by reason of its rotation on its axis. The magnetic field of the earth must be the result of a flowing electric current, which would produce asymmetry. Asymmetry in life, he thought, was the consequence of the asymmetry of the earth or the universe. He tried experiments in which, by means of mirrors, plants were illuminated by a sun that rose in the west and set in the east, and he examined their organic compounds to see if natural symmetry was reversed. Crystals were precipitated out of solution in strong magnetic fields to see if he could artifically produce asymmetry. These experiments failed. It is perhaps just as

231

well that he did not have the chance to continue such direct as-
saults on the secrets of nature. The rich store of new facts that
he uncovered in his practical work on wine making, and the diseases of beer, silkworms, sheep, and man gave him the material
needed to establish the relationship between the simplest forms of
life and the nonliving world, and to delineate some of the main
features of the chemistry of life. Imagination alone is not powerful enough to construct an approach for attacking such problems.
Rich experience also is necessary, and the technological world of
nineteenth-century France gave to the genius Pasteur the opportunity to acquire such experience.

Pasteur was a chemist, not a biologist, but his conviction that
optically active organic compounds could be produced only inside
living organisms led him into open and severe conflict with the
leading chemists of the day. The battleground for this conflict
was the phenomenon known as fermentation. Natural substances
left to themselves sour or rot or otherwise decompose. Grapes,
crushed and killed, become altered to produce alcohol and other
substances. Sprouting barley after being roasted and ground de-
composes in a similar way. This change, fermentation, was naturally of extreme interest to chemists. A large number of compounds—acetic, lactic, and butyric acids, a number of alcohols,
and so on—could be identified in fermentation products. Since the
chemists who worked just before the time of Pasteur had succeeded in banishing life from organic chemistry by synthesizing
organic compounds in the laboratory, they took the position that
the best way to understand fermentation was to consider it a
purely chemical phenomenon, in which the constituents of once-
living organisms were altered by ordinary chemical processes.

Pasteur had been interested in the study of fermentation because it produced the optically active organic compounds that he
had worked on for so many years, and when a wine manufacturer

in 1855 asked him, as a chemist, to look into the reason for souring of wine, he jumped at the chance. Biologists a few years before him had observed that yeasts were always present in alcoholic fermentation, and had seen that these microscopic structures grew and reproduced by budding. Their contention that yeasts were alive, and were responsible for producing alcohol, was treated with the arrogant contempt that the experimental laboratory scientist is prone to hand out to the observing naturalist–biologist. Justus von Liebig (1803–1873), who founded in Germany the first school of chemistry, and Friedrich Wöhler were the most influential voices in the powerful new science of chemistry, and the derision with which they greeted what they called the vitalist theory of fermentation of the biologists effectively discredited it. In a technical journal, they lampooned the theory by figuring, in a ribald fashion, yeast cells shaped like miniature vertebrate animals, eliminating carbon dioxide gas and liquid alcohol. Which, Pasteur was able to show, is exactly what they do.

Liebig could not formulate his chemical theory of fermentation in such a way as to lead to a definite program of experiments. All he could do was to say that the living-germ theory of fermentation was a retreat to medieval darkness; or to use purely verbal argument such as: to say that the yeast cells seen in fermenting liquids are the cause of the chemical change is like a child saying that it is the turning waterwheels that cause a river to flow so rapidly. Pasteur, on the other hand, by minute and patient observation of fermenting mixtures and the development of precise experimental techniques for producing a given kind of fermentation at will, inaugurated a science of microbiology that has flourished to the present day.

To refute Liebig, Pasteur used the unfailing device of the experimenter—to simplify the situation so that relationsips could be identified. The composition of material in a fermenting vat of grape juice is beyond analysis from a chemical point of view, containing hundreds of organic compounds in different proportions in different lots. Pasteur prepared a clear solution containing sugar, ammonia for a nitrogen source, and mineral salts, including a small amount of ash from incinerated yeasts, which hopefully would contain trace elements needed by the living plant. Into this almost completely defined medium he introduced a small amount of yeast. The yeast grew, and as it increased in weight, produced ever larger quantities of alcohol at the expense of the sugar in the solution. He later found that other kinds of microorganisms, recognizably different under the microscope, produced characteristic kinds of fermentation products, and by introducing only one kind of organism into a simple solution, could regularly produce, say, butyric acid from lactic acid, or lactic acid from milk sugar.

A fermentation that particularly interested him was the production of acetic acid or vinegar in wine vats. In these vats a thin scum of a certain kind of bacteria formed at the surface, and if air was supplied, these microorganisms flourished, and the alcohol beneath, which had been produced by yeast fermentation of grape sugar, was converted into acetic acid. This gave him the idea of an ecological division of labor in the microbial world, some kinds of microbes requiring oxygen for life, and carrying out certain types of chemical transformations to obtain the energy they needed for growth, and other kinds being able to live without oxygen, getting energy by the transformation of sugar into alcohol, for example. Pasteur finally restricted the term "fermentation" to this latter process, defining it as life without oxygen.

Yeast, Pasteur found, could live either with or without air, in contrast to some other microorganisms that could not tolerate oxygen. Yeast was a facultative anaerobe; when oxygen was not available, as in the beer or wine vats of the manufacturer, it would get as much energy as it could out of the sugar, leaving alcohol as a residue, but under the more favorable (for the yeast) conditions where oxygen was available, alcohol did not accumulate, and the sugar was broken down completely into carbon dioxide and water, yielding the maximum amount of energy for the growth of the yeast. Pasteur saw certain similarities between the biochemistry of yeast and what little was known about that of animal muscle. This tissue, when contracting, gave off more carbon dioxide than it should, considering the amount of oxygen used, and he thought that this could be explained by assuming that part of the carbon dioxide was produced by fermentation, just as yeast evolved the gas when converting sugar to alcohol. Also, muscle will contract in the absence of oxygen, with the production of carbon dioxide, giving a direct analogy with yeast fermentation.

For some reason, Pasteur's vision of the unity of life, with living cells using a common pattern of biochemical change for extracting energy from foodstuffs, did not lead to any striking developments during the nineteenth century. This fundamentally important concept was to lie dormant until the twentieth century, when it suddenly made sense out of a vast accumulation of detailed knowledge of biochemical processes, and also made it possible to deal with biochemistry from the evolutionary standpoint that had illumined other branches of biology.

So far as the vitalist–mechanist controversy over fermentation was concerned, Liebig had admitted that yeasts were present, and that they were alive, but insisted that the actual breakdown of sugar was purely chemical, and that it was caused by substances released by the dying yeasts. This position could be defended by drawing an analogy with one of the digestive enzymes (pepsin) which, by 1835, had been isolated from animal stomachs, and would decompose meat in a test tube. Liebig's insistent denial that fermentation could be going on *inside* the yeast cell was really a kind of vitalism, for it seemed to say that the process inside a living cell could not be chemical in nature. Pasteur did not get quite so tangled up in semantics, because he merely said that fermentation was always accompanied by and was a manifestation of life, which was true of the fermentations other than digestion (after Pasteur, the term fermentation was no longer applied to digestion). Stripped of the vitalist–mechanist terminology, what Pasteur was saying was that the conversion of sugar to alcohol took place inside the yeast, and furnished the yeast with energy; in other words it was an adaptive, biological process.

Pasteur tried the obvious experiment of extracting from yeast cells something that would decompose sugar into alcohol and carbon dioxide, but he failed, as did others who attempted it. It was not until 1897 that Edward Buchner succeeded, and this without trying. He had ground up yeast cells to make an extract for medicinal purposes. Concentrated sugar solutions (which prevent the growth of the microorganisms of decay) should, he thought, make a good preservative but he found a quite unexpected reaction: the preservative itself was decomposed by the yeast extract, to give carbon dioxide and water. This he recognized as an answer to the mechanist–vitalist controversy of the preceding decades. The active substance in the yeast extract was called zymase, and the general term "enzyme" (literally, *in* + *yeast*) was coined for this and similar substances. As it later turned out, zymase was not a single enzyme, but a system of several enzymes; however, Buchner's achievement did represent a first step towards isolating biochemical reactions from living cells, making it possible to study them in simpler and more easily controlled situations.

In 1859, the year of publication of Darwin's *Origin of Species*, the French biologist Felix Pouchet put before the scientific public a large volume titled *Hetérogénie,* in which he showed that microorganisms arose spontaneously in solutions or mixtures of organic compounds. The fermentations that Pasteur had studied were, in Pouchet's opinion, the first stages in a process inherent in the solutions that led to the production of microorganisms: fermentation was not an activity of microbes—it was the other way around, and microbes were the end product of purely chemical activity. Pasteur had by this time already published a memoir on lactic acid fermentation, as well as a preliminary note on alcohol fermentation, and was far into other aspects of the subject, a subject that, although he was a chemist, he regarded as properly in the field of biology. Although his scientific friends tried to keep him out of the spontaneous generation controversy, as a problem beyond the range of the experimental method, Pasteur realized that unless his point that living microbes arose only from preexisting microbes was established, the whole subject of fermentations (and, as he saw later, the whole field of microbiology) would collapse into nonsense.

In nineteenth-century France, it seemed a logical necessity to many scientists of the powerful mechanist school to assume that nature was continuously giving rise to life, so that the experimental work of Pouchet met with a good deal of support in respected academic circles, as well as among the educated and progressive-thinking public. The idea that life and the rest of nature were rigidly separated seemed to the enlightened to be tainted with mysticism. But the road to enlightenment is not always the easy and obvious one. A reasonable connection between the living and nonliving nature was not to be worked out for nearly a hundred years, as a consequence of the victory of evolution theory and as a result of the efforts of investigators and thinkers in chemistry, physics, astronomy, and biology. As Pasteur saw the situation, the soil and the air is not permeated with a *tendency* toward life, but with actual microscopic, all-but-invisible bits of life, the germs, or microorganisms, that were incredibly abundant and almost ubiquitous. The fact that they were tangible particles should, Pasteur reasoned, make it possible to exclude them by filtering air through wool or cotton, or since they had weight, they would eventually settle out of still air. Since they were alive, it should be possible to kill those already present in the experimental materials by heating, say to the temperature of boiling water or slightly above. In a series of remarkably ingenious experiments, Pasteur was able to show that protected nutrient media would remain free of microbes for months or years, then would support an abundant growth of them if a few microbes were introduced into the media.

In practice, in the hands of different experimenters, the results of experiments on spontaneous generation were variable, because of the mechanical difficulties of excluding the germs postulated by Pasteur, and at the same time admitting air, which was supposed to be necessary for spontaneous generation. The question of lethal heat was also unexpectedly difficult. Very high temperatures could be expected to produce great chemical alterations which might in some way make spontaneous generation impossible. So that it is easy to see that there would be room for argument. Pasteur carried the fight to Pouchet, challenging him to repeat before an academic commission the experiments which, according to Pouchet, invariably produced microorganisms by spontaneous generation. Pouchet declined, and such was the force of Pasteur's polemic, and the elegance of his experimental demonstrations, that the theory of spontaneous generation was defeated. The fact that the defeat was "official" led to the neglect of some of Pouchet's important experimental results. As it eventually turned out, some of the microorganisms he worked with survived high temperatures that Pasteur thought lethal.

Pasteur's results do not exclude the possibility that spontaneous generation is going on somewhere under conditions different from those of his experiments. But his theory does agree well with what is now known about microorganisms. Observations on their biochemistry, and on their structure, as revealed by the electron microscope, make it impossible that they should arise directly from the chemical level of organization. If life of the microbial type does arise spontaneously from nonliving matter, it is by way of intermediate stages of kinds not yet known.

Pasteur had convinced the scientific world that microbes were living creatures that, like other forms of life, come from preexisting individuals of the same kind. He showed that many of them lived in decaying or fermenting organic matter, getting the energy and substance needed for growth and reproduction by chemically transforming this matter. This answered a question posed many years before by Lavoisier: ". . . fermentation, putrefaction and combustion endlessly return to the atmosphere and to the mineral kingdom the principles which plants and animals had borrowed from them. What is the mechanism through which Nature brings about this marvellous circulation of matter between the three kingdoms?"

With his concept of a world of microorganisms, Pasteur answered this basic problem of ecology, establishing a theory comparable in importance to the earlier concept of the relationship between photosynthesis by green plants and respiration. The microbial world, now known to be greater in bulk than all animals combined, is responsible for the final minute subdivision and degradation of the substance of animal and plant bodies that is necessary for its reentry into the living world. Modern ecologists have estimated that as much as 95 percent of the carbon that is incorporated into the biosphere by green plants is each year returned to the atmosphere as carbon dioxide by the microorganisms of decay. When later microbiologists discovered the assimilation of nitrogen from the atmosphere by microorganisms, and its subsequent release to the atmosphere, another major concept was fitted into ecological theory, that virtually the entire atmosphere is a product of, the expression of, the activity of the biosphere.

Pasteur is best known, however, for his part in showing that microbes live not only in decaying substances, but exist, too, in the bodies of living animals, where they may cause disease. This phase of microbial ecology is of extreme importance in human biology: the great majority of human deaths before maturity were, until the twentieth century, caused by microbial disease. Just as specific fermentations were caused by specific germs so, Pasteur was able to demonstrate, a given disease expresses the interaction between a given host animal and a certain species of microorganism. In his classical study of chicken cholera, he found that the causative bacteria, grown in culture for generation after generation, lost their ability to cause the disease when injected into the host animal. But they did have some effect on the host, since it was now resistant to fresh virulent bacteria. From this beginning, with its broader foundation in experience and theory than the earlier development of vaccination against smallpox, the science of immunology developed rapidly within the next twenty years, with hundreds of workers isolating pathogenic bacteria and trying to produce corresponding vaccines.

In summary, besides his uniquely important contributions to

industry, medicine, and agriculture, for which he is best known, Pasteur made advances of comparable magnitude in theoretical biology. By developing the concept of microorganisms, by showing them to be an immense and varied component of the organic world, living everywhere in the soil and water and in the bodies of plants and animals, he made possible a basic outline sketch of the science of ecology. By isolating different species of bacteria and yeasts in different chemical media, he showed that they brought about chemical changes in characteristic and predictable ways, thus constructing much of the framework of biochemistry. And by laying the ghost of spontaneous generation and establishing a lower boundary of the living world, he rounded off the unity of biology as a science, a science that had been named a half century before by Lamarck.

Biochemistry and genetics have fused along a broad segment of their boundaries to produce one of the new interdisciplinary sciences characteristic of the twentieth century—molecular biology, which is concerned with the structure and function of such giant molecules as enzymes and those of DNA (actually organized into indefinitely long strands, rather than into molecules of definitive size), which carry the hereditary units postulated by Mendel. This level of organization, intermediate in size between the cell and the molecule of ordinary chemistry, has been one of the great unknown areas of science, and its study represents a meeting place of physics, chemistry, and biology. The physicists and chemists, having taken up the study of biological materials, in which this level of organization (originally called the colloidal level) is important, have made perhaps the main contributions to molecular biology, often themselves becoming biologists in the process.

The area now called molecular biology was first penetrated on a large scale from two directions: from chemistry by the study of enzymes, and from biology by the study of heredity, which was taken up with new vigor with the rediscovery of Mendelian inheritance in 1900. The reason that the geneticists turned out to be concerned with molecular biology is the remarkable fact that each "molecule" of DNA (that is, the segment of whatever length of the DNA strand can be shown to be concerned with a particular heritable characteristic) is represented effectively only twice in the total DNA complement of each living cell (only once in some organisms, and only once in all sperms and eggs). In essence, the geneticist, when studying the heritable characteristics of the whole organism, is studying effects which can be traced back to a single "molecule," or a single pair of them.

Genetics and biochemistry have been linked up by the one-gene, one-enzyme hypothesis, which has been confirmed in its essentials by a variety of experimental techniques, many of which are still evolving and lie at the frontiers of molecular biology.

Enzymes are biological catalysts. The concept of catalysis was established by Jöns Berzelius, in 1836, for reactions in which a small amount of material brought about chemical transformation without itself being changed. The catalyst could be either inorganic or organic. Best known of the inorganic catalysts was platinum; the ferments, as well as such digestive enzymes as ptyaline, in the saliva, were called organic catalysts.

The similarity between the actions of organic and inorganic catalysis was in some instances very compelling, and Liebig seemed quite justified in classifying fermentations as a purely chemical reaction. In the early 1800s, it was observed that if a finely divided powder of platinum sulfate at room temperature is soaked with alcohol, it spontaneously glows, giving off heat and at the same time converting the alcohol to acetic acid. Other forms of platinum also were effective in catalyzing a variety of chemical reactions, metallic platinum drawn out into fine wires, or made into spongy masses with great surface area being especially effective.

In Germany acetic acid was manufactured by dripping alcohol over wood shavings that were held in a tall column in a tower. Liebig thought that the surface of the wood shavings acted as a catalyst in the same way as did the surface of the platinum, or platinum sulfate. Pasteur, however, who in addition to a fiery eloquence to match Liebig's had a myopic patience all his own, examined the wood shavings most carefully, and found them to be coated with film of the bacterium *Mycoderma aceti*, the same one that formed the scum of the French wine-vinegar vats. So that Pasteur said the supposed catalyst was actually a living microorganism. Later, the contradiction was cleared up when Buchner resolved the problem of alcoholic fermentation by yeast: the catalyst was inside the microbe, and was part of its metabolic machinery.

Determining the chemical nature of these organic catalysts was a task of twentieth-century chemistry. They had already (after Buchner's work on yeast) been called enzymes, and were distinguished from the inorganic catalysts by their extreme sensitivity to heat. Temperatures little over the boiling point of water destroyed their activity, so that they were assumed to be proteins, which were known to be altered by such treatment. This theory was challenged by eminent chemists, who observed enzymatically active solutions that gave negative tests for proteins. The situation was also confused by the close association of metals with some of the enzymes, metals which were themselves catalysts. However, a long period of laborious and exacting work on enzyme preparations has established beyond question that enzymes are protein molecules. It is the fact that they are such extraordinarily efficient catalysts, far more active than anything found in the inorganic world, that accounted for negative protein tests in some instances: they were able to produce detectable reactions without being themselves detected by standard analytic procedures.

Many hundreds of kinds of enzymes are presently known, and each kind is a catalyst for a given chemical reaction or group of similar reactions. Without them, life that proceeds at the tempo we observe in organisms is inconceivable. Besides being specific for the kind of reaction mediated, variants within each kind of enzyme differ in controlling the rate of the reaction. Thus, the hundreds of simultaneous variations that exist within even a single living cell are held in an exquisitely adjusted meshwork of linked reactions. As a most basic generalization, a living system is one controlled by enzymatically mediated chemical reactions. This is not to say that all biochemical reactions are so mediated; there may be whole classes of important reactions that have other catalysts, or none at all.

Associated with many enzymes are small nonprotein molecules that are easily detachable, and are essential to the proper functioning of the enzyme. These are co-enzymes. Some of them are derived from certain vitamins of the so-called B complex, and thus provide an explanation for the requirement of these compounds.

Protein molecules are, compared with most other organic compounds, extremely large structures, composed of some hundreds of component amino acid molecules of about twenty different kinds, arranged in definite linear sequence, which is presumably characteristic of each kind of enzyme. This sequence expresses itself in part in the way the long protein strand folds itself up into a complex, fragile, three-dimensional structure which is the operational enzyme. How the enzyme works is not known, but there is apparently a localized site where the molecule or molecules that undergo reaction are held in place momentarily and perhaps subjected to stresses that alter their configuration in such a way as to facilitate the reaction. The rest of the enzyme has some other function or functions, still unknown.

Ever since systematic analysis of the composition of living matter began early in the nineteenth century, it has been observed that phosphorus is a component of living substance. Even though there was no indication as to its role in biochemistry, one chemist was so impressed with the regularity of its occurrence that he coined the phrase, "There is no life without phosphorus." It is present in living tissue in rather small amounts, and also is one of the rarer components of the earth's crust. One theory of modern ecology is that total volume of the biosphere is ultimately controlled by the amount of available phosphorus. In one of Aldous Huxley's novels, the gloomy scientist predicting the downfall of the human race thinks that it will be shortage of phosphorus that does us in.

One of the first clues as to the role of phosphorus came from observations on the yeast juice and sugar mixture prepared in the manner of Buchner. At first the mixture bubbles cheerfully, as carbon dioxide is given off while the sugar is being converted into alcohol. Activity soon dies down, but is instantly, although only partially, restored if a soluble phosphate is stirred in; and this can be repeated again and again. On analysis of the mixture, the phosphorus can be found attached to certain derivatives of the sugar. In living intact yeast cells, phosphorus does not have to be fed into the cells continuously, so it is being constantly released from combination and reused, in cyclic fashion.

After several decades of work on the behavior of phosphorus compounds in biochemical systems, the function of this element gradually became understood. Just as the unique properties of carbon make possible the large complex and varied molecules that we find making up living substance, so the phosphorus atom has unique properties that make possible the quick transfers of energy that are needed for building up more complex, more energy-rich constituents from simpler and energy-poor building blocks.

The phosphorus atom occurs as the core of a small group of atoms, the phosphate ion. When the phosphate group is attached to an organic molecule, such as a sugar, a second, and yet a third phosphate group can be attached to the first. The structure of the electronic shells of the phosphorus atom is such that when these second and third groups are transferred from one molecule to another they carry with them energy of considerably greater amounts than are involved in most organic reactions. Thus, if a building block is "phosphorylated" with one of these high-energy phosphates, it has the energy needed to combine with another building block. So far as known, the extremely varied synthetic reactions of the living cell are generally powered by a single type of phosphate-bearing organic molecule, which therefore serves as the common coin of energy exchange within the cell. This is adenosine: adenosine di-phosphate, if carrying two phosphate groups, adenosine tri-phosphate if three.

The DNA strips consist of indefinitely long chains of four kinds of nucleotides, of which one is adenosine phosphate and the three others are organic phosphates similar to it. The enzyme molecule, of limited and definite length, is a chain of some hundreds or thousands of twenty or so different kinds of amino acids. It has now been demonstrated that the sequence of the four kinds of nucleotides in a segment of the DNA strip determines the sequence of amino acids in a particular enzyme, which confirms the one gene—one enzyme hypothesis that had earlier been arrived at on the basis of other kinds of evidence. Three nucleotides in a specific sequence are required to specify each amino acid; there are more than enough of such triplet combinations (sixty-four) to specify the twenty kinds of amino acids. DNA thus functions in the manner of a code on a computer tape, storing information used to assemble amino acids into a functioning enzyme.

Molecular biology has thus carried the concept of life as mechanism into the last major unknown realm of biology, the level of organization lying between the cell and the small molecules of ordinary chemistry. It can explain the formation of the extraordinarily complex and functionally ingenious structure of enzyme molecules in mechanistic terms. The vitalist Driesch had once held that the existence of enzymes made it certain that a unique vitalistic force operated in living organisms.

The concept of integrative levels, which assimilates rather then opposes the mechanistic view, recognizes that life is unique, at either the level of the genes and enzymes, or the cell, or the organism, or the biological community. But it points out that it is pattern that is unique, patterns that have an evolutionary history that extends back to the time when life did not exist on the earth.

Although it has been shown that even the simplest microorganisms are of a complexity far beyond anything found in nonliving nature, and arise only from preexisting microorganisms, the modern biologist does not think that this contradicts the prevailing mechanist view of life. He imagines that in the far distant past, some few billions of years ago, there were organisms much simpler in molecular structure than contemporary bacteria. Some may have been fragile watery bags of organic compounds, without enzymes or the nucleic acid mechanisms for assembling enzymes. They could have been called alive because they grew slowly by incorporating organic compounds from the environment and because they reproduced by division. He imagines also that in the nonliving part of the environment were vast accumulations of solutions and suspensions of organic compounds far more complex and diversified than are found in existing nonliving nature. Evidence from astronomy indicates that during an early stage in earth history carbon was present chiefly in chemical combination with iron and hydrogen. Such simple but highly reactive compounds, interacting with ammonia, would produce more complex carbon compounds, which in turn react to produce even more varied and complex organic compounds. There is thus imagined a long period of purely chemical evolution that produced an enormous variety of organic compounds in the primeval sea. The facts of organic chemistry in no way contradict such lines of thinking, and laboratory mixtures of simple carbon and nitrogen compounds interact to produce indefinitely large numbers of complex organic compounds.

At one stage in earth history, then, the wide gap between the nonliving and the living did not exist, and indeed the criteria for life that we derive from a study of existing organisms could hardly be applied to the unending variety of particles and masses of organic compounds that must have existed in the ancient Oparin sea, so named after the Russian biochemist (A. I. Oparin) who was the first to develop this line of speculation to a significant degree. In a general way, chemical evolution was superseded by biological evolution when the kinds of organic aggregates that grew and divided became common. With limited raw materials for growth, competition ensues, with kinds of entities that reproduce more rapidly becoming dominant. The mechanism of natural selection is thus set in motion, with adaptation, which is related to success in survival and reproduction, gradually and imperceptibly becoming a part of nature. Once natural selection has produced such specialized mechanisms associated with reproduction as DNA, the pace of biological evolution swiftens. The enormous variety of half-living or primitive living things was destroyed by surviving efficient types that have given rise to the relatively uniform biochemical systems that exist in modern organisms. The new swarming life of this ancient sea itself devoured the mass of organic compounds that had given rise to it, thus cutting the umbilical cord that had connected life with nonliving nature.

[B I B L I O G R A P H I C A L   N O T E S]

General

There is a large number of textbooks and sourcebooks in the history of science which provide background for the history of biology; only a few are mentioned here. George Sarton examines the methods of the discipline in *A Guide to the History of Science: A First Guide for the History of Science with Introductory Essays on Science and Tradition* (Waltham, Mass., 1952). His massive compendium *Introduction to the History of Science* (3 vols. in 5; Baltimore, 1927–1948) covers material from the time of Homer through the fourteenth century. Charles Singer, whose interests lie mainly in the history of biology, has written *A Short History of Science to the Nineteenth Century* (London, 1941) for the general reader. Another excellent introduction is *A History of Science and Its Relations with Philosophy and Religion* (Cambridge, 1929; rev. 3d ed., 1942) by William Cecil Dampier. A recent account is that of Rupert A. and Marie Boas Hall, *A Brief History of Science* (New York, 1964).

The history of technology, which overlaps that of science, is dealt with in a way both scholarly and interesting in the compendium *A History of Technology* (Oxford, 1954–1965), edited by Charles Singer. The five volumes take up the story with Stone Age technology and carry it through the end of the nineteenth century. Lewis Mumford's *Technics and Civilization* (New York, 1934) is a general reader account of the relationship between technology and the history of culture.

Collections of excerpts from the writings of scientists important from the historical standpoint have been presented, with introductory comments, in such works as the *Harvard Case Histories in Experimental Science* (2 vols.; Cambridge, Mass., 1937), edited by James B. Conant; *Readings in the Literature of Science* (Cambridge, Eng., 1924), arranged by William C. and Margaret Dampier; and *Moments of Discovery* (2 vols.; New York, 1958), edited by George Schwartz and Philip W. Bishop.

Among the more-or-less standard histories of biology there may be mentioned Charles Singer's *A Short History of Biology: A General Introduction to the Study of Living Things* (London, 1931); William A. Locy's *The Growth of Biology* (New York, 1925); and the very complete *The History of Biology: A Survey,* by Erik Nordenskiold (translated by Leonard Eyre). E. Radl's *History of Biological Theories* (Oxford, 1930) is an opinionated but interesting and important account.

Chapter 1
Adaptation in the Living World

The often-reprinted *Natural Theology; or, Evidences of the Existence of the Deity, Collected from the Appearance of Nature* by William Paley was first published in 1802 in London.

Justification for the use of terms, in a strictly scientific context, implying purpose in biological phenomena, is to be found in two letters written to the editors of the journal *Science,* in which the biologist William Powers and paleontologist George Gaylord Simpson, under the heading "On Eschewing Teleology" (129 [1959], 610, 672), reply to an earlier charge that one of them had been overly teleological. In his book *The Ethical Animal* (London, 1960), the biologist C. H. Waddington states the case in this way: "It is by now absolutely conventional and a matter of first principles to consider the whole physiological and sensory apparatus of any living thing as the result of a process which tailors it into conformity with the situations with which the organism will have to deal." This process is, in the Darwinian context, evolution by natural selection. Simpson has discussed the problem in a broader way in "The Problem of Plan and Purpose in Nature" (*Scientific Monthly,* 64 [1947], 481–95). A series of discussions of the same general question by philosophers is to be found in a volume edited by John Canfield, *Purpose in Nature* (Englewood Cliffs, N.J., 1966).

Donald R. Griffin has discussed the adaptations of insect-eating bats for navigating and finding prey in *Echoes of Bats and Men* (Garden City, N.Y., 1959). Hearing in moths is discussed by Kenneth Roeder, "Moths and Ultrasound" (*Scientific American,* 212 [1964], 94–102). Asher Treat describes the mites of moth ears in "A Case of Peculiar Parasitism" (*Natural History,* 67 [1958], 366–73).

Chapter 2
The Human Animal

So rapidly has anthropology been producing new information in the past few years that the more recent texts are necessary to provide a factual background for speculating about the life of primitive man. The third edition of Ashley Montagu's *Introduction to Physical Anthropology* (Springfield, Ill., 1960) is useful. The important question of chronology is discussed authoritatively by Kenneth P. Oakley in *Frameworks for Dating Fossil Man* (Chicago, 1964). A valuable collection of papers on early man that is far more varied than the title might indicate is *Classification and Human Evolution,* edited by Sherwood L. Washburn (Chicago, 1963). Especially relevant in this volume are George Gaylord Simpson's discussion of hominids in "The Meaning of Taxonomic Statements"; Bernard Campbell's "Quantitative Taxonomy and Human Evolution"; John Napier's "The Locomotor Functions of Hominids"; "Behavior and Human Evolution," by S. L. Washburn; "Psychological Definitions of Man," by Anne Roe; "The Taxonomic Evaluation of Fossil Hominids," by Ernst Mayr; and "Genetic Entities in Hominid Evolution," by Theodosius Dobzhansky. Some more general works are A. Barnet, *The Human Species: A Biology of Man* (Harmondsworth, 1957); Dobzhansky, *Mankind Evolving: The Evolution of the Human Species* (New Haven, 1962); and W. E. Les Gros Clark, *The Fossil Evidence for Human Evolution* (Chicago, 1955). In *Prehistory* (New York, 1963), Volume I, Part 1 of the series *History of the Scientific and Cultural Development of Mankind,* Jacquetta Hawkes takes the story up to 8000 B.C.; Part 2 of the same work, by Leonard Woolley, is *The Beginnings of Civilization.*

A short paper on a savage tribe's knowledge of birds is Jared Diamond's "Zoological Classification System of a Primitive People" (*Science,* 151 [1966], 1102–04); a comparable one about primitive botanical classification is by Brent Berlin, D. E. Breedlove, and P. H. Raven, "Folk Taxonomies and Biological Classification" (*Science,* 154 [1966], 273–75).

The book on the bushmen of the Kalahari Desert cited in the text is Elizabeth Marshall Thomas' *The Harmless People* (New York, Random House, 1959).

Chapter 3
The Nature of Science

One of the best ways to understand the nature of the complex human activity called science is to study it in action in various branches of science. The *Harvard Case Histories,* previously cited, exploits this approach. It is done in elegant fashion in Gerald Holton's *Introduction to Concepts and Theories in Physical Science* (Cambridge, Mass., 1953), which although primarily a textbook in physics, has sections set aside, as in chapters 13 and 14, that deal explicitly with the nature of scientific activity. Thomas Kuhn's *The Copernican Revolution* (Cambridge, Mass., 1957), concerned mainly with the influence of astronomical theories in the development of Western thought, has much to say about the factors that come into play during the formulation of scientific concepts. Among the more general writings on the subject is Stephen Toulmin's *The Philosophy of Science: An Introduction* (London, 1953). Gilbert Lewis' *The Anatomy of Science* (New York, 1928) is a widely quoted reference.

Thorstein Veblen's "The Place of Science in Modern Civilization," quoted in the text, originally appeared in the *American Journal of Sociology,* 11 (1906), 585–609.

Bronislaw Malinowski, in his *Magic, Science, and Religion; and Other Essays* (Boston, 1948), discusses the primitive intellectual milieu in which science existed in embryonic form.

The "doctrine of falsifiability" as a test for a scientifically useful hypothesis has been made widely known by K. R. Popper in his *The Logic of Scientific Discovery* (New York, 1961).

Some of the ways in which the concept of integrative levels has concerned biologists are illustrated in a controversial paper by Alex B. Novikoff, "The Concept of Integrative Levels and Biology" (*Science,* 101 [1945], 209–15), and in replies to it by Joseph Needham, and R. W. Gerard and Alfred E. Emerson (". . . Novikoff cuts a wide critical swath, and we are among the frail straws cut down") in the same journal (pp. 582–85). Novikoff gets in a last word in a paper entitled "Continuity and Discontinuity in Evolution" (*Science*, 102 [1945], 405–6). A title not cited in the bibliographies accompanying these exchanges is Needham's *Integrative Levels: A Reevaluation of the Idea of Progress* (Oxford, 1937).

Operationalism has as one of its origins the concept of pragmatism, which is said to have been founded by the famous American philosopher Charles S. Peirce in his essay "How to Make Our Ideas Clear" (Popular Science Monthly, 12 [1878], 286–302). Ways in which this concept, that nouns and adjectives have scientific meaning only when definable in terms of human operations that produce clear-cut results, affects philosophic analyses of the relationship between scientific theory and reality can be discerned, to take one example, in a paper by A. J. Ayer, "On Making Philosophy Intelligible" (*Advancement of Science*, 20 [1964], 406–16).

By force of cultural habit the physical sciences usually are taken as the model sciences. An authoritative challenge to this view, as well as a cogent application of the attitude of operationalism to the question of what science is about, is to be found in George Gaylord Simpson, "Biology and the Nature of Science" (*Science*, 139 [1963], 81–88).

Chapter 4
Greek and Arabic Biology

Of the many books written on Greek science and Greek biology, the following may be listed: Charles Singer, *Greek Biology and Greek Medicine* (Oxford, 1922); Henry Osborn Taylor, *Greek*

Biology and Medicine (Boston, 1922) ; Arnold Reymond, *Science in Greco-Roman Antiquity* (Cambridge, Eng., 1927) ; and Benjamin Farrington, *Greek Science: Its Meaning for Us* (Harmondsworth, 1944–1949). A collection of translations from the writings of important Greek scientists is provided by M. R. Cohen and I. E. Drabkin, *A Source Book in Greek Science* (Cambridge, Mass., 1958).

Four volumes of Hippocratic writings have been translated by W. H. S. Jones and E. T. Withington (London, 1923–1931).

English translations of Aristotle's biological writings appear in *The Oxford Translation of Aristotle,* edited by W. D. Ross (Oxford, 1910–1912). Commentaries on Aristotle's work are provided by T. E. Lones, *Aristotle's Researches in Natural Science* (London, 1912) ; D'Arcy Thompson, *On Aristotle as a Biologist* (Oxford, 1916) ; and Frederick J. E. Woodbridge, *Aristotle's Vision of Nature* (New York, 1965).

Theophrastus' *Enquiry into Plants* (Cambridge, Mass., 1916) is a translation by Arthur Hort.

Galen's *On the Natural Faculties* has been translated by A. J. Brock (London, 1916) and *On Medical Experience* by R. Walzer (Oxford, 1944).

Chapter 5
Roman and Medieval Science

William Stahl, in his *Roman Science: Origins, Development, and Influence to the Later Middle Ages* (Madison, Wis., 1962), has done valuable service in clarifying the relationships between the science of Greek, Roman, Arab, and medieval European cultures. Lynn White Jr., in *Medieval Technology and Social Change* (London, 1962), gives a modern account of the scientifically silent period of intense technological progress of the later Middle

Ages. A chapter by Charles Singer, entitled "Science," is in *Medieval Contributions to Modern Civilization,* edited by F. J. C. Hearnshaw (London, 1921). A. C. Crombie writes on the Middle Ages and its transition into the Renaissance in *Medieval and Early Modern Science* (2 vols.; New York, 1959).

Documentation for the extent of scholarly priestly investigation into human sexual activity will be found in John T. Noonan, *Contraception; A History of Its Treatment by the Catholic Theologians and Canonists* (Cambridge, Mass., 1965) and in G. Rattray Taylor, *Sex in History* (New York, 1954).

Chapter 6
The Scientific Renaissance

General works on the science of the sixteenth and seventeenth centuries, the time of the powerful surge of a renascent science, include Henry Osborn Taylor, *Philosophy and Science in the Sixteenth Century* (New York, 1920) ; George Sarton, *The Appreciation of Ancient and Medieval Science during the Renaissance, 1450–1600* (Philadelphia, 1953) ; and Stephen Toulmin, "Seventeenth Century Science and the Arts," in a collection of lectures edited by Hedley Rhys bearing the same title (Princeton, N.J., 1961).

English translations of some of Galileo's writings are *On Motion,* translated by I. E. Drabkin (Madison, Wis., 1960) ; and *Dialogues Concerning Two New Sciences,* translated from the Italian and Latin by Henry Crew and Alfonso de Salvio (New York, 1914). A biography is that of Ludivico Geymont, *Galileo Galilei: A Biography and Inquiry into His Philosophy of Science,* translated by Stillman Drake (New York, 1966).

William Harvey's *Anatomical Disquisition of the Motion of the Heart and Blood in Animals* has been translated into English by

Robert Willis (London, 1923). A historical discussion of a wider aspect of physiology is Mark Grabaud's *Circulation and Respiration: The Evolution of an Idea* (New York, 1964). Two biographies are Walter Pagel, *William Harvey's Biological Ideas: Selected Aspects and Historical Background* (New York, 1967), which emphasizes the metaphysical background of Harvey's thinking; and Geoffrey Keynes' more straightforward *The Life of William Harvey* (New York, 1966).

Chapter 7
Mapping the Living World

An introduction to the biology of the period in which descriptive aspects were dominant (although the author is concerned primarily with the emergence of experimental biology) is Philip Ritterbush, *Overtures to Biology: The Speculations of Eighteenth-Century Naturalists* (New Haven, 1964). Edward Lee Greene has written a history of botany in which the work of the Renaissance German "Fathers of Botany" is described in detail: *Landmarks of Botanical History: A Study of Certain Epochs in the Development of the Science of Botany;* Part 1: *Prior to 1562* A.D. (Smithsonian Misc. Collections, part of Vol. 54 [1909]). The Renaissance phase of descriptive botany also is illuminated by Agnes Arber's *Herbals: Their Origin and Evolution* (Cambridge, Eng., 1912). The life of an important pre-Linnean biologist is the subject of C. E. Raven's *John Ray, Naturalist: His Life and Works* (Cambridge, Eng., 1942).

Some of the biographies of Linnaeus are Benjamin Jackson's *Linnaeus: The Story of His Life* (London, 1923); Knut Hagburg's *Carl Linnaeus,* translated by Alan Blair (London, 1952); and Norah Gourlie's *The Prince of Botanists, Carl Linnaeus* (London, 1953). The technical aspects of Linnaeus' contribution to the science of classification are discussed authoritatively by William Stearn in a 176-page "Introduction" to a facsimile reprint of Carl Linnaeus, *Species Plantarum* (London, 1957); by H. K. Svenson, "On the Descriptive Method of Linnaeus" (*Rhodora*, 47 [1945], 273–302, 363–88); and by the same author, "Linnaeus and the Species Problem" (*Taxon*, 2 [1953], 55–58).

Alfred Russel Wallace's travel classic is *The Malay Archipelago: The Land of the Orang-Utan and the Bird of Paradise* (London, 1894).

An account of the original discovery of the deep sea *Bathybius* is found in C. Wyville Thomson's *The Depths of the Sea* (2d ed.; London, 1874); Alpheus Packard's notice is in "Life Histories of the Protozoa" (*American Naturalist*, 8 [1874], 728–48).

Chapter 8
The Evolutionary Outlook

In a collection of essays edited by Bentley Glass, Owsei Temkin, and William Straus Jr., *Forerunners of Darwin, 1745–1859*, is an extensive discussion of the evolutionary biologists of the century preceding Darwin.

Charles Gillispie, *Genesis and Geology* (Harvard Historical Studies, Vol. 18 [1951]), takes up the development of geology, enlivened with an account of the conflict between the scientific outlook and the theological bias of certain prominent scientists. James Hutton's *Theory of the Earth, with Proofs and Illustrations* (Edinburgh, 1795) has been republished in facsimile in two volumes (New York, 1959). Hutton's analysis was rewritten in plain English by John Playfair, *Illustrations of the Huttonian Theory of the Earth* (Edinburgh, 1802), and this also is available in facsimile reprint (Urbana, Ill., 1956).

The many volumes of *Histoire Naturelle, générale et particu-*

laire of Georges Buffon and his collaborators were published in Paris in the years 1749 to 1804; among the English versions may be mentioned one edited by John Wright (Boston, 1831).

Alpheus Packard has written a sympathetic biography, *Lamarck, The Founder of Evolution: His Life and Work* (London, 1901). Lamarck's *Philosophie Zoologique* has been translated into English by H. S. R. Elliott (London, 1914). The *Biologie; oder die Philosophie der lebenden Nature* (6 vols.; Göttingen, 1802–1822) of Gottfried Treviranus has been neglected.

Chapter 9
Evolution by Natural Selection

A popularly written book by Loren Eiseley, *Darwin's Century: Evolution and the Men Who Discovered It* (Garden City, N.Y., 1958), has placed the major historical and scientific events preceding and surrounding Darwin's work in perspective in a very effective way.

There are many biographies of Darwin. The most famous written by a literary figure is Geoffrey West's *Charles Darwin: A Portrait* (New Haven, 1938), with its chapter entitled "The Fragmentary Man," which compares Darwin with the "fragmentary" businessman of Werner Sombart's *Quintessence of Capitalism* (London, 1915)—the captain of industry collects money; Darwin collects scientific knowledge. Gavin de Beer's *Charles Darwin: Evolution by Natural Selection* (New York, 1964) is a biography written by a leading biologist. The very interesting attacks on Darwin in the writings of Samuel Butler are beyond the scope of the present book, but the existence of this literary episode should be called to the attention of the reader.

In the numerous books written by Charles Darwin may be found not only the theory which dominates all biology (Charles

Singer writes that "the whole of modern biology has been called a commentary on the *Origin of Species*") but also the germs of leading ideas in many of the modern subdisciplines of biology, particularly in ecology. There is a complete bibliography of Darwin's writings—his books are widely available in larger libraries —in the *Life and Letters of Charles Darwin*, edited by his son Francis Darwin (2 vols.; New York, 1896). A reprint of the essential first edition of the *Origin* (most of the available versions are of the final sixth edition) has been published, together with a foreword by C. D. Darlington (London, 1950); and there is a facsimile reprint of the first edition of Darwin's *Journal of Researches into the Geology and Natural History of the Various Countries Visited by H. M. S. Beagle* (New York, 1952). Darwin's two preliminary versions of the *Origin* (the "1842 sketch" and the "1844 essay") and the Darwin–Wallace papers of 1858 have been brought together, with an introduction, by Gavin de Beer, *Charles Darwin and Alfred Russel Wallace: Evolution by Natural Selection* (Cambridge, Eng., 1958).

Robert Chambers' *Vestiges of the History of Creation*, published anonymously in London, 1844, is discussed thoroughly by Milton Millhauser, *Just Before Darwin: Robert Chambers and Vestiges* (Middletown, Conn., 1959). The anecdote of the *Vestiges* and Abraham Lincoln, who "grew into a warm advocate of the new doctrine" of evolution is found in William Herndon's *Abraham Lincoln* (New York, 1892), II, 147.

The criticism of Darwin by Alfred Burnett cited in the text appeared as "The Theory of Natural Selection Taken from a Mathematical Point of View" (*Nature, 30* [1870], 30–33).

Probably the first technical paper in professional biology to demonstrate the likelihood, on grounds other than similarity in appearance, of an organic connection between distinct species was Alfred Russel Wallace's "On the Law Which Has Regulated the Introduction of New Species" (*Annals and Magazine of Natural History* [1885], p. 184), which pointed out some relevant facts of geographic distribution. It has been said of Wallace's series of essay, entitled *Contributions to the Theory of Natural Selection* (London, 1870), that "Probably, next to the *Origin of Species,* no single work has done so much to promote clear understanding of natural selection and confidence in its truth." Some Wallace memorabilia have been assembled by James Marchant, *Alfred Russel Wallace: Letters and Reminiscences* (New York, 1916). A brief but important biography is by Loren Eiseley, "Alfred Russel Wallace" (*Scientific American* [Feb., 1959], pp. 70–84).

Chapter 10
Units of Life

A history of the study of cells is A. Hughes, *A History of Cytology* (New York, 1959). Matthias Schleiden's *Contributions to Phytogenesis,* important in the history of cell theory, was appended to Theodor Schwann's equally important *Microscopical Researches into the Accordance in the Structure and Growth of Animals and Plants,* in a translation of both by Henry Smith (London, 1847). The *Cellular Pathology* of Rudolf Virchow, which made the study of cells an important part of medical science, was translated into English by P. Chance (London, 1860).

Some general histories of genetics are Elof Carlson, *The Gene: A Critical History* (Philadelphia, 1966); L. C. Dunn, *A Short History of Genetics* (New York, 1965); and A. H. Sturtevant, *A History of Genetics* (New York, 1965).

August Weismann's *The Germ Plasm: A Theory of Heredity* (1893) was translated from the German by W. Newton Parker and Harriet Rönnfeldt (New York, 1893). The *Natural Inheri-*

tance of Francis Galton (London, 1894) was an early statistical treatment of heredity. A standard biography of Mendel is Hugo Iltis, *Life of Mendel,* translated by Eden and Cedar Paul (reprinted New York, 1965). The circumstances surrounding the rediscovery of Mendelian inheritance in 1900 are dealt with by *The Birth of Genetics: Mendel, De Vries, Correns, Tschermak, in English Translation,* by the editors of *Genetics* (Supplement to *Genetics,* Vol. 35 [1950]); and by Robert Olby, *Origins of Mendelism* (New York, 1966). The statistical analysis of Mendel's work referred to in the text is R. A. Fisher, "Has Mendel's Work Been Rediscovered?" (*Annals of Science,* 1 [1936], 115–37).

Two histories of embryology may be cited: Joseph Needham *A History of Embryology* (Cambridge, Eng., 1934) and A. W. Meyer, *The Rise of Embryology* (Stanford, 1939). Extracts from the writings of the pioneers of experimental embryology, with introductory notes, are found in Benjamin Willier and Jane Oppenheimer, editors, *Foundations of Experimental Embryology* (Englewood Cliffs, N.J., 1964).

Chapter 11
Life As Mechanism

Some titles in the history of chemistry, a subject that provides part of the background for the history of biology, are Eduard Farber, *The Evolution of Chemistry* (New York, 1952); *Crucibles: The Story of Chemistry,* by Bernard Jaffe (Greenwich, Conn., 1930); and Isaac Asimov's *A Short History of Chemistry: An Introduction to the Ideas and Concepts of Chemistry* (Garden City, N.Y., 1965).

Two major biographies of Louis Pasteur are *Louis Pasteur: Free Lance of Science,* by the microbiologist René Dubos (Boston, 1950), which gives good insight into the concept of microbes as living chemical mechanisms as it developed in the nineteenth century; and the more personal *The Life of Pasteur,* by René Vallery-Radot, translated from the French by R. L. Devonshire (Garden City, N.Y., 1926). A wide view of the field of biochemical microbiology, hence of biochemistry in general, is given in *The Microbe's Contribution to Biology,* by A. J. Kluyver and C. B. van Niel, based on a series of lectures for a nonspecialist university audience (Cambridge, Mass., 1956).

Although it belongs to a later period than that explictly covered by the present book, A. I. Oparin's *The Origin of Life,* translated from the Russian by Sergius Morgulis (New York, 1938), is worth special mention because it brought an evolutionary approach into biochemistry in a basic way, and also tied biology in a meaningful fashion to astronomy.

A collection of lectures by the physicist Erwin Schrödinger, published in 1944 under the title *What Is Life?* (Cambridge, Eng.), probably has done as much as any single book to bring a mid-century crop of theoretical physicists into biology. It is concerned mostly with some physical features of biological materials that would interest a physicist relatively naïve about biology, but naïveté is not always a disadvantage in an invasion of a borderline field, as that between biology and physics. The following generation of molecular biologists, with its rich infusion of physicists, is highly sophisticated regarding the outstanding characteristic of living things—a pervasive adaptiveness in which may be found analogues of the most ingenious human technological advances.

[I N D E X]

INDEX